THE
MURDER
OF
SOPHIE
PART ONE

HOW I HUNTED AND HAUNTED
THE WEST CORK KILLER

MICHAEL SHERIDAN

First published in Great Britain by Gadfly Press in 2020

Copyright © Michael Sheridan 2020

The right of Michael Sheridan to be identified as the author of this work has been asserted by her in accordance with the Copyright, Designs and Patents Act 1988. All rights reserved

No part of this book may be reproduced, stored in a retrieval system or transmitted in any form or by any means (electronic, mechanical, photocopying, recording or otherwise) without the prior written permission of the author, except in cases of brief quotations embodied in reviews or articles. It may not be edited, amended, lent, resold, hired out, distributed or otherwise circulated without the publisher's written permission

Permission can be obtained from gadflypress@outlook.com

This book is a work of non-fiction based on research by the author

A catalogue record of this book is available from the British Library

Typeset and cover by Jane Dixon-Smith

Cover photo by Michael Mac Sweeney @ Provision Photography
https://www.provision.ie/

SPELLING DIFFERENCES: UK V US

This book was written in British English, hence US readers may notice some spelling differences with American English: e.g. color = colour, meter = metre and = jewelry = jewellery

"The paradox of destiny: This young woman was solitary, elegant, she did not like show and took refuge in this beautiful country Ireland is. She was caught by a criminal who was the exact opposite to everything she was: obscure, barbaric, media attention-seeking. Her name should not be reduced to being a sole reference to this affair and today justice must be rendered for her."

Jean-Pierre Bonthoux
Advocate General
Paris, May 31, 2019

*"Thus thee thyself in themes like these alone,
Can hunt from thought to thought and keenly wind,
Along even long and to the secret places
And drag out the truth."*

Lucretius (55 BC)

"The dead are invisible they are not absent."

Saint Augustine (354–430 AD)

"For nothing is hidden that will not be made manifest, nor is anything secret that will not be known and come to light."

Luke 8.17, the Bible

DEDICATIONS

*"But O for the touch of a vanished hand
And the sound of a voice that is still."*

Tennyson

This book is dedicated to the memories of my late parents Martin and Patsy Sheridan, who inspired me in all aspects to the possibility of writing but also by their sense of justice in the society in which they lived in. And of course, their love of their children.

Also to the Bouniol family, Georges, Marguerite, Bertrand and Stephane; Pierre Louis-Vignaud and his family; to Jean-Pierre Gazeau and Marie Madeleine Opalka; to Alain Spilliaert and Jean-Antoine Bloc; and to the memory of Sophie, a light in all their lives and so cruelly taken away from them.

And to the West Cork witnesses who stuck steadfastly over the years to the cause of truth; not to specifically pick out any of them but in particular to Bill Hogan, Bill Fuller, Amanda and Malachi Reed, Richie Shelley and to the memory of the late Rosie Shelley.

Finally, to members of the Garda murder investigation team alive and dead who were wrongly and maliciously slandered and criticised over the years before being finally vindicated by numerous public inquiries and by the High Court Dublin in 2015. And who along with the Bouniol family and ASSOPH provided an unwavering voice for justice for Sophie.

CONTENTS

Preface		1
Prologue In the Still of the Night		5
PART ONE		15
Chapter 1	A Devil in the Hills	15
Chapter 2	A Person of Interest	33
Chapter 3	Murder He Wrote	53
Chapter 4	The Arrests	75
Chapter 5	A Craving for Attention	101
PART TWO		127
Chapter 6	The Plot Thickens	127
Chapter 7	The "Poet" is Nailed to a Literary Cross	147
Chapter 8	The Psychology of Evil	163
Chapter 9	The "Murder" Trial Sensation	186
Chapter 10	The People vs Bailey	216
Acknowledgements		236
Bibliography		237
Other Books by Gadfly Press		240
About the Author		261

PREFACE

Having read *Death in December*, Michael Sheridan's first book published on the case in 2002, I came to realise the stakes and the extent of the judicial procedure surrounding the murder of my niece Sophie. This book played an important part in the decision made in 2007 to create the association (ASSOPH) to establish the truth about the murder of Sophie Toscan du Plantier, née Bouniol.

The reading of this new publication by Mr Sheridan was for me terrifying yet provided clarity. Awe at the inconceivable passivity of the DPP and of his inert reaction to the stagnation of the case in his department. Clarity on the justification of Ian Bailey's conviction for murder on May 31, 2019 by the Criminal Court in Paris.

In actual fact, this book explains the guilt of the accused much better than all other publications, by highlighting two facts. Firstly, the truth prevails when a person who is not subjected to physical or moral constraint proclaims his innocence. On the other hand, where is the truth in the shocking succession of lies by Ian Bailey? He, from the start, and with the benefit of leniency and tolerance of the DPP, continuously changed his version of events.

In addition to that, there were the lies of Marie Farrell once she retracted her statement, at the end of 2005, in the wake of a vile campaign of intimidation by Bailey in an effort to get her to change her statement. Earlier, legal threats were issued to her by him after she gave an interview to Michael Sheridan about how she lived in fear of him.

These lies were mercilessly exposed by Paul O'Higgins' defence counsel for the Gardai and the State in Bailey's failed High Court action of 2014–15.

What is to be expected now? Precisely that this book of evidence incriminating the failures of justice will make the public aware of the denial of justice in Ireland. This jurisdiction, despite a thorough and exhaustive Garda investigation, which would have resulted in a charge and trial in any other jurisdiction in the world, never made any acceptable solid arguments to justify its passivity. On the contrary, during these long and cruel twenty-three years, there has been silence and more silence.

The only exception is the well-known document entitled "Analysis of the evidence to link Ian Bailey to the Sophie Toscan du Plantier murder", not officially signed nor dated, which was pulled out of a hat before the hearings of the Supreme Court of Ireland in 2011.

This document, a one-sided accusation of the Gardai, is flagrantly biased – enough to be declared inadmissible evidence by the Irish High Court. Even to the extent of casting doubt on Sophie's words, which mentioned the name of her killer in November 1996, and I quote, "The statement of Guy Girard contains hearsay evidence only." Guy Girard, whose evidence is dated and signed, has never varied in his statement, which was direct as opposed to hearsay evidence.

On the other hand, the absurd interpretation of Bailey's confessions of responsibility for the crime to no less that eleven witnesses as some form of black humour, when not one of those witnesses experienced the confessions as anything but admissions frightening to many, which prompted the witnesses to give statements to the Garda investigators.

Michael Sheridan has accomplished in his imposing and captivating publication an extraordinary work, eminently salutary in its denunciation of the errors of justice and with the undeniable distinct demonstration of Ian Bailey's guilt.

In Ireland, Bailey suffered humiliating defeats in the libel trial of 2003 and his High Court action against the State in 2014–15, where in the latter his slanderous attack on the Garda murder investigation was roundly rejected. His complaints were also rejected by the Fennelly Commission and the GSOC inquiry. In France, eight superior court judges rejected his appeals against the 2016 indictment for murder and finally he was found guilty of the crime by the Paris Criminal Court in 2019.

Jean-Pierre Gazeau – Sophie's uncle and President of ASSOPH

PROLOGUE
IN THE STILL OF
THE NIGHT

Paris/West Cork, December 1996

On the evening of Thursday, December 19, 1996, television producer Sophie Toscan du Plantier and her husband, French film mogul Daniel, attended a party at a well-known Paris club – *Les Bains Douches*. Her husband noted that she was in great form, looked beautiful and did not waste time on the social niceties, but instead engaged in a long and intense conversation of creative nature with another filmmaker. Without any sense of foreboding, it did concern him that she was travelling alone for the first time to her West Cork holiday home, and he made a gentle suggestion that it might not be a good idea, but she was determined to, and not sure of the exact day of her return had bought two tickets – one for December 23 and the other for the following day. On Friday, December 20, Sophie took the 11.30 a.m. flight from Charles de Gaulle Airport, arriving at Dublin Airport at 1 p.m. Before boarding at CDG, she rang her mother to say goodbye. Unusually, she used the words "Adieu, Maman" instead of "Au revoir". It struck Marguerite as odd and made her slightly uncomfortable.

Sophie was on the way to her holiday home in a remote region in West Cork in Southern Ireland for a short break. It was the first time since purchasing the house some years before that she had travelled alone. Normally she would go with friends or family.

The flight later continued to Cork Airport, arriving at 2.25 p.m. There she hired a Ford Fiesta car from Avis and drove towards West Cork. Sophie first stopped at Hurley's Garage in Skibbereen to buy firelighters. The gas station attendant noticed a man in the passenger seat. He was tall, his head nearing the roof of the car, he had medium-to-long brown hair and the collar of his coat was pulled up. The attendant asked Sophie what she wanted, but she did not seem to understand, possibly because of his distinct Cork accent.

The passenger repeated it to Sophie in clearer English. He appeared to be Irish. Sophie asked the attendant to fill up the car. The passenger paid the ten pounds owed. The car then drove in the direction of Schull. It next stopped at a Texaco filling station in Ballydehob, where Sophie bought firelighters before driving away. The attendant there noticed that Sophie was alone. By the time she reached Toormore, darkness had fallen in the valley. She parked the car beside the house.

Josephine Hellen, the caretaker of the house, rang at 4.45 p.m. to check that Sophie had arrived and that all was in order. Josephine had cleaned and aired the house, prepared the fire and added a festive touch by placing bunches of holly in the living room. Sophie was delighted and thankful and indicated that she would spend the New Year in Dakar with her husband Daniel and friends Jerome Clement and his sister Catherine. Later, having settled in and having had something to eat, she rang Josephine, who happened to be out, and instead spoke to her daughter, saying that she would ring back the following day.

At 11.15 p.m., she answered the phone, a call from her best friend Agnes Thomas, and they spoke for twenty minutes. Sophie told her that everything was fine in the house thanks to Josephine and informed Agnes that she would be sleeping not in her usual bedroom but the one above the kitchen, as it was so cold in the former. In that room there was a plug-in heater. She had been made aware before her journey that there was a problem with the heating, which she intended to sort out during her short stay.

This room was the largest of the upstairs accommodation and perhaps being located above the kitchen was the warmest, apart from the heating facility and a bathroom off to the gable end. The sparse furniture was, as in Sophie's usual bedroom, old and simple in construction. There was no bed but a mattress on the floor. It typified the owner's approach to the house as a whole – to maintain the spirit of the original almost as an antidote to the Parisian luxury she was now used to as the wife of a famous film producer.

The upper floor is accessed by an eleven-step wooden stairway; to the right, if ascending, is the largest space – the living room – with a large open fireplace which would have been the focal point of the occupiers of the farmhouse over generations, the source of the greatest heat and also more than likely used for the business of cooking. There were old pokers and a bellow beside it, in front a table and wooden chairs, and a sofa against the end wall.

The next day, Saturday, December 21, she drove to the nearest small town, Schull, stopped at the Courtyard bar on the main street between 2 p.m. and 2.30 p.m. and shopped at the Spar supermarket at around 3.40 p.m. Later, she took £200 from an ATM of the Allied Irish Bank and browsed in an arts and crafts shop nearby. Her activities had been watched by a man wearing a distinctive long black coat who saw her in the Spar shop and followed her when she left, standing opposite the arts and crafts shop while she was in there and again following her when she left to walk around the town.

On Sunday, she drove to the home of friends, the famous international illustrator and artist Tomi Ungerer and his wife Yvonne at their home in Dunlough, Goleen, having first visited the local castle. Ungerer was born in Strasbourg during the Nazi occupation before leaving at twenty-five years of age for New York and a career of fame and fortune. Sophie admired his huge talent but also his fierce independence as a creator, and there was some discussion about a collaboration with him, most likely a documentary.

This was about lunchtime and the couple got the impression that she was relaxed and happy, and she told them that she would be returning to West Cork at Easter. However, uncharacteristically she did reveal that she had a strange sense of foreboding about something on which she could not be specific.

She then drove to Crookhaven, where she called into the bar and restaurant owned by Billy and Angela O'Sullivan. They invited her over on Christmas Day, but she said she was not sure of her return date to Paris. After about fifteen minutes, she left and drove back to Toormore.

The local postman, Thomas Hodnett, passed by Sophie's house at 6 p.m. to deliver letters to Alfie Lyons's post-box and noticed lights on in the first and ground floors. Sophie made several phone calls from her landline that evening. The first was to Josephine Hellen at 7.10 p.m., which was answered by her daughter Catherine, who said that her mother was out again. Twenty minutes later, she called Pat Hegarty, who did regular maintenance work on the house. He was also out, and his daughter Joanne said she would pass on the message to him.

When Josephine returned, she rang Sophie back about 9.10 p.m. They arranged to meet at Sophie's house at noon the next day to discuss matters in relation to the house, including bills to be paid. Sophie said she had been trying to contact local builder Pat Hegarty about payment and to arrange further renovation work and suggested that he should also attend their arranged meeting. In common with other people whom she had encountered during her short stay, Josephine got the impression that Sophie was in excellent form. Later, just before midnight, Daniel returned a call from Sophie which he had earlier not been able to take as he had been on a conference call in relation to UniFrance business. They had spoken by phone numerous times since her arrival and this time had a good conversation. She said she was not sure when she would be back but was joking and confirmed that she would travel back to Paris on Christmas Eve.

She had booked a seat on an Aer Lingus flight to Toulouse arriving at 8 p.m., where Daniel would collect her at Toulouse-Blagnac Airport. They made plans to spend Christmas Day at the country house in Ambax and to travel to Dakar for the New Year, where they would celebrate with friends and film colleagues.

It was, according to Daniel, a relaxed conversation that concluded at 1 a.m. (midnight Irish time), in which he told her that it would be nice to have his wife back for Christmas, to which she replied that she loved to be alone and would stay on to study and read. She was again joking and then went on to consider what sort of present she would give him. Sophie had already decided without telling him what it would be and had beforehand contacted the gardener in Ambax to order a linden tree to be planted outside their bedroom window in the house.

It might have appeared to be a most unusual gift – a tree outside a bedroom. But it was most likely chosen with an informed and careful significance. The linden or lime tree shares common symbolism with any sacred tree in European lore. The presence protects against ill luck; the strike of lightning and the bright nature is supposed to repel those spirits that might cause harm to the household.

The tree has been used by poets through the ages as a metaphor for the beauties of nature, a tree of grace with romantic associations of love and protection, also good luck and fertility. Lovers were encouraged to stand under it and to swear to never end their relationships, but to follow their hearts and dreams with the power of fidelity and love. As a gift, the message seemed to be clear.

Her best friend Agnes Thomas later confirmed that Sophie was in a good place at the time; she loved her work and she had been reconciled with Daniel after a separation, and they hoped to have a child together.

Over the valley and the house, the full moon hung, suspended in the cloudless sky, a giant orb bestowing the earth and the sea with its bright presence, and illuminating the contours and banishing the shadows of the night that normally held sway even as winter began to retreat. The sun and the moon faced off directly, making the latter shine even more dramatically and seeming bigger with the aid of the solar rays. Toormore and the valley were bathed in light, and reflecting starry shapes danced on the surface of the sea in Roaringwater Bay.

Four and half miles out in the Atlantic, the Fastnet Lighthouse flashed its beam and illuminated Sophie's usual bedroom like a visual metronome. She was fascinated by this historic protector of seaborne men and vessels built on two rocks, the larger stretching to a height of 147 feet above the crashing waves of the sea. She may well have been acquainted with the words of Sir Robert Ball, the scientific adviser to the Commissioner of Irish Lights, who described its effect just after completion:

"As to the beams of the Fastnet during all the time of our return to the harbour I can only describe them as magnificent. At 10 miles distant, the great revolving spokes of light, succeeding each other at intervals of five seconds gave the most distinctive character possible ... each flash as it swept past lighted up the ship and the rigging like a searchlight."

She elevated her bed to watch it before she slept. She kept a model of it and several framed photographs including one stunning aerial shot which hung in the corridor outside the bedroom. It would have made a great subject for one of her documentaries with its mesmeric location, character and history.

Inside the house, Sophie must have been comforted by the moon that illuminated the valley, and the atmosphere of preparation and bonhomie typical of the approach to Christmas that she had witnessed during her latest trip and conversations in the area. There was a perfect sense of peace, tranquillity and safety, and confirmation that her choice of the house and location was the right one, far from the madding crowd in Paris.

As the night wore on, the temperature began to fall towards minus, enough to conjure clouds of breath from a walker's mouth. The moor and the bogland and the rough heathered terrain would normally, at this time, be buried in impenetrable darkness, and a source of danger for the fittest midnight rambler. Not that there should be any abroad at this time of year in a remote and freezing cold area, even when bathed in moonlight.

The wild animals in the valley, in hibernation, were well ensconced in their lairs, protected from the inclement elements. There was one of the human species equally protected in the bars of Schull, drinking heavily with dark thoughts on his mind, buried from the attention of his pub companions. There is no art, the Bard wrote, to find the mind's construction in the face.

In Toormore, some domestic animals showed signs of agitation which the owners considered unusual. A man minding a wolfhound noticed that the dog was upset between midnight and 1 a.m., while another woman's dog was continually barking from 10.30 p.m. for three hours. A couple's dog showed signs of agitation between 10 p.m. and 2 a.m. It is not unusual for domestic animals to display restlessness and upset during a full moon, which may well explain the agitation that can be magnified by the collective barking.

Animals are not alone in being affected by the lunar pull. Humans, particularly those with unbalanced minds, can show such signs and there had been two instances in the area. A woman in the valley had been awoken one night by a local man in the grip of full-moon fever, standing below her window howling her name. On another occasion one full moon night, a man driving on a nearby road had caught sight in his headlights of the same man, this time dressed in women's attire, running along also howling.

Daniel had the impression during the call that Sophie was either in or preparing for bed. Earlier, before his phone call, she was on the ground floor near the kitchen area, sitting at the small table. As she was reading, she pulled a chair close to the one she was sitting on and rested her legs on it. She was wearing white leggings, a shirt, a blue dressing gown and walking shoes, which she was in the habit of removing when going upstairs.

Behind where she sat was the tiny kitchen, and directly under the window another small table next to a porcelain sink on a brick base, a legacy of the former life of the house. A wooden door with a latch led out of the kitchen into a small room that doubled as a pantry and utility room containing a fridge, washing machine, shelves for foodstuffs and tools including a small kindle hatchet. The rear door led out to the side of the house and a roughly paved stone patio. Opposite was rough ground and rock, with no through path.

The door faced an old shed surrounded by thick, impenetrable bushes with thistles and briars. The field below in front of the house was typical of the surrounding rough terrain. It was sloping and steep, the surface uneven and displaying the odd jutting rock. Any local with mild motive of robbery would have recognised such physical detail as a form of trap if things went wrong. There was no immediate exit or any escape route of value.

Behind that was the neighbours Alfie Lyons and Shirley Foster's house, and a further distance away another holiday home. The sloping laneway to the gate entrance was shared with the neighbours. From the road, at a vantage point called Hunt's Hill, the house could not have presented on this night a more peaceful aspect. Or for someone with other things in mind a more appropriate opportunity. The white exterior reflected the natural beam from the sky with the gable light on, providing confirmation that the occupant was present in the house.

Sophie was, while reading at the table, occasionally eating olives from a bowl. She had a broad reading taste. Her bookcase contained a collection of her favourite poet W.B. Yeats, Canadian author Paul Auster and a collection of short stories by the Irish master of that medium, William Trevor, and J.M. Synge's plays were also represented, as well as books by Thomas De Quincey and Théophile Gautier. On another adjacent shelf, there were more poetry collections and a couple of Agatha Christie murder mysteries. It was the W.B. Yeats collection that lay in front of her.

She opened a page that contained a poem with a French connection. It had been written in 1891 for the subject of his great unrequited love for Maud Gonne, who had lived in France, where she had borne two children with a Frenchman. She had been ill and was recovering in the South of France, and his concern for her health had inspired the poet to write about his worst fear – her death. It had first been titled "An Epitaph" and later changed to "A Dream of Death".

A DREAM OF DEATH
W.B. Yeats

I dreamed that one had died in a strange place
Near no accustomed hand;
And they had nailed the boards above her face,
The peasants of that land,
Wondering to lay her in that solitude,
And raised above her mound
A cross they had made out of two bits of wood,
And planted cypress round;
And left her to the indifferent stars above
Until I carved these words:
She was more beautiful than thy first love,
But now lies under boards.

This different solitude from the fifth line of the poem must have seemed like some sort of heaven for her and utter confirmation of the peace she had sought in this haven.

Sophie was overcome by a wave of tiredness. She placed a jar of honey on the page of another book she had been reading on the table as an improvised bookmark, took off her walking shoes and left them at the bottom of the wooden staircase, and went up to her room. It involved turning left at the top of the stairs instead of right to the room she normally occupied. Crucially, the room was not just above the kitchen but adjacent to the rear door.

Sometime after her conversation with Daniel she had fallen asleep, and she was awoken by a knock on the rear door. Sophie was not sure if she heard it at first. There was a pause and then the knocking became more insistent. Who could it possibly be at this time of night? If she did not answer it then perhaps whoever was outside would go away. She hesitated but then pulled the bed clothes aside, got on her dressing gown, descended the stairs and put on her walking shoes.

Sophie possibly thought it might well be Alfie or Shirley, but only if an emergency had arisen. Still, wouldn't either call out her name? If you heard a neighbour's voice, you would react much quicker. She gingerly walked to the kitchen. The knocking was rattling the door. She opened it suddenly. He stood there with his hand raised to strike the door again.

She recognised him as someone she had been introduced to before and had been contacted by, but was also shocked by his state – wild-eyed, agitated and drunk. He stepped into the kitchen. There was a moment of silence. She asked him why he was there and what he wanted, and he replied with a roughness. What did she think he wanted, and he told her. She stepped forward and she had no interest in his proposition, urging him to go home. He felt the blood boiling in his veins and the anger bursting in his head.

The valley and the bay waters were bathed in the brilliant light of the moon. Everything seemed quiet and not even the distant barking of dogs could be heard. People slept deeply in their warm beds free from the cares of the world.

The metronomic blinking of the Fastnet Lighthouse flashed seawards and landwards. All was at peace in Toormore. Then a scream shattered the silence and was soon gone, but the echo would last for decades.

PART ONE

CHAPTER 1
A DEVIL IN THE HILLS

West Cork/Paris – December 1996

The bright moon had faded and the grey dawn was breaking in the valley. Nobody in West Cork could have predicted that it would be replaced by the morning star of evil. Lights were being switched on in the silhouetted houses in the area, and in the nearby villages and small towns from Goleen and Schull to Ballydehob and beyond. Most householders would soon be in the feverish grip of the final preparations for Christmas Day. Some would be more advanced in their plans than others, but last-minute Yuletide tasks were on the lists of even the most punctilious and organised of shoppers.

It was a crisp, dry and cold day, and soon the sun would shine in a bright clear sky, unusual but welcome at this time of the year. In Toormore, the normal rhythm of nature – the sheep and cows that dotted the landscape, the twittering birds in the trees and bushes – created a peaceful atmosphere. That aura of solitude would soon be shattered, even if nature would remain indifferent to human tragedy.

Just before 10 a.m., Sophie's next-door neighbour Shirley Foster left the house, got into a white Peugeot car and eased towards the S bend in the laneway, intending to drive to Schull. As she rounded the bend, something struck her as unusual. The gate at the laneway was open. As she slowed the car, she saw a piece of white clothing flapping from a barbed wire to the left of the concrete gatepost. She stopped the car, got out and was overcome with a sickening feeling. A crumpled shape, that she first thought was a mannequin, she soon recognised as a human laid on the grass margin near the gate.

She fled back up the laneway to her house and alerted her partner Alfie Lyons. He rushed down the lane to confirm her suspicion that there was a corpse near the gate which led to the valley and saw the body. He went to Sophie's house to warn her not to go out, but not getting any reply thought the body might be hers and immediately rang the emergency line for help.

Alfie's call was put through to Bandon Garda Station, which is the divisional headquarters of the area and was handled by Garda Eugene McCarthy, who made notes of the conversation and then rang the nearest station in Schull, where the call was answered by Garda Martin Malone. Two colleagues on patrol, Sergeant Gerard Prendeville and Garda Billy Byrne, were told at 10.15 a.m. to go straight to the location in Toormore. They arrived at the scene twenty minutes later and quickly established that the body was that of a woman with extensive head injuries.

Garda Byrne was tasked to cordon off the area where the body lay while Sergeant Prendeville went to Alfie and Shirley's house to make initial inquiries. The shocked and shaken couple informed him that the house next to theirs was owned by Sophie Bouniol, who had arrived some days before. The silver Ford Fiesta parked in front of the house was a car she had hired at Cork Airport, confirming the fact that she had not returned to Paris.

Sergeant Prendeville rang Bantry Garda Station, spoke to Superintendent Twomey and requested help to secure the crime scene and make preliminary inquiries. As well as guarding the body of a small woman, her long blonde hair tied back, Officer Byrne also took notes of details he witnessed at the scene, including multiple injuries particularly to the head and neck. There was a bloodstained slate rock near the body and a bloodied concrete block, lying on the blue dressing gown which the victim wore over torn white leggings, and brown walking shoes. A portion of the leggings were caught on a barbed wire fence.

There were large amounts of blood on her hair, face and neck. The white shirt she wore was pulled above the stomach.

Schull-based Dr Larry O'Connor was summoned to the scene, arriving at 11 a.m. and taking notes of injuries, before pronouncing the victim as deceased and noting that rigor mortis had set in, while Catholic priest Fr Denis Cashman arrived to administer the last rites to the then formally unidentified victim. At around 12.35 p.m., and in the presence of the officers and Superintendent Twomey, Josephine Hellen and her husband Finbar, he identified the body as being that of Sophie Toscan du Plantier.

While officers talked to Alfie Lyons and Shirley Foster for background on the victim, back in Paris the Bouniol family were unaware of the unfolding investigation, not to mind the terrible death of their beloved Sophie. As the local person closest to the victim, officers took a statement from Josephine Hellen. She recounted her communications with Sophie before and subsequent to her arrival. She revealed that relations between Sophie and her neighbour Alfie Lyons had been fractious in the past.

There had been a quarrel two years previously over water seeping from Alfie's garden onto Sophie's property, an issue concerning an adjoining structure and another time she had accused Alfie of using her bath and leaving it dirty. To the best of the caretaker's knowledge, those disputes had been settled. She said that Sophie most often used the front door and always left the rear door open, only locking it when she went to bed. There was a small axe for chopping wood, usually kept in a pouch under the porch, that was missing.

Nothing in the local officers' experience of crime matched what they were now attempting to deal with, through no fault of their own given the absence of a forensic pathologist. There is little doubt that the traffic of people in and around the crime scene under normal circumstances provided the distinct possibility of contaminating evidence there. But that evidence had already been compromised and contaminated in advance of any single person's presence. The late arrival of a forensic pathologist did not help matters.

There was a ludicrous situation where there was, apart from a locum, one chief state pathologist in a year in which there was not just a huge spike in violence and murder of women, but also a huge surge in gangland killings, a victim of which in June of that year was my colleague, investigative crime journalist Veronica Guerin, with whom I had been working on a screenplay about her work, which became the movie *When the Sky Falls*.

The consequence was that Dr John Harbison, the chief State pathologist, was run ragged with a huge number of cases, and having been socialising the night before the murder, could not travel to West Cork until the following day, as the usual practice of Gardai driving to the scene of a crime was not in operation. In crime-scene investigation, the speed of the examination is invaluable for gathering evidence as quickly as possible to establish the cause and time of death of the victim.

The latter is often linked to two factors: the state of rigor mortis and the ambient temperature. Tissues in the human body begin to break down almost immediately after death, and delay in getting the body to a morgue can make it harder to determine the time of death, a process that at the best of times is not an exact science.

Post-mortem rigidity, which usually sets in between two and four hours after death, is caused by chemical changes in the muscles. Under normal conditions, it lasts from eight to twelve hours, but could be present for another eighteen. It can be helpful in establishing an approximate time of death. The ambient temperature has an influence on the post-mortem process. In extreme heat, body changes are more rapid, while the opposite is true in extremely cold conditions.

In freezing conditions, which was the case in Toormore, the progress of rigor mortis is considerably slowed and therefore could not provide a reliable guide to the time of death. That in no way excuses the delay; it is a scientific fact. Forensic aid was provided to the investigation from the National Forensic Laboratory in Dublin for the normal but expert crime-scene investigation, including photography, gathering of trace evidence and samples of blood at the scene and around the body, but not on it – this was the pathologist's area.

But the only problem that might occur, as it would transpire, was the inability to preserve small blood samples in an open environment as opposed to a closed one, for example within the house. Not in relation to the victim, but rather the perpetrator. The body had been lying near the gate and exposed to the elements for approximately eight hours before the arrival of investigators, and a further twenty-eight hours passed before the arrival of the pathologist.

The weather factors included wind, an extremely cold temperature and sun. During this vital period at a crime scene in the open, and one which stretched back from where the body lay to the rear door of the house, vital trace evidence such as fibres and hair could be dispersed by the wind and blood evidence contaminated.

Any blood left by the killer, especially in contact with the briars and barbed wire near the body, could have been compromised by the temperature, literally frozen and further diminished by the wind and the sun, all of which play key roles in the destruction of such evidence on a crime scene exposed as in this case to the elements for so long before the discovery of the body.

In such a situation, accurate laboratory testing of small quantities of such blood samples is rendered virtually impossible. Therefore, the investigation of this horrendous murder began at a distinct disadvantage most pertinently in the matter of gathering vital forensic evidence at the crime scene. This, among the many myths that would emerge about the case, had nothing to do with the lack of expertise on behalf of the forensic team who gathered evidence at the crime scene.

The basic pattern of what had happened at the scene was quickly established by the crime scene investigators. There were bloodstains on the jamb and the knob of the rear door, indicating this was the location for the first stage of the assault. There was further bloodstaining on a flat rock halfway down the incline of the garden. This indicated that the victim had fled the first site and was hit by a projectile thrown from behind, most likely a flat rock, which was then picked up by the attacker with the intention of using it again.

* * * * * *

Sophie had then fled to the gate on which blood spattering indicated a prelude to the third and the most violent attack, in which the perpetrator was intent in finishing the kill in an orgy of violence. She was pulled back from the gate fell to the ground and attempted to crawl through the briar bush like a desperate animal fleeing from the hunter. There was a distinct possibility that the killer sustained scratches and wounds while pulling the victim away from the briars and barbed wire.

It would be posited that the first weapon employed was a missing kindle hatchet, which had been in a pouch inside the rear door. Its position indicated that Sophie may have taken it to protect herself. A slate rock was also used. Her body had been pulled back from the bushes, where part of her leggings were caught in the barbed wire. It had appeared but to be confirmed that a concrete block was dropped on her face and head. There was no sign of the kindle hatchet.

This weapon had the most potential evidence linking the killer to the crime scene, including latent prints, biological and trace material and transfer evidence from the victim. The fact that it was missing, obviously disposed of somewhere else, provided proof that the attacker had some forensic knowledge. The general pattern also established that there were multiple crime scenes stretching from the side door of the house into the sloping field below and leading to the final location in front of the gates and beside the bushes and briars and barbed wire of the border fence.

A blue plastic covering had been placed over the body to preserve it from the elements and contain any trace evidence of foreign blood, DNA or fibres deposited on the corpse or the clothes worn at the time of death. There is a common and repeated misconception that there was no forensic evidence at the scene to provide a link to or match with the perpetrator.

According to the famous French criminalist Dr Edmond Locard's Exchange Principle, the perpetrator of a crime will bring something to the scene and leave with something from it, and every contact leaves a trace. In this instance, there had been a frenzied contact between the killer and the victim, who had fought with every ounce of her small frame for her life.

While the killer, in this case say if a tall man or even one of average height with a long reach, may have had less direct contact with the tiny victim than a smaller man, he had moved the body when pulling it out of the briary bushes close to the barbed wire. It would be impossible to complete this action without leaving trace evidence on the body and particularly the clothes, if only fibres from his own clothes.

The American forensic scientist and criminalist Paul Kirk translated Locard thus: "Wherever he steps, whatever he touches, whatever he leaves even unconsciously will serve as a silent witness against him ... This is evidence that does not forget, it cannot perjure itself, it cannot be totally absent. Only human failure to find it, study and understand it, can diminish its value."

So, it is utterly clear that the killer must have left trace evidence both at the scene and on the body and clothes of the victim, and blood evidence, which had most probably been dispersed and contaminated by the elements. But its value in more ideal circumstances is only realised by matches with the killer, particularly blood evidence from the victim on his boots and his clothes.

If he washed himself thoroughly over time and destroyed everything he wore on the night – the duvet, sheets and mattress of the bed he slept in –there would be nothing left to provide the vital link. Therefore, it would be incumbent on the investigation team to move as quickly as possible in the circumstances.

An initial examination of the interior of the house revealed nothing out of the ordinary. There was no sign of a break-in or any struggle. The keys of the house were found in the locked main front door. The rear door was unlocked. Inside all appeared normal. The lights were off. There were two washed wine glasses beside the kitchen sink and an unfinished glass of wine in the living room. The book with the honey pot as a bookmark lay on a table with a bowl containing olives.

Now the lights were off? This might be explained in the context of loud and rapid knocking of the door, which caused Sophie to rush to open it to a daylight effect from the rays of the full moon.

Upstairs in the room which the victim had occupied, the sheets were pulled back from the mattress on the floor, with a cordless telephone next to it. Sophie's passport, a wallet with ten bills of twenty Irish pounds, several bank cards in her name and the keys of the hired Ford Fiesta car were also found in the room. The scene indicated clearly that Sophie had been in bed when the killer had called to the door. She had descended the stairs, put on her walking boots, went to the door, unlocked and opened it.

There is little doubt that she recognised the midnight rambler and wondered what had brought him to the house at such an unearthly hour of the night. Some introductory conversation must have ensued, during which he had revealed the purpose of the visit and was rejected out of hand. This rejection alone does not explain the explosion of rage and violence that followed. He may have laid hands on her in the act of making a pass and forcing his lascivious intentions on her.

The kindle hatchet in the pouch was close and possibly Sophie grabbed it and in an act of self-defence hit the attacker, who possibly pulled the weapon from her and struck the struggling woman, who then escaped through the door and ran into the garden in a vain effort to save her life. In the grip of explosive anger, he determined, as he had done before to another, to beat the living daylights out of the French woman, who not only had the gall to reject him but had also hit him.

The Bouniol family in Paris were totally unaware of what a terrible event had occurred, while by mid-afternoon in Toormore there had been a large media presence gathered outside the gate at a distance from the crime scene. The first journalist to receive information about an incident in the area was West Cork correspondent for the Cork-based *Examiner* newspaper, Eddie Cassidy. The tip-off gave him little detail other than that there had been a fatality in Toormore, the nature of which was not communicated other than the victim was a foreign national.

That gave him no clue, as West Cork had become a haven for foreign nationals of both means and none at all, such as a contingent of New Age travellers, a member of which Cassidy assumed could have figured. He had no idea of the import of the story and contacted several colleagues who worked for other media outlets, rightly assuming that there was safety in numbers in the matter of eliciting more information.

Among them was an out-of-work journalist, Ian Bailey, who had been contacted at 1.40 p.m. by Cassidy to check out a death in the area and who with this minimal information had driven straight to the crime scene. While he was on that short journey, journalist Cathy Farrell revealed in a 2 p.m. news bulletin on local radio station 98FM that the victim was a French national.

Shirley Foster told investigators later that on that day between 2.15 p.m. and 2.30 p.m., while outside the Garda protective cordon at the crime scene, she had come across Ian Bailey and Jules Thomas in a car, and when she told them that police had installed a barrier in the area, Bailey had replied that he was there on official business for the newspaper *The Examiner*.

As the day wore on and darkness fell, teams of officers took turns to protect the crime scene while other members of the investigation team were putting together the details of Sophie's movements and people she had met in the days since she had arrived. By now, the limited details of the murder had spread through the rural community like a wild-fire, causing shock, disbelief and fear, and reporters attempted to add some flesh to the bare bones of the story.

By mid-afternoon, a larger gathering of local and national media had assembled near the crime scene but were kept at a distance by the Gardai assigned to protect it. All had by now realised that this was in fact a huge story with international dimensions, as the victim was the wife of a famous French film producer, and a familiar figure in West Cork and frequent visitor to her holiday home which was now part of the crime scene. Soon it would become an international story, with the arrival of reporters from France and England.

Still neither the Irish police nor their French counterparts, for some reason, had managed to reach the family, a dreadful state of affairs which would magnify the grief both in the present and the future. Marguerite, Sophie's mother, was watching the 8 p.m. news bulletin which carried a small report about the murder of a Frenchwoman in West Cork. She was overwhelmed by the feeling that the then unnamed victim was her daughter. When Schull was mentioned, she knew for certain that it was Sophie.

Daniel was in Ambax, in the company of his good friend Gilles Jacob, distinguished chairman of the Cannes Film Festival, when he saw the same bulletin and said to him that it could not have been Sophie and then in fright began to try to work out what had happened. About 10 p.m., his son rang the house. Josephine Hellen answered but said as instructed by the police that she could not talk. Sophie's cousin Alexandra took on the task of trying to confirm her aunt's worst fear.

She managed to get hold of a member of the investigation team but was told that he had no authority to name the deceased. She eventually spoke to Josephine Hellen and asked her if Sophie was alive. The devastating answer which Josephine could not have avoided was, "NO." Her sister Patricia passed on the news to their mother Marie Madeleine, who in turn informed Georges and Marguerite, Sophie's parents. Daniel had received independent confirmation from the French Minister for Foreign Affairs.

The immediate family began making plans to travel to Cork. It was approaching midnight. Daniel decided not to travel as he had been given some details of the attack on his wife and could not bear to witness the horrible injuries on a woman he wanted to remember as her last saw her. This would later draw negative media comment but suffice it to say that people's reactions to bereavement differ; some confront and take charge whilst others withdraw.

The following day, December 24, after disembarking in Cork after a flight from Dublin, the State pathologist Dr John Harbison was driven to the crime scene, where he performed a preliminary examination of the corpse in situ starting at 3.57 p.m., just thirty hours after the discovery of the body.

He noted that the victim was a small woman measuring 1.66 metres in height, whose body was covered by a canvas sheet. She was lying on her back along the sidewalk near the entrance gate, the head slightly tilted towards the wall, left arm stretched over the body and the right elbow bent at a right angle at forty-five degrees from the body.

The right hand was under the corpse, and the head, shoulders and the right arm were covered with blood. Blood also stained the left arm, the abdomen and the region of the right hip. The victim wore a cotton T-shirt, long johns, socks and shoes with thick soles; her long johns were attached to an iron wire that marked the boundary of the lot and were partially torn at hip level.

The tear exposed the lower part of the abdomen, the pubis and part of the right hip and thigh. The bloodstains on her clothes were mostly circular in form, which suggested that they had fallen vertically over the long johns, instead of dripping from the head to the legs.

Gaping wounds were visible on the right side of the forehead – showing a depression on the skull from the eyebrow to the temporal bone – the lower part of the right ear was seriously cut and the right cheek had several abrasions. Beside the left shoulder and head was a stone that looked like a slate and was stained with blood. Between the body and the barbed wire was a prefabricated hollow building block with two cavities through its length, measuring eighteen inches long and nine square inches.

Moreover, similar blocks constituted the top part of a structure built around an electric pump 20 to 30 feet from where the body lay on a hill. They were not cemented together; one full block and a half were missing, and two others were displaced. The block that was beside the body seemed to come from this structure.

After assisting the investigator who was on site in covering the head with a plastic bag, a process that was revealed to be difficult because of the many tangles on the victim's hair, the pathologist noticed that rigor mortis had particularly set on the neck and right elbow. This indicated the slow progress of rigor mortis caused by the weather conditions.

It usually starts in the smaller muscles of the face and neck, and makes its way down, and could only be used as a guesstimate of the time of death.

Once the body was carefully removed, a blood-filled depression under the head was noted and the pathologist deduced that the body had already been in that position when the final blows were administered, as the spot contained the largest amount of blood pooling.

Samples were taken from under the nails of both hands; around a dozen hairs were attached and coiled around the right-hand fingers and two were attached to the back of the left hand. Similar samples were taken from the buccal, vulval, vaginal and thigh areas.

Afterwards, Dr Harbison and members of the investigation team followed the hearse containing the body to Cork University Hospital, where the pathologist performed a detailed post-mortem. This examination revealed further evidence of the brutal and horrific attack on Sophie Toscan du Plantier.

There was a tear on the upper lip, abrasions and a long laceration on the lower lip, a bone fracture on the face and there were multiple lacerations on the right temple and cheek. On the neck there was a grazed zone showing nine parallel scratches that suggested traces made by Dr. Martens-type boots or a jagged object that could have been used to slice the neck.

There was a linear abrasion under the stomach, and multiple scratches on the back – two clusters of which could correspond to blows from the concrete block – scratches on the buttocks and left arm, and two incisions on the base of the index finger, the former of which could have come from thorns and brambles and the latter from a sharp weapon.

On the right arm, there were two series of scratches which could have come from the Dr. Martens-type boots, an incision of the skin at the base of the right thumb and contusions at the back of the hand; on the legs there were isolated clusters of scratches at the back of the right thigh, the back part of the knee and behind the calf.

Dr Harbison concluded that death had been caused by multiple lesions on the head, with fractures to the skull and injury to the brain. The wounds to the hands were considered to be signs of defence, which demonstrated the fact that the victim had fought desperately hard for her life, prompting the attacker to inflict even greater injuries.

Most of the wounds were caused by blunt objects, one of which was light and the origin of minor wounds, and at least one other heavy and the origin of fractures on the skull and its base. The hollow block and large slate-like stone discovered near the body could have been used to inflict further wounds on the head.

There was the use of a Dr. Martens-type boot to inflict additional injuries to the neck area and the pathologist determined the time of death to be the night of December 22 or at the first hours of December 23.

The extent of cuts, lacerations, bruises and deeper wounds spoke of a frenzied and brutal attack, and included broken fingers sustained in a protective reaction, as well as hair from her head in a hand that had been caused also by an effort to protect injury from blows to the head. When a person is facing a strike in the face, he or she will automatically lower and turn their head away from the blow to protect their face and eyes. They will automatically place their hands in a protective gesture to shield the face, and thus will sustain severe injuries to the hands.

Some lighter wounds were caused by a missing weapon, the kindle hatchet, which the perpetrator had taken away and disposed of, while the extensive trauma to the face, head and shoulder areas were caused by the rock slate and the concrete block. Information on all of which was not released and was only known to the top tier of the investigation team.

All of the weapons had already been on the scene outside the house, therefore they were defined as weapons of opportunity utilised by an attacker in the grip of a deadly rage, probably sparked by rejection when he had been looking for sex and fuelled by alcohol and drugs. It would not be necessary to be a graduate of the FBI Quantico unit for an investigator of this crime to arrive at the conclusion that it was the work of a psychopath.

But even in the absence of a profiler who would provide a psychological portrait of the killer, the apparent random nature of the crime, the use of weapons of opportunity and the use of the rear door indicated a person with local knowledge and who had some knowledge, however slight, of the victim, her movements over the previous days and information that she would be alone for the first time at the location. It was not and could not have been the work of a stranger to the area or the location. The killer was also familiar with the layout of the house and surrounding grounds and countryside.

Since there had been apparently no sight or sound of a car in the area in the early hours of the morning, the killer would have faced making his way home by foot. But one woman in the area had heard a car driving by in the late hours of the morning.

But one way or another, there would have been no portion of his clothes, shoes, hands and hair that would not have been exempt from the blood of the victim.

Blood velocity from the impact of such an attack could travel up to 10 feet. Blood spatter on clothing does not drop away unless it is water repellent, and it was unlikely on a cold, dry day and night that the killer would have been wearing waterproof clothes.

There is no doubt that the attacker would have sustained cuts and grazes when pulling the victim away from the briar bushes and barbed wire, possibly on the face but certainly on the hands and forearms, which would have been difficult to conceal.

The backward arc of the sharp-edged hatchet used during striking would have deposited blood drops in the hair on both shoulders and on the back of the attacker's coat. It would have been considerably less than the front and sleeves, which would have absorbed more because of the position of the killer while attacking the victim.

Blood travels in a trajectory which is essentially parabolic or curved as a result of gravity, so there would be a large concentration of the victim's blood on the perpetrator's mid to lower coat, the exposed portion of the trousers and on the boots, which had to be close to where the greatest intensity of blood pooling was found next to the victim's head and one of which would have been used in a kicking action to the arm and neck. When a significant amount of blood is transferred to boots, even if the killer immerses them in water, evidence of the original blood will remain, especially on boots with ridged soles.

Blood is so viscous and sticky that even a high concentration on the soles would provide, depending on the terrain, a trail of no greater than 50 feet. The ground on and around the crime scene, given the temperature and weather conditions, was rock hard, so it was highly unlikely that sole impressions would have been left as might be the case in soft and wet conditions.

The most direct concentration of blood, tissue and fingerprint evidence would have been on the hatchet, so it would be a simple matter of ensuring that this was disposed of in conditions where it would be impossible to find until that evidence dissipated for the killer not to be connected with the scene or the crime.

There were a lot of factors in favour of the killer that night, including the location, the light of the full moon, the temperature, the underfoot conditions on rock-hard ground and the unlikely chance of being witnessed before, during or after the crime, and most importantly the lapse of time in weather conditions, which resulted in dissipation and contamination of forensic evidence.

This was also true of the nature of the two other weapons employed, the slate rock and the concrete block. Unless the user was losing blood from a deep wound sustained in the struggle, there would be little to connect or match him to the weapons. Fingerprints would not easily adhere to the slate surface, which could in any event be easily wiped, while this would be virtually impossible on the surface of a concrete block.

Had he sustained less severe wounds, for example a semi-deep head wound or surface lacerations to his hands or arms, it would be easy to stem any light seepage with a coat sleeve or handkerchief, as there would be no gushing or spattering without the velocity of blood incurred by more serious trauma. Even blood on a weapon like the hatchet is not easily displaced, and even vigorous shaking and swinging will displace only small drops. Blood drips from the face and hands act in the same way as from the weapon.

But the fact remained that the killer would never have been able to immediately get rid of the extensive blood evidence when he eventually arrived home, and he would have been well aware that he had left at the least fibre evidence on the scene and the body. Bloodstained clothes can be compromised as evidence in a limited manner by the application of a detergent such as bleach. The only completely effective way to dispose of them would be to burn them to ashes.

Members of the Bouniol family, including Sophie's parents Georges and Marguerite, Aunt Marie Madeleine and brother Bertrand, arrived in Cork on December 24. They were interviewed separately by police officers without an interpreter, which must have been trying, the difficulty emphasised by the fact that the parents didn't have anything like a comprehensive grasp of the English language.

Daniel Toscan du Plantier did not travel because he said that after conversations with the police, he knew the disfiguring extent of the injuries and wanted to preserve his memory of her beauty. Gilles Jacob would confirm that he had never seen someone so upset and Daniel had not got the courage to go to Ireland. Still, the stance is hard to understand or accept, particularly from a man of such status and power.

It was not a privilege her family could or would have chosen. They had to face the awful physical evidence of the nature of the killing. It was not until St Stephen's Day, December 26, that they were given permission to visit the funeral home in Cork where Sophie's body had been laid out. The prospect would have been emotionally difficult enough had they been viewing their beloved in her coffin with her beauty intact even with the assistance of the mortician's art.

That was not possible, such was the impact of the crushing injuries to the face and to her beautiful hands, with her shattered fingers encased in bandages.

Devastated by the loss, the savagery of her death and the contemplation of the terror of her last moments on Earth, the family's suffering was magnified by the fact that they could hardly recognise Sophie, and they had all been plunged into a waking nightmare. Inevitably, the grief of family and friends was accompanied by a sense of guilt that they had not been there to protect their beloved Sophie, and that had even one of them travelled with her to West Cork then this tragedy would never have happened.

Daniel later said in an interview that there was "a devil somewhere in the hills of Southern Ireland", and in his interaction with the press and family displayed more than adequate evidence of his grief. He said that the tragedy was too much for many of his colleagues, and that the film-maker with whom Sophie had such an intense debate in the Paris club the night before her departure had never spoken to him since.

"I think he just cannot bear to experience the emotion and grasp the reality of what happened. Nobody imagines that it happens to their friend or relative, but to Sophie ... it was inconceivable that such a bright, talented, ambitious woman could suffer this fate. Nobody could speak of it without emotion."

The famous French film director Maurice Pialat lived next

door to their country home in Ambax. Daniel had produced his Cannes award-winning film *Under the Sun of Satan*, and the director had become friendly with Sophie and was naturally devastated by her death. As a measure of his affection for her, he told Daniel that he may have lived with great French actresses, but that Sophie was the star.

For the Bouniol family, that experience would not be limited to one jurisdiction, and the sense of alienation that it produced had already begun during their first contact with the Irish authorities, where they were greeted with scepticism and officious coldness that characterises the establishment and progress of a criminal investigation.

CHAPTER 2
A PERSON OF INTEREST

West Cork – 1996–97

On the afternoon of December 24, Josephine Hellen was brought to the house by detectives to ascertain if she noticed anything unusual in the interior of the home with which, as the caretaker, she would have been familiar. After close examination of the kitchen area and the living room, she could not find anything amiss. Everything appeared to be in order. However, she did notice that a pouch inside the rear door was empty. It normally contained a small kindle hatchet that might be used to chop wood. This confirmed that it was highly likely that the killer had gained entrance to the kitchen even just by a few steps. Sophie would not have allowed this to happen if the visitor was a total stranger to her, indicating that she was aware of his identity and had had some interaction with him, however fleeting, in the past. The killer would also have had knowledge of the immediate interior, including the kitchen area and the table where Sophie had been sitting.

The Bouniol family returned to Paris on December 26. The following day, Sophie's body was brought from Cork to Dublin, then flown to Paris, and then on December 28 transferred to Toulouse to await a ceremony and burial. It is almost unimaginable what the impact of this ghastly tragedy was having on the members of the particularly close-knit family.

This was a huge story for the media, both nationally and internationally, and once Christmas Day was done there was a flurry of activity. Ann Mooney was the southern correspondent of the *Irish Daily Mirror* based in Cork at the time.

"I was in Cork city doing last minute Christmas shopping when I received a call from a colleague asking if I had heard about a woman being killed in West Cork near Schull. I had not, so I began to make calls to numerous contacts and to other journalists, including those working in local radio stations. No one appeared to have heard any details, but it emerged soon after that the woman was not Irish and had been killed near her holiday home in Toormore.

"Because it was the day before Christmas Eve and there would be no newspapers published on Christmas Day, we really did not get working full tilt until St Stephen's Day. The name and circumstances began to emerge, and I headed to West Cork but could not get near the scene because of the Garda presence. I spoke to locals and followed the usual type of news gathering associated with a murder."

On December 27, two members of the investigation team, Garda Bart O'Leary and Garda Kevin Kelleher, were in Tom Brosnan's supermarket in Schull, where they saw Ian Bailey, the freelance journalist who was now reporting on the murder for several newspapers. Garda O'Leary did not know him but was informed by his colleague of his identity. Bailey was pale, rattled-looking and unshaven, and pushed customers aside to get to the counter.

When he asked the shop assistant for a copy of *The Irish Times*, the officers noticed the top of his hands and wrists were covered in scratches.

When he saw the officers, he made a hasty exit from the shop while looking back at them all the time. A journalist under normal circumstances would have approached the members of the Garda and enquired about updates in the investigation; instead, he spurned the opportunity and fled the premises.

This encounter was sufficient to arouse suspicion and it was decided to pay him a visit at the home Bailey shared with his partner Jules Thomas at the Prairie, Liscaha, some 12 kilometres outside Schull. In local geographical terms, the house was located about 4.6 kilometres from the crime scene.

They were not the only members of the investigation team to be struck by certain behaviour manifested by Bailey. Garda Martin Malone from Schull Station was at the crime scene when Bailey turned up at 2.30 p.m. Bailey was well dressed in a long black coat and instead of hanging around with the rest of the media posse, he made a hasty departure, which struck the officer as strange.

"He departed too quickly, and this made me suspicious of him. I heard that some days later he was back at the crime scene. He had gone up the lane past the Garda cordon to Alfie Lyons's house and told Gardai that he had a message for him. This made me furious and suspicious, and I wondered if Bailey was trying to compromise the crime scene. I nominated him as a good suspect at the incident room in Bandon Garda Station."

It is one thing to harbour suspicion but quite another to develop reasonable suspicion. There is, in addition, the considerable legal implications of fingering a suspect, sticking dangerously to the script if the decision is mistaken in terms of not just damage to the immediate case but possible future negative consequences including considerable financial damages. Thus, caution on the part of an investigation team is entirely understandable.

Nonetheless, failure to identify a suspect in a timely fashion can afford the opportunity to dispose of vital evidence, provide a false alibi and ultimately provide the route to evade prosecution. Murder investigation, in common with any human activity, is not free from the matter of risk-taking. Sometimes, instinct can supplant and triumph over the rules of reason and science, and banish caution to the vault of weakness and inaction. This inherent dilemma would prove to have a huge and complex role to play in the future of this case.

On December 28, as part of neighbourhood inquiries, Gardai Kelleher and O'Leary visited the house shared by Ian Bailey and his partner Jules Thomas. They asked them to fill in a questionnaire prepared for the investigation which required an account of their movements before, during and after the date of the crime.

While there, Garda O'Leary asked Ian Bailey where the wounds on his hands came from and he replied that he sustained them while cutting the top of their Christmas tree.

When he removed his coat, the police noted that the cuts and scratches extended up to his elbows. They appeared to the investigators the type of wounds that might have been caused by contact with thorns, brambles or barbed wire. They also noted a deep cut on the right side of Bailey's forehead.

In the answers given in the questionnaire, Bailey stated that on the night of December 22, 1996 he went to the Courtyard bar in Schull with Jules Thomas and remained there until the closing hour, and they went home at midnight. (This was incorrect; they went first to the Courtyard for a drink and then to the Galley pub, where they stayed until closing time.)

He said that he had never met the victim except once eighteen months previously. Jules Thomas in her answers said that they had left the pub at 11.15 p.m. and collected her daughter before driving home. Bailey called into the police station afterwards to change some details of his answers.

As a result of some contradiction between Bailey's and Thomas's accounts, it was decided that investigators would call round to them at their home to interview them once more.

Two different Garda officers, Detective Garda Paul Culligan and Detective Garda Denis Harrington, went to the house at the Prairie on December 31, as part, they said, of their door-to-door enquiries. The Cork city-based detectives had been drafted in to help with the investigation and were detailed to concentrate their attention on everything to do with Ian Bailey.

They asked him to explain the cause of the wound above his right eyebrow and the scratches on his hands. He answered that he had sustained the injuries chopping the top of a pine for a Christmas tree and from killing three turkeys, which he said he had to deliver to customers on the 23rd. All these actions, he said, had happened on the morning of December 22, the turkeys having been killed around noon and both in the company of Jules's daughter Saffron Thomas.

He gave a sketchy account of his movements and said that on December 22 he had been at the Courtyard pub, where he had stayed until about midnight. This was again wrong, as he had spent most of the evening at the Galley pub. He had returned home and slept all night. In the morning, he brought coffee to Jules at about 9 a.m. and went back to sleep until 10 a.m.

He did some housework and at around 2 p.m. he got a call from Eddie Cassidy about a murder. He and Jules went to the site then but did not stay for long. They went to the local post office and found the name Bouniol in the telephone directory. They returned to the crime scene with photographer Mike Brown and met Eddie Cassidy at around 4 p.m.

The statement from Jules Thomas in relation to their movements on the night of December 22 was much in line with her partner's, including the error about being in the Courtyard pub all evening. There was a fleeting reference to some violence that she had suffered at his hands, but they had been reconciled afterwards and had a good relationship. They had both travelled to the scene of the crime, as he had stated, after Bailey had received a call from news reporter Eddie Cassidy from *The Examiner* to check a death in the area.

The most important issue in Bailey's account was in relation to his explanation for how he had sustained the wounds. It should have and did arouse suspicion, to the extent that demanded an immediate response. The pertinent fact to establish was when exactly those wounds were sustained, either before or after the crime. There were also several other statements he had made in the interview that required further investigation.

The investigators were not at all convinced that Ian Bailey had sustained the scratches in the manner he claimed, nor on the date he had nominated. As he had been out drinking most of that night in a packed pub, customers or people in his company must have noticed the scratches or not.

It is a rule of thumb that the investigation of a murder should not focus too early in an exclusive way on any single suspect. In most cases, the widening and narrowing in the selection process of suspects makes sense in large towns and cities. In a small rural area where such a crime is a rarity, it is arguable that a narrower focus is more appropriate to a sparsely populated area. A person with a history of sadistic violence towards a female would stand out in the area of Toormore and justifiably be deserving of quick attention as a suspect.

Furthermore, it had been abundantly obvious that the killer had knowledge of both the remote region and the house and the immediate surroundings, and more than likely of the victim and the fact that she had travelled alone for the first time. Even a local flatfoot would not need to be Sherlock Holmes to deduce from the brutality of the murder and the sequence of attacks that the perpetrator might have sustained cuts and grazes, as it was obvious that the victim had attempted to escape through the thorn bushes beside the gate and had been pulled back by the killer.

On December 31, while Bailey and Thomas were being interviewed by investigators, Sophie was being laid to rest in France in the Mauvezin Cemetery in Gers, in the south-western region where her husband had a property. The service and eulogy incensed the Bouniol family, who felt marginalised as Daniel stood centre stage and the priest delivered a speech on cinema. Where, the family were entitled to ask, was Sophie in all this?

It was traumatic for them, according to a close family friend, Jean-Antoine Bloc: "It was difficult for them when the funeral, such an important personal ceremony, became the platform for the emotions of Daniel Toscan du Plantier's friends and family, an opportunity for the priest Joseph Marty to deliver a lecture on the science of cinema and an attraction for a horde of journalists. For the family, the memory of that day remains unbearable. Some regret not having walked out on a eulogy in which Sophie was almost a side note."

It was only the beginning of their journey of pain and suffering, Jean-Antoine added: "They felt pushed aside and excluded and suffered a new and different kind of pain. This could not be said to be the fault of any particular institution, although the Government was represented at the funeral. Looking back, that was the day they started to feel that they had been left alone with their loss, that beyond lip service to their suffering the responsible institutions were not doing their duty. Occasionally, condolences were expressed, but Sophie's friends had enough sadness without suffering the compassion of others. What they needed was action."

It appeared from the circumstances that the victim in advance of the ghastly crime was on a life trajectory of an upward curve, with personal happiness and professional success in the future, while the killer was on a downward arc, with an accumulation of life reverses, disillusionment and anger as a consequence. A ticking psychological time bomb waiting for a destructive emotional release.

So, who was the man that slipped outside the shop in Schull, evading the attention of the two officers inside and becoming a person of interest in the crime, and who would soon become the expert on the murder to whom news agencies and reporters would defer for vital information on the case?

Ian Bailey was born in Manchester, England in 1957, but grew up in Gloucestershire, where he attended the Crypt Grammar School and proved to be a promising pupil. His towering athletic physique was ideal for rugby and he played second row for a local club. He trained as a journalist and secured a position working for a local news service, the Gloucester and County News Service, in 1975, which provided stories for national newspapers including *The Times*, *Daily Mirror*, *The Sunday Times* and *The Daily Telegraph*, as well as TV stations HTV and BBC West.

John Hawkins was the editor of the agency and remembers Bailey joining at nineteen years of age. "Even as a fresh young reporter he was confident and brash. He quickly learned the trade but soon became bored with the humdrum day-to-day routine of local journalism. He seemed more interested in the social opportunities the job offered and never missed a chance for a party or lunch. He did his fair share of drinking and socialising at Gloucester's Old Cryptians Rugby Club, where he played as a second row forward."

He left the agency in 1978 after qualifying as a journalist and began in opposition to the agency where he had trained from Cheltenham, 10 miles away. He specialised in espionage stories with links to the nearby Government Communications Headquarters in Cheltenham, where he was based for eight years. He was one of the reporters involved in breaking the story of the Geoffrey Prime spy scandal at GCHQ, the top-secret eavesdropping base. Prime, who had been selling secrets to the Russians, was jailed for thirty-eight years.

Journalist George Henderson, who worked with him at the time, remembers him as a man who liked his pints and the ladies, and who was confident of his ability. "He always talked big. He was bursting with ideas for making his fame and fortune and was ambitious."

He married journalist Sarah Limbrick in 1980, the daughter of a wealthy property developer and former journalist Malcolm and Jill Limbrick. They moved into a large house, but the marriage ran into difficulties and they separated four years later; the divorce process, which was not finalised until 1988, was described as bitter and acrimonious.

During the court proceedings, she gave evidence of violent tendencies, not involving beating her but smashing household items, an addiction to drink and drugs, and having extramarital affairs. She described him as being selfish, mean and dishonest, and alleged that he had falsified her signature for a life insurance contract. She would go much further later about a life-threatening incident.

The promising start to his career had been undone, as well as his marriage, by unstable behaviour which would continue to be manifested in the future. He drifted in search of new horizons between London and the U.S. before going to Dublin, briefly to West Cork, then to Wicklow and finally to Schull back in West Cork in 1991. There he worked in a fish factory for a short time, where he met a local artist of Welsh origin, Jules Thomas, and later moved into her home outside Schull, where she lived with three daughters from two previous relationships.

By any manner or means, it could be said that the drifter had landed on his feet. Jules was a beautiful woman, a talented artist who specialised in land and seascape paintings, with a comfortable abode unencumbered financially. Bailey was a striking figure, with long, lank, jet-black hair, an aura about him which had he been an actor could have provided ideal casting as Heathcliff. They could have been perceived as a golden couple in the making.

He had ambitions to be a writer, a poet in particular, and was possessed of undoubted intelligence, based in a region, however remote, containing like-minded people of creative skills who found the surroundings conducive to their work. Here was an opportunity for Ian Bailey to turn the past negatives of his life into positives and productive activity. But any creative pursuit is not founded in indolence but rather the application of discipline and hard graft.

For that purpose, he would have to leave behind the inclinations noticed by his former colleagues in journalism to talk big and fantasise about becoming rich and famous, and temper his appetite for both alcohol and drugs. In fairness to him, he also realised that he had to bring in some money, so he began to do some work in gardening, which may have caused him some resentment about his status, but he did it. He also had a need to be accepted by the new community he had joined, so he developed an interest in Irish traditional music.

It appeared that he was craving acceptance in the artistic community at least and had attempted to adopt a Celtic persona by changing his first name to Eoin and his second name to O'Baille. He then learned to play a traditional Irish percussion instrument, the bodhran, which no more than others like the accordion, fiddle or harp required considerable time to acquire even basic competence. Bailey, as with his gardening and poetry, was not prepared to put in the time and work, and yet would attempt to play the goatskin instrument in O'Sullivan's pub in Ballydehob in front of an audience.

John Montague and his then partner and later wife Elisabeth Wassell, whom I interviewed many years ago at length in their home in West Cork, had by chance become well acquainted with Bailey. They first met him in O'Sullivan's pub in Ballydehob in the winter of 1994, when he introduced himself and passed on his card, mentioning that he had an interest in gardening. A poet, John was much in demand, such was his reputation on the international literary circuit, so much so that they needed someone to tend their garden, which became wildly overgrown during their frequent absences. John rang him and asked Bailey to cut it back and keep it in shape.

As the Englishman also had creative aspirations as a poet, the job provided an opportunity on a casual basis of securing a mentor for a fledgling writer sitting at the table of a master. He would first have to prove himself competent regarding the job for which he had been hired.

Later, the couple returned from a foreign trip to find the grass overgrown, weeds thriving and bushes and trees with no sign of having been attended. The gardener was obviously disorganised, neglectful and indolent, deficiencies which in the matter of tending such horticultural necessities are impossible to conceal. His employer was patient and was introduced to the gardener's creative ambitions with what Montague described as scraps of songs and poems which "lacked the tedious, concentrated work of a serious writer".

During the early years of their acquaintance, John and Elisabeth displayed tolerance and patience towards Bailey; they had plenty of reason to do otherwise but decent people as they were, they held their counsel. That would change when, some years later, they would collaborate for an article on the case for *The New Yorker* magazine.

So, Ian Bailey was a man of unfulfilled ambition – a poor gardener and bodhran player and lacking the discipline that might have improved the doggerel that masqueraded as poetry. His adoption of a Celtic persona would not have met the approval of locals and was considered more than faintly ridiculous when accompanied by a distinct English accent.

He got involved in a State-funded training course (FAS) and tried documentary film scriptwriting in 1995 for a project entitled "Changing Times" about the region. It got nowhere, as did his attempt to renew his journalism career at the start of the following year, with him just having a few small pieces published by the *Irish Examiner* and a local paper, *The Southern Star*.

But the murder, as he would boast to locals and journalists, had resurrected his career, and he was fast becoming the self-appointed expert on the crime, writing articles and supplying information to Irish and French national newspapers. So intense was his self-aggrandisement and concentration on his career that he talked of continuing his investigation in France having established a French connection.

In the grip of hubris, he did not recognise the danger of elevating his status to ringmaster of the media circus and unwittingly revealing damning facts in between the fiction and the facts.

Meanwhile, back in Sophie's beloved West Cork, police officers kept up the relentless pace of the investigation into the murder. But there was another jurisdiction – as a result of the complications of the case – also involved, albeit for the moment in a more limited fashion.

Under the laws of France, the French courts have jurisdiction to prosecute and put on trial an accused person in relation to the murder of a French citizen even when the crime takes place in another country and jurisdiction. Article 113.7 of the Penal Code states:

"*French criminal law is applicable to any felony as well as any misdemeanour punished by imprisonment, committed by a French or foreign national outside the territory of the French Republic, where the victim is a French national at the time the offence took place.*"

The jurisdiction is exercised under what is known as the "passive personality principle", which is one of the five bases recognised under customary international law whereby a state may exercise extraterritorial jurisdiction where the victim of a crime is a national of that state. While both Ireland and France had on that basis equal interest in prosecuting the crime, there would naturally be a question as to whether the former would intrude on the sovereignty of the latter where the crime took place whatever the valid interests of both.

It would be important in the early stages that the domestic investigation should not be undermined by premature action on behalf of the birth State of the victim. It was in the ultimate interests of both countries that a prosecution of an accused person should be carried out both successfully and fairly on his behalf and also that of the victim and her family, despite the clarity or otherwise of international legislation. If the home state decided not to prosecute the crime, then a whole new scenario would unfold which would somewhat diminish the complexities of the issues involved.

Nonetheless, the investigation of the murder of Sophie Toscan du Plantier would require co-operation between the judicial authorities of both countries. At the time, the only formal manner to pursue this was by the issuing of a letter or request for co-operation and gathering of evidence. It was tenuous to say the least, and obviously there would be the matter of the local investigation not being compromised in any way.

Yet it was in the interest of both jurisdictions in the pursuit of justice to facilitate interviews with witnesses and the gathering of evidence which would involve both countries despite radical differences in legal and practical approaches to murder investigation. In France, the procedure is more direct, with the crime under the authority of an examining magistrate who controls the investigation, meets with police officers, evaluates evidence and hears the testimony of witnesses.

If there is conclusive or corroborating evidence implicating a suspect, the magistrate may place the suspect under "*mise en examen*", a procedure which focuses on the suspect and the equivalent in France of an indictment or pressing charges. When that process is completed, the file is handed to a public prosecutor who guides the case in the criminal courts.

In Ireland, the crime is investigated by the relevant police authorities, and when the file is complete it is sent to the office of the Director of Public Prosecutions (DPP), where it is evaluated and a decision is arrived at whether to either prosecute the case in the courts, leave it open in the event of new evidence or drop it altogether. The assessment of the DPP has no evidential value; its officers never go to a crime scene or in any way replicate the work of an examining magistrate. The decisions are made without leaving the desk and are based on a legal opinion and as such are open to error.

The shaky framework for co-operation was exposed when in January 1997, members of the Irish investigation team arrived in Paris to question Sophie's associates; their letter of request was deemed invalid by the French judicial authorities and the officers were confined to their hotel. The iniquities of red tape would not be confined to one side; the Irish Department of Justice would subsequently not respond to letters of request from French magistrates and would fail to inform the Garda authorities of the communications.

However, there was evidence of some co-operation in the domestic inquiries, including interviews with a French native and possible suspect, and with friends and colleagues of the victim. During a rocky passage in her marriage, Sophie had met a man at an arts event in Paris and embarked on an affair in 1992. Bruno Carbonnet was an artist and professor of painting and had travelled to Toormore three times in 1993. He was interviewed by police in Rouen on December 28, 1996. Later, he was arrested and placed in custody on January 16, 1997 as requested by the Irish authorities. He was released the following day when his presence in Paris on December 23, 1996 was confirmed by a receipt signed by him for a telephone installation and corroborated by a France Telecom technician.

During his questioning, Carbonnet claimed that Daniel Toscan du Plantier had known about the affair and he said that Sophie was tough but fragile, secretive and discreet.

He told investigators: "Madame Toscan du Plantier for me was an intimate friend during 1992 and 1993. I have known her since the spring of 1992, when she was introduced to me at a meeting of the workshop of the arts centre of the Ephemeral Hospital in Paris. We afterwards became lovers. We went to Goleen together to the simple house where I stayed and helped to set herself up.

"The last time I went to the house was in the summer of 1993. She finished it (the relationship) without any warning. This end was hard for me. The last occasion I saw her was at her funeral in Père Lachaise Cemetery in Paris in March 1994."

He obviously had a greater commitment to the relationship than she did, as he related that when she abruptly ended the affair without apparent explanation at Christmas 1993, he took it hard, so badly that he allegedly attacked her on a Metro and the police had to be called to intervene. He was in France at the time of the murder, his alibi stood up and he joined a list of ten early suspects to be eliminated.

Agnes Thomas, the best friend of the victim, provided a narration of her contacts with Sophie before and during her fateful trip to West Cork. She had a conversation with her on December 20, 1996 while Sophie was at Charles de Gaulle Airport and recounted that she was in good form and looking forward to the journey to Ireland. Later that day, at about 11.15 p.m., they conversed again, and Sophie said that she had arrived safely and everything in the house in Toormore was in order thanks to Josephine Hellen, the caretaker.

Sophie confirmed that she would be sleeping in the bedroom above the kitchen as the house was so cold. On December 22, which was the birthday of Agnes, she rang past midnight and listened to a voice message left at 6.32 p.m. Paris time, one hour later than Irish time, in which Sophie wished her happy birthday and asked her to call back later that evening. Agnes did not, as it was already so late. On December 23, at about 10 p.m., she rang Sophie several times, but her calls were left unanswered.

Agnes said that Sophie was a romantic and lovable person who conversed comfortably with anyone she met in the street or in a pub. She added that Sophie wore warm long johns when going to bed, underclothes which they had bought together on a trip to Schull in 1993–94.

Alexandra Levy, Sophie's cousin, stated that several days before her trip to West Cork, Sophie had received a phone call at Les Champs Blancs, her production office in Paris, from a man who lived in the region of her holiday house. According to Alexandra, the man claimed to be a journalist and writer, and wanted to meet her for cultural purposes, and Sophie was both surprised by the call and by the man's refusal to reveal where he had obtained the telephone number of the company, but it did not worry her.

Alexandra could not recall the name of the man as communicated by Sophie but said that it certainly did fit Ian Bailey in many respects.

With these exceptions, a shadow of lassitude, inaction and incompetent bureaucracy would be cast over the case which would unfortunately persist for many years. On January 17, 1997, Daniel Toscan du Plantier, and Georges and Margaret Bouniol, filed a complaint under the status of *parties civiles* which under law allows injured parties such as the family of victims to be integrated into the criminal prosecution procedure. The counts were intentional homicide, murder and premeditated murder under the French criminal code.

There was no immediate response to the complaint, and it appeared that the French authorities were dragging their heels, perhaps for diplomatic reasons and the fear of being seen to interfere or intervene with the Irish investigation. Such concerns, however understandable, were unjustified given the bare fact that by law they were enabled to investigate the murder, however limited the framework for co-operation.

Even without trampling over the Irish investigation, the French action could have continued more actively on native soil. For example, in the matter of inaction there was no second autopsy before Sophie's burial and neither her belongings, diaries, phone and computer records nor personal effects were obtained and examined. When eventually, after pressure from the family, an examining magistrate was appointed, the case file was empty.

The Bouniol family lawyer Alain Spilliaert explained: "In the present case, the responsibility for initiating an agreement lay with the French political authorities. The law in France contains certain provisions virtually unknown in Ireland, which meant the French Government was in a unique position to take the first step, to lay the foundations for a bridge over a legal gulf. The lack of determination on the part of the French authorities was reinforced by a kind of complacency towards their Irish counterparts. Around the end of 1996, the Irish Minister for Justice and the Gardai reiterated their commitment to leave no stone unturned in the investigation and asserted their confidence that the matter would soon come to a satisfactory conclusion."

Time, though short enough in terms of an investigation at this stage, was still running out to realise the aspiration of the Irish authorities. Already there had been a long delay of five days between the officers noting the wounds on Bailey and the visit to his house. Even with the necessity to make certain enquiries in the interim, it was still too long. They returned to take a sample of his hair in order to establish DNA and comparison with blood samples taken at the scene. He willingly co-operated for a good reason which only he knew.

There was an atmosphere of fear and paranoia in the local community which across the region amounted to about 2,000 people. One of the aspects of life there that had appealed to Sophie was the open-door policy and long-standing Irish rural practice whereby neighbours left their doors unlocked so that if they needed anything like household goods – milk, butter or sugar – they were given free access. Such trust was endemic and there had been no reason to have it challenged over the years.

Journalist Ann Mooney captured the mood: "The murder impacted greatly on the people of Schull, Goleen and the surrounding areas because they always prided themselves in welcoming people into their areas and crime was always at a low level. For such a brutal murder in their midst cast a shadow over the communities in the region."

The atmosphere in the region had changed utterly and trust through fear of the monster was blown away like branches in a storm, and doors were padlocked and chained. Local people were under no illusions despite fictional newspaper reports, and knew that the murderer lived amongst them and was more than capable of killing again. It was the depths of winter, and darkness reigned. Women living alone were obviously the most vulnerable and some sold up and moved out.

The tragedy was an affront to the decent values of people and the horror seeped into every household like the floodwaters of a river that had burst its banks. Peace and tranquillity had been the order of the day in the region for over two decades since the assassination of the Irish patriot Michael Collins in 1922. Schull was a town, as Agent Cooper describes the town Twin Peaks in David Lynch's show of the same name, where "a yellow light means slow down, not speed up".

Yeats's lines from "The Second Coming" summed it up:

The blood-dimmed tide is loosed, and everywhere
The ceremony of innocence is drowned;
The best lack all conviction, while the worst
Are full of passionate intensity.

The caretaker Josephine Hellen and her family lived only a mile away from the crime scene and she was terrified. She had not slept since the body was discovered and under no circumstances would she remain in the house on her own. There is little doubt, given her relationship with Sophie, the fact that she and her husband had to identify the body at the scene and that the sheer enormity of the event would have led to her suffering from post-traumatic stress.

Bill Hogan, who sold cheese to Sophie, found as the weeks passed that the feeling of emptiness, loss and fear increased, and he could not keep the savage destruction of the stylish, elegant and beautiful woman he knew out of his mind and imagination, especially their last meeting just four months before, when she looked as if she had stepped out from the pages of *Vogue*. Leo Bolger, who maintained the house for her, felt the loss acutely and said that the place and the people would never be the same again.

It was as if the blood at the crime scene had spread across the spiritual map of West Cork, staining the valley, the moors, the rocks, the fields and the rivers, seeping from the branches of trees, bushes on mountain paths, the sky, the sea and the land everywhere that captured the imagination and inspired the love and devotion of a beautiful, intelligent and talented Frenchwoman, destroyed by a devil who also took away the lightness and the wonderful appeal of the area and replaced it with a sickening and toxic overhanging cloud.

The fright and terror of the people was intensified by the knowledge that the killer was still among them, walking the streets of Schull, Goleen and Skibbereen at will and wherever he wished, visiting the pubs and shops. In a big city, he would have melted into the crowd and disappeared into another street, house or suburb. But not in West Cork, where no one had suddenly fled or moved out as would be expected, proving that this was a brazen and uninhibited monster not possessed of remorse and therefore likely to kill a woman again, as he was a coward in the company of men.

This "poisonous atmosphere", as John Montague described it, also induced a sense of shame amongst the inhabitants as a result of the nature of the killing and the personality of the victim and her attachment to the area. It was as if they could or should have done something to prevent it or anticipate the bloody intentions of the perpetrator. It was an entirely natural reaction in a place where murder was unknown and where peace had reigned for such a long time.

The initial investigation was based in Bantry Garda Station, where the district officer was in overall charge of the management of the case, assisted by detectives from West Cork divisional quarters. A team of detectives from the National Bureau of Criminal Investigation (NBCI) was also sent to assist in the investigation. Headquarters of the investigation would in the following year be moved to Bandon Garda Station, as the facilities proved inadequate for the scale of the inquiry.

The incident room was a hive of activity, with members of the investigation team sorting through completed questionnaires, notes of door-to-door inquiries and interviews with potential witnesses. The name of Ian Bailey was beginning to loom larger, as officers began to review and cross-check the results of various enquiries. There were inquiries pursued to check his version of how he sustained the wounds. Denis O'Callaghan, owner of a small store at Lowertown, Schull, told investigators that Bailey had come into the shop around noon on December 24.

When the storeman asked him how he was, he replied, "I hope it will get better in a few hours." He appeared pale and anxious, and O'Callaghan noticed scratches on the back of his left hand that seemed to have been caused by brambles. He asked for a new saw blade. He left and went back half an hour later to collect the tool and bought chicken food, two bales of briquettes and a litre of bleach. The purpose of the last item could have been legitimate, but it just so happens to be an agent also utilised for the removal of stains, including blood from clothes.

Investigators then concentrated on interviewing staff and customers who were in the Galley pub on the night of December 22 and who had seen or encountered Ian Bailey during the approximately two hours he had spent there, to establish if anyone had seen the wounds he said had occurred that day cutting the fir tree and killing the turkeys. Bernadette Kelley had been there from 11 p.m. until midnight. A man who she later identified as Bailey was sitting beside her telling a story and playing the bodhran.

He appeared drunk, unshaven and dishevelled, but she did not notice any scratches on his hands or arms while he was playing. Chris Lynch, who had worked with Bailey in the fish factory, saw him in the Galley pub on the night in question and they had talked. He had not seen any scratches on the hands of his former co-worker.

John McGowan, the barman, had served Bailey five times during the evening and obviously had a close view of his hands, but also did not see any scratches. Bailey had rolled up his sleeves to play the bodhran and nobody saw evidence of the wounds he had claimed to have sustained earlier that day.

David Galvin, the owner of the bar, said that the interior was brightly lit, with five 60-watt lamps over the location where Bailey played the bodhran. He stated that Bailey and Thomas had left at half past midnight.

It was abundantly clear to the investigation team from those witness statements and the observations of Gardai O'Leary and Kelleher that Ian Bailey had not sustained the wounds on the date he claimed. The way he said he had got them would later be tested.

CHAPTER 3
MURDER HE WROTE

West Cork – 1996–97

Meanwhile, over the following weeks, Bailey – without any Garda sources – was working overtime supplying stories to newspapers which liberally mixed fact with fiction, so determined was he to demonstrate that he was the journalist on the spot, with the unrivalled insight into the crime and everything surrounding the dreadful event. In this hasty pursuit, he revealed details about the crime scene and injuries to the body of the victim that only a person who was there on the night of the murder could have known.

He went as far as to tell some reporters that he was investigating the crime as the local police officers had not a clue what they were doing and knew nothing about murder investigation. An attitude that would be foreign to any crime reporter hoping to get vital information from police sources when this was also patently untrue. Top crime investigators from both Dublin and Cork had been brought in from the beginning to assist local police.

Bailey had apparently first been contacted by acting news editor and reporter Eddie Cassidy from *The Examiner* at 1.40 p.m. on December 23, to check out a death in the area. Cassidy had received a phone call from a contact earlier saying there had been an incident down west. He then rang Bantry Garda Station and was referred to Schull Station.

He was told by a police officer that a body had been found, a woman's body. While he had also contacted local priest Fr Cashman at 12.15 p.m. and Superintendent Twomey some minutes later, neither would give any details.

Cassidy was unequivocal about the nature of the call: "He [Superintendent Twomey] didn't give any specific details about the nationality, age or anything about her other than the fact that the body had been found. There was nothing suspicious mentioned, nothing to give me any indication that we had a murder on our hands. I made some general checks but got no formal details. About twenty minutes later, I phoned Ian Bailey because he lived in the immediate area. I said there had been a body found somewhere and said it was on the road."

In possession of this sparse information, Bailey was able to decipher where the body lay and the identity of the woman, and was driven by his partner Jules Thomas straight to the crime scene, arriving at 2.30 p.m. It was noted by Gardai that he asked no questions of the two uniformed officers present, including anything about the victim. Which was strange for a journalist, seeking no information about anything related to the case. He departed shortly afterwards.

He returned after 4 p.m., by which time Eddie Cassidy was there and filed a report to his own newspaper while Bailey, using the first name Eoin, began to file regular reports to the *Irish Daily Star* and the *Sunday Tribune*, and provide information on the crime to French and English publications.

On the surface and in the rush to print of a major story, it appeared that Bailey was just doing the job with a renewed efficiency that he had displayed over two decades earlier when first working in England.

News editors who commissioned his copy were glad at first to have a local correspondent with good knowledge of the area and seemingly the inside track on the story which, like any high-profile murder and this with international dimensions, prompted huge rivalry between news organisations.

Ian Bailey was promoting himself as not just a hack but an investigative reporter who was breaking exclusive stories and who was the first port of call for foreign outlets such as *Paris Match*. He first contacted the *Star* on December 23 and his contribution provided the bulk of the local part of the report which ran under a full-page headline the following day:

WOMAN IS BATTERED TO DEATH YARDS FROM HOME

On December 26, his name or by-line as it is known appeared as Eoin Bailey on a story in the *Star* newspaper under the main headline:

QUESTIONS ON VICTIM'S FINAL HOURS

And the sub-headline:

HUNT INTENSIFIES

He re-wrote a Garda press release appeal for information. Just days after the murder, on December 23, when Bailey had no sources in the investigation, he had been told by a Garda protecting the perimeter near the crime scene, when he presented himself as a journalist for *The Examiner*, to contact the Garda Press Office. He had details in the small article that were only known to a select few of the top echelon of investigators, who confirmed that they never gave him information at that time or any other time during the investigation.

"Ms Du Plantier had been beaten to death with a blunt instrument. A post-mortem revealed that she died of multiple head injuries and was not sexually assaulted."

With the first sentence, giving the benefit of doubt, he could have made a calculated guess. But not with the second. The post-mortem had only been carried out on the day of Christmas Eve, the details of which he could not possibly have known, specifically about the absence of a sexual assault. It would take weeks and laboratory tests on vaginal swabs to establish that fact. On the other hand, a detail that he could have easily checked, and which was in the public domain he got completely wrong:

"*Local farmer Finbar Hellen found her body while out checking his stock.*"

The body was discovered by neighbour Shirley Foster as she drove towards the gateway. This was a ridiculous mistake by a journalist who supposedly had a superior knowledge of the event and contacts in the immediate local area, and evidence of a sloppiness and laziness he had manifested while working as a gardener and later as a journalist in England.

Two days later, on Saturday, December 28, Bailey was given another *Star* front-page splash under the headline:

MURDERED SOPHIE'S TANGLED LOVE LIFE

This piece was a remarkable example of an emerging pattern in his reporting of the crime: a mix of the fabrication of facts and the invention of quotes and sources, along with revealing details of the murder, body and crime scene which only someone who was present during the commission of the crime could have known.

On page one, beside a photograph of Sophie and Daniel at a high- class function, it read:

"*Twice-married Sophie Toscan du Plantier brutally murdered near her isolated hideaway - used the home as a love nest.*

"*Locals said Sophie (38) brought a number of male companions to the West Cork holiday home.*

"*Gardai who found two used wine glasses in the kitchen want to know who was with her last Sunday night hours before her murder.*

"Film-maker Sophie had planned to divorce her second husband Daniel and rejoin her first husband."

There was a two-page spread inside on pages four and five under the banner:

FILM MAKER'S TANGLED LOVE LIFE SPARKS A NEW MYSTERY

The main article had the Eoin Bailey by-line. The opening paragraphs read:

"The complicated love life of murdered French documentary film-maker Sophie Toscan du Plantier was revealed last night.

"Ms Du Plantier, whose badly battered body was discovered yards from her isolated holiday home near Schull, West Cork on Monday, made frequent visits to the area – often with different male companions.

"The 38-year-old film-maker had just decided to divorce her present husband Daniel – who had been married three times – and to rejoin her first husband.

"She used the white-painted converted farmhouse as a hideaway love-nest, neighbours said. 'Sophie would often visit with a different man each time,' one local, asked not to be named, said."

This looked like what might be considered in the trade a sensational piece, a "great story" evidenced by the prominence it received and likely greeted with great enthusiasm in the newsroom. That is if the main angles were true, which was not the case. They were complete fabrications.

Sophie and Daniel were getting on well and were planning to have a child together. A fact confirmed by her family, best friend Agnes Thomas and caretaker Josephine Hellen. Bailey made up the angle of the planned divorce, adding the outrageous and false suggestion that Sophie was getting back with her first husband.

This was not even "faction", the phrase coined by famous American author Norman Mailer to describe a mixture of fact and novelistic licence; it was pure fiction. Nasty fiction.

The marriage had gone through a bad patch in 1993 and Sophie did bring Bruno Carbonnet to the Toormore home several times that year, but not a procession of men as the piece suggested, backed by an invented quote from a local who "asked not to be named". None of the locals said anything of the sort or had even spoken to Bailey.

"Gardai are still trying to discover if one of her male friends was with her when she travelled to West Cork before Christmas – and if he had been in the house with her on the night of the murder."

Here was another invention. It had been established on day one at the scene, after the interior of the house had been inspected, that there was no evidence of the presence of anyone else there. The Gardai had no concern in that regard; it was the killer they were interested in, not another phantom of the reporter's imagination.

Then, switching tack, Bailey without a source inside the investigation began to include true facts and details:

"Meanwhile, the search was continuing last night for the murder weapon and for clues Gardai hope will lead them to her killer.

"Miss Du Plantier may have held the most vital clue of all in the palm of her hand as she lay dying in the boreen beside her house.

"She had a clump of hair in her hand from the head of the attacker. Traces of skin were also found under her fingernails, suggesting she scratched her attacker in a desperate fight for life."

The Gardai were in fact searching for one of three murder weapons; the other two were at the scene – the flat rock and the concrete block. The kindle hatchet was missing, disposed of by the killer either during his flight from the scene or afterwards.

Sophie did have a clump of hair in her hand, a fact which Bailey could not have elicited from any other source at the time. Writing that it came from the killer's head was a fabrication. It was her own hair pulled out of her head in a defensive reaction as the blows rained down. She most likely did try to scratch the attacker but failed with such a small reach. She certainly did put up a desperate fight for her life, evidenced by defensive wounds to her hands, but this was only known at the time by the pathologist and a small number of top investigators, none of whom had spoken to the reporter.

In any event, the origin of the clump of hairs – even though maybe obvious by the colour of the strands – remained to be confirmed by DNA comparison with the victim, which would take considerable time.

There was a side piece on the page-five spread under the "*Star Reporter*" by-line, but consisting of information supplied by Bailey, a practice of hiding his authorship he would continue to use in future in both Irish and French publications. This appeared under the headline:

GLASSES CLUE TO THE KILLER

"*Sophie Toscan du Plantier almost certainly knew the person who bludgeoned her to death in a frenzied attack near her holiday home. Sophie was in her nightclothes when she ran from her luxury holiday home last Sunday night. Her bed had been slept in and two empty wine glasses were in the kitchen.*

"*There was no sign of a break-in at the five-bedroom house and nothing had been stolen.*"

This was neither speculation nor fabrication but pure fact.

Only a person who had stepped a few paces inside the rear door would have seen the wine glasses on the drainage board beside the sink. Only the investigators who had checked the house knew that fact. The use of the word "bludgeoned" and of the description "frenzied attack" are a perfect description of the attack that reveals specific knowledge of what went on that night, which the reporter could not have gleaned from any other source.

Bailey then reverted to fabrication by means of an invented quote:

"'Either her attacker was in the house with her at the time, or she let him in or he had a key to let himself in. We don't know yet,' a Garda said yesterday."

No Garda spoke to him on the matter and he was already under suspicion and visited at his home by Gardai Kevin Kelleher and Bart O'Leary the same day as the article was published to answer some questions. But he persisted with the deception of his media bosses and the public, but again revealed facts of the murder without the help of any Garda source:

"Gardai said that the diminutive Sophie tried to defend herself as she was viciously bashed with a blunt instrument in the boreen beside her house. As she ran from him in the dark she tripped. Her head was bleeding heavily and her arms had been injured as she tried to protect herself.

"The murderer dropped a heavy stone or concrete block on her head before fleeing."

The physical details are correct and again read almost like a witness statement, which in essence it was, with a transparent attempt to put it into the voices of non-existent Gardai sources. Investigators had no idea or proof that Sophie had tripped during her flight from the house. But Bailey's observation was entirely consistent with the discovery of the victim's blood on a stone halfway down the sloping garden after having been felled either by a slate rock or a blow to the back of the head with the kindle hatchet by the pursuing killer.

Also, the reporter reveals that as the victim was fleeing, she had been attacked from behind. Only the top investigators and the pathologist were privy to that information. As the body had been found face upwards, this was only discovered when it had been turned over on the hospital gurney and it became obvious that she had been hit from behind with a blunt instrument. The full post-mortem report would not be written, including this detail, for close to another three months. Ian Bailey already knew it and was careless enough to put it in writing.

On January 2, 1997, he wrote a story for the *Star* saying that the Gardai were searching a disused mine for the weapon used to bludgeon Sophie to death and that the hunt for her killer had been extended to the wider area of Mizen Head. The next day, he wrote a front-page piece saying that several men had been asked by the Gardai to provide hair samples for DNA testing. He specifically requested that his name would not appear on the article.

On January 4, he assisted without even a shared by-line *Star* crime reporter Senan Molony with a story that claimed the fingerprints of the killer might have been left on two wine glasses on the sink in the cottage, which suggested that the killer had been a guest the night of the murder: a fact backed by no evidence whatsoever.

SOPHIE'S KILLER MAY HAVE LEFT PRINTS

It was clear from the substance of the article based on a speculative angle that Bailey's mark was all over the piece. It was an elaboration of his earlier revelation that there were two wine glasses on the sink. The killer could have easily spotted them on the draining board on the night and concluded they must have been washed, which was the case. That fact would have been established quickly after the police examination of the interior of the house. There were no prints of anyone's on the glasses. But to enable another story, he just had the wine glasses as empty.

What Bailey did not know was that there was an unfinished glass of wine in the living room, which contained the victim's fingerprints.

So, the whole angle and the statement that the Gardai were waiting for tests and believed that these could lead them to the killer was wrong. The great deceiver Bailey was pulling the wool over the unsuspecting eyes of the *Star* crime correspondent Senan Molony, who would subsequently realise the nature of the deception.

Bailey's name was entirely absent from the inside full-page spread, but his imprint was everywhere within the pieces under Molony's by-line and containing detail that would arouse the crime reporter's suspicion.

The lead on page four mentioned three aspects that were puzzling the crime investigators. The victim was wearing nightclothes but also boots that were laced up; the bed upstairs had been slept in and the bedclothes rumpled, with investigators wanting to know if she had been awoken by her killer demanding admittance; and she had closed but not locked the door and the lights were off.

A side piece concentrated on the fact that the murder weapon may never be found; the source of the information was suggested to be the Gardai, as was the lead, but it was not. Bailey was again putting into the mouths of the investigators facts he already knew and recycling those facts from news reports. But Senan Molony could not understand why the man who was supplying this information did not want his name on the articles.

"I first met Ian Bailey at this time when I was assigned to go with photographer Martin Maher to West Cork to write about the murder. The news desk told me to link up with the local stringer Bailey, who had been reporting on the crime for the *Star*, the *Sunday Tribune* and other media outlets.

"When we arrived in Schull, I made contact with him and we picked him up in Martin's van and drove to the crime scene in Toormore. He was a tall, powerful man wearing a long black coat but looked dishevelled. My first impression was that he was someone who had embraced the bohemian lifestyle of West Cork.

"During the journey, Bailey provided me with a series of details about the killing which were, to my mind, impressive in their breadth and scope. I was able to fill a couple of pages in my notebook even before we arrived at the crime scene. There were two aspects of his version of the case which appeared to show particular insight.

"The first was when he spoke of the lights going on or off in Sophie's house and the time on the night of the murder. The second was his description of two wine glasses which had been resting on the draining board in the kitchen of the house. Both of those details, I felt, could only have been known to someone who was close to the investigation, which I found impressive but unusual at such an early stage of the enquiries.

"I distinctly remember suggesting to Ian Bailey at one point that I would not feel right transmitting the material under my own by-line since the details provided by him were so impressive. I suggested that I would do so under his name, but he demurred, as he did when I suggested a joint by-line with his name appearing first. I thought that his deference was altogether unusual, given that he had already told me that as a former journalist in the West of England he planned to begin freelancing in the New Year."

Molony quite rightly was suspicious of his reluctance to push his name given the fact of Bailey's existing output for the *Star* and the *Tribune*, and the accepted perception from both titles and also French publications including *Paris Match* that the reporter was leading the media pack with an insight not matched by the rest. The *Star* crime correspondent at the time did not know that there was a perfectly good reason for Bailey's sudden and uncharacteristic attack of humility.

"When we arrived at the crime scene, Bailey hung around in the background and did not make any introduction to the Gardai – despite my assumption that his level of knowledge must have been the product of his relationship with the local law enforcement officers. I made my own efforts to link up with the Gardai, but they were less than forthcoming. I also tried to interview neighbours in the locality, but I found them reluctant to talk.

"Much of Ian Bailey's work formed the basis of a detailed catalogue of clues about the killing published on January 4, 1997, including the fact that Sophie was wearing nightclothes and boots which had been laced up. Also, that the bed upstairs had been slept in and the bedclothes were rumpled, the back door of the house was closed but not locked and the lights were off."

Despite Molony's suspicions on this matter and including the dawning realisation that Bailey had neither Garda or local sources, he had no solid evidence or a way of corroborating the fact as neither investigators nor locals were co-operating with the media. This enabled Bailey to continue his deception and fabrication, pumping out articles for the *Star* and the *Sunday Tribune*.

On January 5, he wrote a front-page piece in the *Sunday Tribune* under the heading:

WOMAN'S KILLER THOUGHT TO BE LOCAL

He had obviously played enough with the "French connection", a theory that he had been propounding to anyone who would listen but for legal reasons dare not write. This was the extension of his fabricated story about the impending split between Sophie and her husband. Bailey's theory was – as he told Bill Hogan among others – that Daniel would lose half of his estate in a divorce and so, to avoid that eventuality, he had hired an assassin supplied by the Corsican mafia to kill his wife.

Most of the population of Schull would find it difficult to know and how to get to that isolated spot, not to mind a Corsican hit man who had to rely on what was lying around the ground to carry out the assassination.

"There is a growing belief that Sophie Toscan du Plantier was brutally murdered by someone living in the locality. A French connection has not been ruled out but Garda sources indicate that an arrest might be made today. The hunt for the killer of the French television documentary maker whose body was found on Tuesday, intensified this weekend as Gardai carried out house-to-house inquiries in the isolated townland surrounding Schull."

The French connection and not the one Bailey referred to was inquiries in relation to Sophie's one-time lover Bruno Carbonnet, who would be taken off the suspects list. This was proof positive if needed that the reporter had no Garda sources. The reporter of course knew that house-to-house inquiries were happening because the previous day he had been visited by two detectives to account for his movements in and around the time of the crime.

There was no intention by Gardai to arrest anyone at this time, a fact that Bailey could have guessed without a source, but instead he reported that an arrest was imminent.

The reporter, in the absence of sources, had to rely more and more on making up facts, hoping and relying amid a media frenzy that no one would challenge the fictional narrative as it unravelled.

"Ms Plantier had spoken to her house-keeper Josie Hellen on Sunday night, saying she had changed her original plans and intended returning to France on Monday rather than her original departure date of December 27. Mrs Hellen who had known the victim for several years, said something had occurred to make Ms Du Plantier, known locally by the name of her maiden name Bouniol, change her plans."

Nothing of this was true and Bailey had never spoken to the caretaker. Josephine Hellen told me that Sophie never discussed anything with her about her return plans, which was not unusual. During the conversation on Sunday night, she told the caretaker of her plan to get more renovation work done on the interior of the house. The final arrangement discussed was that Josephine would call to the house the following day at noon. When she arrived, she was faced with the shocking sight of a crime scene.

The heading on a large centre-page piece on page five read:

VICTIM'S FAMILY ASSIST MURDER HUNT

There was more unsourced and accurate description of what had happened to the victim:

"Ms Du Plantier was hit by a blow to the back of the head and then brutally battered, the cause of death was multiple fractures to the head."

More fabrication followed:

"Extensive search of the area with metal detectors have so far, failed to produce any sign of the weapon. Fingerprints on wine glasses are being checked against locals as are hair samples as a clump of the assailant's hair was found in the clasped hand of the victim."

The details of the physical attack on the victim were entirely accurate but known at that stage only to the pathologist and leading members of the investigation team, none of whom had any contact with Bailey. How could he have possibly known?

One metal detector had been employed during the search of the crime scene which had been shown on a television news clip. The majority had been conducted by a team of Gardai who combed every inch of the field below the house and surrounding areas. There were, as the reporter knew, no fingerprints on the wine glasses, but to write stories and get paid, Bailey needed to continually stretch even the invented facts.

If the hair of the assailant had been found, the game would have been shortly over. That may have been visually obvious at the scene to the pathologist, but lab tests not yet conducted could only provide confirmation. Yet the reporter knew that the victim had hair strands gripped in her hand and that they were hers. Perhaps he thought that by transferring them to the attacker, it might distance himself from suspicion about knowing such correct detail. Ian Bailey was more and more relying on himself as the source of both incriminating fact and transparent fiction.

The clump of hair was again featured in an article in the January 17 edition of the *Tribune* with an extra invention:

"But forensic experts were unable to confirm a link and it is now suspected that the fibres were strands of organic non-human material. A search by twenty-five detectives has, so far, failed to reveal the murder weapon, believed to be a blunt instrument like a poker."

Whatever "organic non-human material" meant was a mystery known only to the reporter, whose invention of the poker as the weapon gained widespread currency in the media and was supported further by information Bailey supplied to *Paris Match* and a quote from Josephine Hellen saying that a poker had been missing from the living room of the house. She never provided the information or the quote, as she confirmed to me, and the poker was still in place by the living room fireplace. Bailey continued to invent facts and quotes.

What Josephine Hellen had told investigators was that the kindle hatchet was missing from its usual spot inside the rear door. Was the kindle hatchet a bridge too far for the reporter in terms of fact? He might have done better than the poker, as the killer would have had to traverse the ground floor to retrieve it from the living room, which never happened.

WOMAN AMONG SOPHIE SUSPECTS

There was another *Star* page-one story on January 8 without his name attached. He wrote that a young mother was among five suspects detained for DNA testing in connection with the murder. The main article inside by a fictitious reporter named Emer Healy was simply a female cover for Bailey. The young mother, the story claimed, was a suspect who had complained during a procedure to get a hair sample from her that the hair had been hacked from her head with a blunt razor blade.

Of course, she was not identified; another bogus story followed, saying that Gardai in Bantry admitted, despite a big-scale hunt, that there had been no significant breakthrough.

"The Garda investigation did not get into full swing for four days as a result of the Christmas break during which time the trail went cold."

This was total nonsense and Healy aka Bailey knew full well that the trail had led straight to his door.

The same day, he filed another story straight from the drawer of his overworked imagination. This one stated that Interpol had unearthed several non-nationals in the area who were known to international police.

"They included a number of robbers, embezzlers, drug dealers and even a paedophile who had been found guilty of abusing children."

By now, Bailey was also telling local people that he was conducting his own investigation into the murder, and considering he had already been questioned by investigation officers, made the extraordinary move of contacting detectives Culligan and Harrington and inviting them to his house on two occasions to discuss his theory about a French connection to the crime.

The officers visited him at the house on January 9, where he referred to matters in France. On the second occasion, Detective Harrington and two other officers went to the house on Bailey's invitation and he again concentrated on France and spoke of Daniel Toscan du Plantier having an influence on the French media.

In and around this time, a crew and actors from the RTE television programme *Crimeline* were in the area filming a reconstruction of Sophie's movements before the murder. While they were on location at Three Castles Head, Bailey appeared and approached the crew. Anne Cahalane, who was playing the role of Sophie, was present when Bailey "bounded over, said that he was a news journalist covering the story and said that he knew Sophie and he had met her while on a walk to Three Castles Head". Anne's partner at the time also heard what Bailey said.

The director Bernard Rogan told me that Bailey literally stalked the crew during the shoot. It is possible that the purpose of his intervention was to be asked for an interview, but that was not going to happen because the producers of the programme were aware that he was a suspect. He had from the start steadfastly maintained to the investigation team that he did not know Sophie, but he was now telling complete strangers the opposite.

Ironically, when the *Crimeline* programme was broadcast later, Bailey would write about it for the *Star* newspaper. He was also telling some senior journalists the same, probably in order to get more work. Paul Webster, *The Guardian*'s correspondent in Paris, got a call from Bailey, who told him that he knew Sophie more as an acquaintance as opposed to a friend. Webster said he made it absolutely clear that he had talked to her before and that he had seen her on the day that she had died.

Ian Bailey was climbing the ladder of the suspect list but – in the throes of his self-appointed role as ringmaster of the media circus, chief expert and investigator of the crime – was blinded to the danger of being found out by his media employers.

But he had resurrected his career and there was no stopping him from reaching the heights of journalism that he had long aspired to and in his view warranted. He had left behind the lowly status of bad gardener and bodhran thumper; he was now

Mr Reporter, and all would bow before his skill, knowledge and expertise. He had come back from the dead on the back of the dead, and at last a future and perhaps a fortune was on the horizon.

There was an extraordinary scenario unfolding, unprecedented in the history of a murder case, where the man who was emerging as a suspect for the crime was not just reporting on it for numerous publications but also engaging members of the investigation team with his theories about who might be responsible for the crime. At the same time, he was not informing his media commissioners of his interaction with the police and embarking on his own "investigation".

He had told a local man he was thinking of extending his investigation of the crime to France, based on his new theory that Daniel Toscan du Plantier – because of his alleged impending split from his wife and the prospect that it would involve the loss of half of his estate – had sent an assassin to West Cork to murder her.

One of the people he visited to discuss this scenario was Bill Hogan, at his house. Bill, who ran a cheese-making business, had known Sophie well, as she was during her trips a regular customer of his, for whom he held in high regard not just for her style but also her decency and modesty.

"He first came to see me within a week or so of the murder and wanted to know what I knew about Sophie, what she was like; he said he was used to crime scene reporting and wanted to know as much as he could about her. I told him that I would help him about what I knew about her as she was a customer of mine. He kept coming back and asking more questions and repeating them.

"Then he fabricated a story attributed to a local cheesemaker (me) in a *Sunday Tribune* article reporting that I said that she was going to divorce her husband, which I never said and knew nothing about. I confronted him about it, and he said that he was going to flush out the real killer and it was her husband who did it. He said that Daniel got the Corsican Mafia to do the job.

He said he needed to go to France to talk to people in the film industry there to make some headway in his investigation."

Bill thought despite the misquote that he was genuine and offered to give him a contact, a food writer he knew in France that might be able to help. Bailey told him that he needed to get the money to go to France and Bill offered to pay his fare. Bailey did not react and went away, returning some days later.

He took two wine glasses and placed them on the table of the kitchen and attempted to give a reconstruction of the crime, and was told in no uncertain terms that Bill was not going to listen. His final visit in early to mid-January was both revealing and astounding to his now reluctant host.

"Bailey told me that he could not go to France because he was now a suspect for the murder, and my reaction was that you are the reporter, not the murderer. He was obviously agitated and nervous. He told me that he could not remember anything about that night and that he needed to be hypnotised. 'I will go down for mental,' he said, 'just like that guy in Sligo.' I was shocked and had to get him out of my place."

This was the first of several admissions that Ian Bailey would make for being responsible for the murder. The reference to Sligo was a case in which a man had murdered his ex-girlfriend and her mother in the car park of Sligo Hospital and was subsequently found to be insane and incarcerated in the Central Mental Hospital in Dublin, a facility for the criminally insane, before later being released.

Bailey was obviously beginning to think about what sort of plea he would advance as a defence if he were arrested for the crime and later put on trial and found guilty. He was aware that if an insanity defence was successful, he would be incarcerated in the only facility for the criminally insane in South County, Dublin, and there was the possibility as happened in other cases that he would be released when he was declared mentally fit to be returned to society.

Bill Hogan had the impression that Bailey was under psychological pressure and probably depressed. This could be explained by the fact that the investigation net was tightening on him, and his best efforts through his reporting to deflect attention from himself were failing. It was a measure of his desperation that he would attempt to propagate a story that proposed that an assassin was sent to kill Sophie.

Once he was officially nominated as a suspect, he knew that he would be dropped like a hot potato by the media outlets he had been reporting for, his remuneration would cease, and his revived career would be over. So, all in all, Ian Bailey was under a lot of pressure, but continued to pump articles out. On January 21, he wrote in the *Star* that Daniel Toscan du Plantier had hired a lawyer to launch his own inquiry into the murder, which was not accurate; it was in relation to the *parties civiles* action on behalf of himself and the family, and any inquiry would be carried out by an examining magistrate.

Senan Molony began to realise Bailey was not just careless with the facts but given to inventing quotes, as he had no sources. At the time, his carelessness might have been put down to a long period away from reporting and an overweening arrogance and the necessity to live up to the self-appointed role of being the expert on the crime. The West Cork stringer was also increasingly avoiding having his name on material he was supplying, to the *Star* in particular, and had it replaced by "Star Reporter" and in one case "Emer Healy", an invented name of a person who did not exist.

Around the end of November 1996, a journalist had contacted Helen Callanan, the news editor of the *Sunday Tribune* newspaper in Dublin, and asked to "give a chance" to a West Cork freelance reporter by the name of Eoin Bailey. She had never met him and knew little about him, but gave him a couple of assignments and he provided a couple of stories. He was not on contract or a regular freelancer.

When news of the murder broke, Helen Callanan rang him and asked if he had any information about the crime. Bailey told her that he had spoken to Sophie Toscan du Plantier, which Helen interpreted as establishing a connection to the story and being of benefit to him. She was totally unaware of the fact that Bailey, apart from trying to get work from news outlets, had denied to the investigation team that he ever knew or had contact with the victim.

He supplied the newspaper with all the Irish material in the reporting of the crime on a non-exclusive basis. Callanan excised some parts of his stories, including one in which he reported that the victim had several lovers. Apart from that, she was content to have someone covering the crime who was based in the area. A phone caller at the beginning of February 1997 informed her that her West Cork correspondent was in fact a suspect for the murder. Helen Callanan, as she would testify in future court hearings, was shocked by the news and realised that she was the unwitting victim of a massive deception. She decided to confront Ian Bailey about the matter.

"This was probably the single biggest fiasco I had encountered, that the reporter I had on the story was in fact a suspect. It was inappropriate in so many ways that I had to take it up with him." She picked up the phone and rang him and said that this was a serious situation and she had been told that he was the suspect in the case. She found his response incredible.

"He was cool and calm and asked who had told me. He was unable to see the mess he was in and that he had effectively duped me." He then dropped a bombshell. Bailey told the news editor that he was responsible for the crime. "It was me. I did it. I killed her; I did it to resurrect my career."

Helen Callanan did not detect any hint of irony or black humour; his statement came across as matter of fact and in essence a confession. She had started out to challenge him about the information she had received that he was a suspect, and far from a denial she had been given an admission of guilt by a man she had hired to report on the murder. After the conversation was over, she was flabbergasted, did not know at first what to make of it but decided that she would inform the investigation team of the conversation and Bailey's reaction.

It struck the news editor, in retrospect, that the reporter had not grasped the idea that he had deceived the person who had employed him to cover the story. "The idea did not occur to him to extricate himself from the scenario which had been presented to him and that the moral compass was broken. He had not apologised, did not seem to appreciate the issue and had never addressed it during our conversation. He later rang and requested a meeting if he happened to be in Dublin. I declined," she said.

Bailey would have now realised that his newly renewed career was grinding to a halt, but he kept supplying articles on the crime to other outlets, most notably the *Star*, whose crime reporter was privately convinced of the guilt of Bailey.

Senan Molony was at the same time in a state of suspended disbelief from the fact that a journalist who had reported on the crime had possibly committed the savage murder and was now profiting from this ghastly deed – a scenario unheard of not simply in his own extensive experience but hardly at all in the history of murder, not just in Ireland but anywhere in the world.

An upcoming dramatic event would prompt the *Star* crime reporter to delve further into the conundrum and investigate in detail the former career and background of a man who would shortly become the prime suspect for the murder.

CHAPTER 4
THE ARRESTS

West Cork – February 1997

On January 11, 1997, under the radar of the media horde, a development promised a major break for the investigation. A woman naming herself Fiona, who had made several previous anonymous calls in relation to the case – the first one on Christmas Day 1996 – rang Bandon Garda Station and was put through to a member of the team. She told him that while she was driving towards Kealfadda Bridge between 3 a.m. and 4 a.m. on December 23, 1996, she had seen a man in her headlights. He was tall, wearing a long black coat, and was stumbling along the roadside and holding his head in his hands. The location was less than 3 kilometres from the crime scene.

She had seen a man of similar build and wearing a long black coat on the afternoon of Saturday, December 21 at the top of the main street in Schull and again on the morning of Sunday 22nd at 7 a.m., apparently hitching a lift near Airhill, outside Schull. Detective Garda Jim Fitzgerald was given the task of tracing the woman "Fiona", which was presumed to be a pseudonym.

After an appeal for information from the public about the murder on the *Crimeline* television programme, which guaranteed the anonymity of callers, "Fiona" once again telephoned the police on January 21 and agreed to meet investigators four days later at Bandon Station, but did not turn up.

On the instructions of a superior officer, Detective Fitzgerald made inquiries related to the call from "Fiona", which was traced to a private house in Schull, and the phone subscriber was identified as a Christopher Farrell. The voice on the call which was recorded was identified by Garda Kevin Kelleher based at Schull Garda Station as that of Marie Farrell, the wife of the subscriber, who ran an arts and crafts shop in Schull. At the evening conference, it was decided that Garda Kelleher would go to the house on January 28 for the purpose of speaking to her.

Garda Kelleher subsequently rang Bandon Station and Detective Fitzgerald along with Garda Jim Slattery drove to their colleague's house, where they met Marie Farrell. Garda Kelleher asked her to outline what had happened and she recounted that she had made the phone calls and said that she had seen a man at Kealfadda Bridge. She had been out with a friend that night and was not supposed to be out.

She did not want to make a statement on that occasion as she had personal difficulties (her husband Chris was not aware of what she had been up to on the night), but she took Gardai to the location where she had seen Bailey in the early hours of December 23. The Gardai informed the incident room at Bandon Station about the meeting and on February 7, Detective Jim Fitzgerald wrote a memo on the conversation with Marie Farrell and he and Detective Slattery signed it.

Shortly afterwards, she was reading a newspaper at the counter of her shop and saw a photograph of a man who bore a strong resemblance to the one she had seen at the bridge and the other locations. What particularly resonated with her was the incident on the Saturday while Sophie was browsing in her shop and the man was standing on the opposite path looking in. When Sophie left, the man followed her towards the lower end of the main street.

Gripped by a sense of fright, she took the newspaper and ran out into the street where she met a police officer and showed him the photograph, which he identified as Ian Bailey, who had told investigators that he had stayed at home in the Prairie on the Saturday night. It emerged that this was not true; he had in fact stayed at a friend's house after consuming a large amount of drink and drugs, as was his wont at the time. That explained why he was on the road the next morning trying to get home to the Prairie when he was spotted by Marie Farrell.

Further investigation established exactly where Bailey was on that Saturday night and he was not at home as he had asserted in questionnaires and statements to investigating officers. He had gone to the home of Mark Murphy, who resided there with his mother Patricia and her companion Tony Doran, with Mark and Robert Shelley arriving about midnight. They drank some beer and Mark went to bed, leaving Bailey chatting with his mother.

Bailey left the house at around 2 a.m. and then returned shortly after and asked if he could stay the night. Patricia agreed and said he could sleep on the couch. Someone heard the front door being opened early the next morning but fell asleep again. The walking distance from the house to the road is less than five minutes, where Marie Farrell was driving towards Cork and saw a man which she would later identify as Bailey on the opposite side hitching at 7.15 a.m. By what could be considered a remarkable coincidence, Bailey was in Murphy's house, less than 100 metres from the road.

The next day, Mark got up after noon and drove Bailey to Liscaha around 2 p.m. Robert Shelley awoke after eight o'clock and left the house at 9.30 a.m. He said that Bailey had slept on the couch. Tony Doran went to the ground floor at 11.30 a.m. and met Bailey coming out of the living room and followed him into the kitchen.

He told Doran that he should have already left for Bantry to de-feather some turkeys. Doran got the impression that Bailey wanted to drive him there but ignored this and said that Bailey would be late. He left the house after midday but later recalled that he thought he had heard someone leaving the house at 7.30 a.m. but had never heard anyone coming back.

Patricia Murphy stated that about a week after this event, Bailey had arrived at the door of her house and asked her if she had told police that he had stayed at her home on the Saturday night. She told him she had and asked him if he had said the same. He replied that he had not and said, "I've forgotten with everything that has happened." Once more, Bailey's version of events was both inconsistent and in error. He had not forgotten anything. He knew well that he had said to investigators that he had spent that night at home.

The following night, he said that after a tour of pubs in Schull he had returned to the home he shared with Jules Thomas in her company; they went to bed and neither left the house on the morning of December 23. This account would be contradicted by several local witnesses. He would later change this account but continue his facility for lying not just to investigators and newspapers, but also in the future to courts.

Additional inquiries into the ongoing investigation unearthed further contradictions in the statements given by Ian Bailey and Jules Thomas about their movements before and after the crime, and those provided by local witnesses, many of whom were familiar to and had previous contact with the couple.

Between 10 a.m. and 11 a.m. on the morning of December 23, Mr and Mrs Camier encountered Jules Thomas at their Christmas stall in Goleen. She told them that she had just dropped Ian off: "Because there was a murder in the West End, and he has gone on to investigate. It is sad, but it is part of his job." She struck the couple as being agitated, worried and nervous about something.

On February 4, 1997, fourteen-year-old schoolboy Malachi Reed, who lived with his mother Amanda close to Liscaha, had been given a lift home by Bailey, who in the course of the journey told him that he was responsible for the killing by bashing the victim's head in with a rock. Both the boy and his mother gave statements in relation to the incident to a member of the investigation team.

Detective Superintendent Dermot Dwyer and senior members of the investigation team were legitimately and justifiably beginning to concentrate on Ian Bailey as not just a person of interest but an emerging prime suspect for the commission of the crime. More local people with some knowledge of and connection to the journalist were questioned and revealed further contradictions in Bailey's accounts of his whereabouts and actions on the morning after the murder and in the following days and weeks.

There was already in existence a dispute about the phone call from Eddie Cassidy to Bailey requesting him to check out an incident of death in the area. It was obvious to the investigation team that Cassidy could hardly have a negative agenda in his version, which was that at the time of the call he said he had no detailed knowledge of the event or of the identity of the victim.

Even if he had some prior detail which he might withhold to protect his sources, he could have presumed that a local journalist living in the area should have little difficulty over time to establish with normal enquiries what had occurred. Other facts in the journalistic process added to the suspicion about Bailey's actions in the immediate aftermath of the murder.

Cork city-based photographer and principal of the Provision agency, Michael McSweeney received a phone call from the photo editor of the Dublin-based newspaper the *Irish Independent*, Padraig O'Beirne, before 1 p.m. on the day of the murder. He told his Cork colleague that he had been contacted earlier by Ian Bailey, who had offered him pictures of the murder scene taken by a friend when they visited it between 10 a.m. and 11 a.m., an impossibility unknown at the time by the Dublin editor.

It had to have occurred earlier. O'Beirne refused the offer but the photographs must have been taken much earlier, which again indicated a knowledge of the event by Bailey long in advance of it coming into the public domain, and more pertinently before the call from Eddie Cassidy.

Further statements obtained by the investigators corroborated the accounts provided by Eddie Cassidy, Michael McSweeney and Padraig O'Beirne.

Their statements, along with those from local people who had spoken to both Bailey and Thomas on the morning of the murder, proved beyond a shadow of a doubt that the reporter had knowledge of the murder long before he had been contacted by

Eddie Cassidy, and without a source in the Garda investigation or anywhere else in the area. Quite the reverse – news of the murder was being given to locals who had no previous knowledge of the event by Ian Bailey.

Caroline Leftwich said that she had an arrangement to meet Bailey on the same morning in Skibbereen. She was contacted by him between 11.30 a.m. and 12.30 p.m. He said he had to cancel the meeting as he had to cover the "murder of a French woman, someone who was on holiday". Bailey was also due to deliver a turkey to Paul O'Colmain the same morning but he also cancelled, telling the prospective customer at around 11.30 a.m., and said with an excited voice that he was going back into journalism and told O'Colmain that there had been a murder in the area.

Detective Culligan arrested an old bachelor farmer who had been robbing houses of gas cylinders and batteries, but quickly realised that the man – who lived in poor circumstances – was incapable of carrying out the murder and eliminated him as a suspect. Ian Bailey now dominated the subject of the evening conferences at Bandon Station and was first nominated as a suspect on December 27.

The superintendent in charge gave the reasons why Bailey should be arrested and questioned as the prime suspect for the murder.

"His accounts of his movements in the period of the murder were not correct; there were scratches on his arms; he had been seen by Marie Farrell at Kealfadda Bridge; he had been violent towards his partner Jules Thomas; he had told people not only that he had committed the murder but how he had done it." The rationale was straightforward and the suspicion under the circumstances was reasonable.

There was no disagreement about the course of action at the incident room in Bandon. There was agreement that there would be a considerable media reaction to the arrest, not just for the simple reason that a member of the fourth estate who had reported extensively on and was conducting his own "investigation" into the crime was now the prime suspect.

It was an unprecedented scenario in the history of national and international murder investigation, where a reporter who had filed numerous reports on the crime was being arrested and the team at Bandon would not underestimate the sensational nature of the media reaction.

This instilled an extra caution on behalf of the investigation team in every aspect of the impending arrest. The fact that Bailey had reported on the murder and would have an awareness of his rights and the general protocol of the arrest process not possessed by the average crime suspect would dictate such an imperative. It was also obvious from the contradictions in his statements that he had already lied about his movements around the time of the crime. He was therefore likely to invent details of the arrest to reflect well on himself – a man hard done by members of the investigating team.

Tom McEnaney, a *Sunday Tribune* journalist, contacted Bailey a week before Christmas and arranged that Bailey would send an article on Internet advertising to the newspaper; the deadline was on the morning of December 23, as the staff would then be due to start their Christmas break. When the deadline passed, he and the business editor Richard Curran thought they might need a replacement article. After being contacted, Bailey eventually dictated it over the phone at 4 p.m. the following day.

On the morning of February 10, 1997, detectives Culligan, Harrington and Liam Hogan travelled to Bailey's home at the Prairie. He was asked to account for his movements at the time of the murder and the days afterwards, and notes were taken of his account. The content of the interview contained further discrepancies. Then at 10.45 a.m., Detective Culligan told him that he was being arrested for the murder of Sophie Toscan du Plantier, contrary to Common Law, and cautioned him.

Bailey appeared shocked and replied: "You can't be serious. You can't do this to me." The arrest had taken place in the studio near the house, and Detective Culligan asked him if he wished to clean himself up. He replied that he wished to see Jules Thomas, and the officers took him to the main part of the house to fulfil his wish. Bailey was handcuffed, which although a normal practice of the procedure of arrest seemed hardly necessary.

As they were leaving, Jules Thomas put her hands to the window and said: "Remember, they have nothing on you ... I love you and I will say that in court."

The journey to Bandon Station was uneventful, according to Detective Harrington, and without any undue unpleasantries. Bailey would later disagree with this account, alleging that he was threatened that if he did not confess to the crime, he would end up in a ditch with a bullet in the back of his head. Nothing in his demeanour during his custody and interviews suggested that there could have been an ounce of truth in that allegation.

His rights were read and explained to him. At 11.58 a.m., he requested a solicitor, Con Murphy, who arrived at 12.26 p.m. He was provided with food, drinks and cigarettes. At 4.34 p.m., the superintendent authorised the taking of his blood, photograph, finger and palm prints. The superintendent gave authorisation to extend his detention for six hours and three minutes later, the prisoner was medically examined.

Throughout his period of custody, the normal arrest protocols such as the Garda interviews, prisoner checks and rest/hygiene breaks were meticulously carried out in accordance with the rules and regulations.

In the interim, Jules Thomas had also been arrested at the house in Liscaha at 12.22 p.m., on suspicion of being an accessory after the fact to the murder of Sophie Toscan du Plantier, contrary to Common Law. The reason for the arrest was based on information the Gardai had at the time and the account she had given to the team outlining the movements of herself and Bailey at the material time of interest to the murder investigation.

She was taken to Bandon Garda Station, arriving at 1.30 p.m. She was again informed of why she had been arrested and was asked if she understood. She was offered the services of a solicitor but declined at that time.

The same meticulous routine was followed, with the Garda member in charge stating that he believed that her detention was necessary for the proper investigation of the offence for which she had been arrested and she was detained under the same section of the 1984 act. She was given notice of her rights and signed for them. She was given water and coffee, and offered food, which she declined.

At 2.30 p.m., she requested the attendance of a specific solicitor, but as he was not available at the time, he did not arrive at the station until 4.30 p.m. At 6.17 p.m., the appropriate superintendent authorised an extension of her detention for a further six hours. During the period of the detention, Jules Thomas was given refreshments, cigarettes and rest breaks. At 10.15 p.m., the superintendent authorised photographs to be taken of her.

Bailey was released without charge at 10.44 p.m. At 12.14 a.m. on February 11, Jules Thomas was released from custody without charge and it was recorded that she made no complaints. Neither had Ian Bailey made any complaints.

The huge media attention ensured that this appeared to be a sensational development in the case, primarily with Bailey, the reporter on the crime whose role had been transferred to prime suspect.

Since there was no forensic evidence connecting Bailey to the crime, the interrogating team would concentrate on the contradictions in his accounts of his movements and actions before and after the crime, and hope that his partner might further emphasise those contradictions and add others. The team were building what appeared to be a strong circumstantial case.

Bailey had purchased bleach from a shop in Schull the day after the murder. Bleach, of course, is a detergent commonly applied to clothes to remove stains including blood. Information would later be obtained from a friend of one of Jules's daughters, Ariana Boarina, who had seen dark clothes soaking in the bath around that time. Two other neighbours also witnessed a large bonfire on the Liscaha property on St Stephen's Day.

In the interview room at Bandon Station, Bailey was asked where he had been on the Sunday night, December 22, 1996.

"I was drinking in the Galley pub with Jules. I left, went down to the car and drove it around, came back to pick up Jules at the pub."

He had in fact previously been in O'Reagan's pub, where he had played the bodhran and, according to witnesses in both pubs, consumed a large quantity of alcohol, mixing Guinness, whiskey and wine.

"Did you leave the house after going home with Jules?"

"I went to bed, I stayed in bed all night until the next morning. I never left the house all night. Jules will tell you."

He had previously told investigators that he had also been at home all night on the evening of Saturday, December 21 and the morning of Sunday, December 22. This was not correct; he had been at an impromptu gathering at the Murphy household. To put it mildly, he had lied when he made that statement, although at the time it did not seem to have much advantage for him. Later, having spoken to Mrs Murphy, he went back to investigators and changed his previous statements about that night.

"You were seen on Sunday morning at 7 a.m. on the roadway."

"I didn't leave Mark Murphy's until 11.30 a.m. and I went to Brosnan's shop for the paper."

"You were seen again on Monday morning, the 23rd of December, at 3.30 a.m., near Sylvia Connell's place on the roadway. Is this correct?"

"I don't agree with it, being on the roadway on Monday morning. I know I had nothing to do with it. I didn't murder her."

The contradiction of the account of the contact by journalist Eddie Cassidy to check out a death in Toormore was raised.

"Eddie asked me where Toormore was. He wanted me to find the scene, he told me it was a French national that was murdered. I went off to the scene."

"How did you know where to go?"

"I had knowledge there was a house sometimes occupied by a French national."

"How did you know her name?"

"I knew she was in the phone book as Bouniol."

The interviewers were aware this version was contested by Eddie Cassidy, who said he did not have that detail of nationality and if he had he could have checked it himself and driven straight to the crime scene without any necessity of contacting Bailey.

Meanwhile, Jules Thomas was being questioned regarding the couple's movements and actions before and after the crime.

"Went to Schull with Ian around 9.30 p.m. on Sunday night. On the way home from Schull we stopped the car at Hunt's Hill. Ian got out of the car and said nothing, he looked up at the moon and commented how beautiful the reflection of the moon was on the bay. I was very tired and wanted to go home to bed. The bay was very beautiful, but I was tired. We went home and got to bed about 1 a.m. We went to bed together."

It just happens that from Hunt's Hill, Bailey had a good view of Sophie's house as plain as daylight under the full moon and could see the gable light at the side of the house. It was also possible he could have established that the neighbour Alfie Lyons's house was in darkness, indicating that he and his partner Shirley Foster had retired for the night, which was the case.

In her account, Bailey also asked her, "Isn't that Alfie's house over there? There is a light in his place."

There was no light on in Alfie's house as he and his partner Shirley had long since retired to bed, so the house was in darkness.

The reason for stopping at Hunt's Hill was hardly to wax poetic but more likely a form of reconnaissance. But had he told Jules the truth about Alfie's house being in darkness, he would not have any excuse to call over to him later. He would hardly tell his partner that he was in fact going to call to Alfie's neighbour.

"Could Ian have left the house?"

"I'm a light sleeper, he never got up all night, I'd have heard him. I don't remember him getting up to go to the bathroom. Even if Ian was going to the toilet, he would tell me."

"Is it possible, Jules, you are getting the nights mixed up?"

"No, I'm definite about the Sunday night. Ian didn't get up during the night. I would know if he did."

Jules Thomas appeared to be less assured than her partner while being interviewed. This would have been entirely understandable under the circumstances, the fact of being upset as she was by the media presence outside the station and not aware of how his interview was going. It was obvious to the officers that Jules Thomas was becoming more vulnerable as the questioning progressed. No doubt this had something to do with the daunting experience, however straightforward, of being in custody.

"Since the first time we interviewed you, you've changed your statements on several occasions. In the first questionnaire, you said you left the Courtyard bar at 11.15 p.m., collected your daughter home. This isn't true."

"I was mistaken. It was difficult to remember at the time, all the different nights until we sat down and went through the days step by step."

This was a statement that would not have surprised the officers, as what she was saying was that the couple were creating a narrative to cover all the angles, so that in relation to the events they would be singing from the same hymn sheet. Understandable under the circumstances. Certainly, Jules Thomas had no incentive to lie. The same did not apply to her partner. If there had been a rehearsal, it would have been at his behest and under his direction.

When the truth is being told, the story never varies. An event such as the savage murder that had taken place in a local setting like West Cork would have fallen into the category of the assassination of JFK when people's memories of where they were and what they were doing at the time would become unusually clear and accurate as a result of the heightened impact and significance of the occurrence.

"You're mistaken about every other thing. I put it to you that you are mistaken about Sunday night."

"I'm sure about the Sunday night, had Ian got up and gone out, I'd have heard him as I am a very light sleeper. I'd know if he had left the bed, I'd have felt him not there in the bed with me."

A break was taken after less than an hour had passed early in the afternoon. Perhaps Jules was feeling a bit insecure and she requested a consultation with a solicitor. When the interview was resumed, there was a noticeable shift in her position.

"Did Ian leave the house after *Prime Time*?"

"I think he stayed in all night. He may have gone out to the kitchen for a while. I'm not sure. He may have gone out. He doesn't tell me every time he goes out."

This was a different version of what she had related earlier, with what seemed a great deal of certainty. Jules was now admitting to the possibility that her partner had gone out.

"I do not believe you are telling the truth about the Sunday night. Did Ian leave the house at any time?"

"No, Ian was with me all night. I had my period all that week and was sleeping light. I would have known if he had left the bed."

Her resolution on the point was weak. She had said before that she was a light sleeper. She then mentioned her period was the cause of not sleeping soundly. Whatever rehearsal of the events her partner had imposed on her and had been conducted to cover Sunday night was not as consistent as it should have been.

"The two of us then went home and very little was said except some words to the effect that he was going over later some time, if I wanted to go and I said I was too tired. I got the impression he was going over to Alfie's, but I wasn't too sure if that was right or not ... I did a few small jobs like putting on the electric blanket on the bed at 1.30 a.m. I remember Ian coming into the bedroom and getting into bed ... I took two tablets for period pain, these were pain killers. I was in a sleep and Ian was tossing and turning and then he got up from the bed and I would estimate he got up an hour later."

So now the narrative changes somewhat but with the mantra that little was said, echoing the stop at Hunt's Hill. For a man as typically effusive as Ian Bailey, particularly under the influence of alcohol, this appears strangely out of character, unless there was something else on his mind that he wished to keep from his partner. The mention of going over to Alfie's is entirely consistent with the lie Bailey told her about the lights being on in the house.

"He got up easy so as not to wake me up; even though my recollection was poor I am almost one hundred per cent sure. He did not say anything to me. I don't recall his absence during my further sleep. I can't recall Ian coming back to bed. I remembered him getting me coffee at nine o'clock and as far as I can honestly remember he did not come back to bed all that morning."

While having a second coffee in the kitchen, she noticed something on Bailey's forehead. "I saw a scratch on his forehead. I am sure and have no recollection of seeing this scratch on his forehead on the Sunday. The scratch was raw, and I asked him what happened as it was fresh and a bit bloodied and he said he got it from a stick, it was a jagged bit of a mark."

"What was the answer?"

"He did not elaborate where he came into contact with the stick."

Jules Thomas then appeared to break down, perhaps less under the pressure of questioning but more with the realisation of the implications of her changing narrative. She returned to the topic of Hunt's Hill, where she related that Bailey had said little other than remarking on the beauty of the bay. She now said he had said something in addition.

"Ian got back in [the car] and said that he had a bad feeling about something."

She then went further, unwittingly revealing somewhat the true purpose of the stop at Hunt's Hill and a lot more.

"From what was said at Hunt's Hill, the fact that he said to me he was going over to Alfie's, the mark on his face and now he is put at Kealfadda Bridge, my concluding remark is there is strong evidence to link him to the murder of the French lady."

Apart from stating the obvious, Jules Thomas had just stripped her partner Ian Bailey of an alibi from the missing hours between the couple going to bed and seeing him in the morning around 9 a.m., and in doing so contradicted his long-held version of being at home all of the night of the murder. In addition, other questions arose which the detectives would sensibly avoid at this juncture.

She then made further statements of damning fact.

"Following the days after the murder happening, Ian spoke to me about the case. He told me he knew her by sight and had seen her while he was up at Alfie's. He said he had seen her at Brosnan's supermarket in Schull on the weekend, he did not elaborate whether she was on her own or not."

This statement contradicted Bailey's contention that he did not know Sophie and he had not seen her in Schull on the weekend before the murder. He had in fact been introduced to her by Alfie Lyons in the summer of 1995, while he was working on his friend's garden.

She then discussed travelling to the crime scene after the phone call from Eddie Cassidy. "Following Eddie Cassidy's ringing, I subsequently drove Ian to the scene, and he said we will try Alfie's road and we drove straight there and into the scene of the murder without asking anybody. He said my hunch was right, it's up here."

It was of course not her hunch at all. He knew well where to go and didn't need a hunch but was deflecting from himself by telling Jules it was her hunch. The implication of his duplicity struck her forcefully.

"Ian mentally manipulated me. Ian used me."

It was typical of Bailey's arrogant and ruthless character that he was passing on the responsibility for driving straight to the scene of the crime to his partner without even bothering to check in advance with any other possible source given the scant information he had been provided by Eddie Cassidy.

"After Gardai had called on the questionnaires I said and Ian said that we were in the Courtyard bar on Sunday night and this was incorrect, this was said because there were three nights out and looking after three daughters. Following the Gardai calling Ian asked me 'Where did you say we were?' and when I answered him, he said, 'Okay, stick to that.' He also started saying, 'What else did they say, what else did they say?' He then insisted on sticking to my story."

So, on the evidence of this statement and the earlier reference to the couple sitting down to go over the events of the three-day lead-up to the murder, it indicated that Bailey was coaching his unwitting partner to get a coherent and consistent narrative to distance him from the crime. This gave the detectives the ammunition to take a harder line of questioning with Bailey.

One of the questioning officers put it to Bailey that there was certain evidence available and urged him to tell the truth. Witnesses said they saw him at Kealfadda Bridge.

"These people are mistaken. I was in bed."

It was then put to him that Jules stated he had left the bed and returned the following morning with a mark on his forehead. He replied that this did not happen.

"We got home between one and two and went to bed."

Bailey then admitted meeting Sophie at Alfie Lyons's house one or two years earlier but denied seeing her in Schull on the weekend before the murder. He was sticking to the story of being at home all night despite the glaring and damaging contradiction provided by Jules Thomas. He had not counted on the possibility that his partner would tell the truth about the matter.

Following a break in questioning, he was again asked to tell the truth, an action so foreign to Ian Bailey that the detectives must have thought they were wasting their breath.

"I didn't kill that lady; I didn't kill her."

Bailey was beginning to realise he would have to invent another scenario to explain the chasm between his statements and those he had directed and rehearsed with his partner about the night in question.

"You have told us several times on this day that you went away from the Galley pub with Jules, then went to bed and did not get up until the following morning. Now you have told the other officer that you did in fact get up that night and left Jules's house."

This was a reference to an earlier sequence of questioning

conducted by Detective Superintendent Dermot Dwyer and Detective Inspector Michael Kelleher which commenced at 8.40 p.m. Dermot Dwyer had spoken to him several times, including at the house in Liscaha, so the atmosphere was relaxed. It was put to Bailey that there was evidence that he was involved in the murder and he was urged to tell the truth. He denied any involvement and said that he was in bed with Jules. He was told a witness saw him at 3.15 a.m. at Kealfadda Bridge.

Bailey replied that those witnesses were wrong and repeated that he had been in bed with Jules. It was put to him that she stated that he had left the bed. He then admitted he had got up sometime after 1 a.m. to write an article in the kitchen. He then went down to the studio. It was dark and he had no watch, so he did not know what time it was. He had an article to write about the Internet. He was supposed to have it finished by the morning (of December 23) but the deadline had been changed to the following day. He returned to Jules's house and got up at 11 a.m.

Inspector Kelleher put it to him that he had told someone he had committed the murder. Bailey replied that it was a black joke. It was anything but a joke and the person he had told had not been amused.

He had told Yvonne Ungerer and it was suggested that not only had he told her that he had committed the murder but actually how he had done it. Bailey replied that it was a block and that this fact was all over the Courtyard bar on the night (of the murder). He was asked if he knew Sophie and he replied that he had seen her from Alfie Lyons's property the previous year.

He had thought she was quite plain. He had been in Schull on Saturday, December 21 when she had been there but had not seen her. He thought he had been wearing his long black coat that day.

The interrogation by those officers finished at 10.05 p.m. The notes of it were read to him and he signed them as correct.

"Yes, now I remember that I did get up and go to my studio and do some work."

"Why are you now changing your story regarding that night,

is it because you are aware that Jules is now saying you did get up?"

"No, I remember now."

What Bailey "remembered" was getting up at 4 a.m. to write an article in the studio, a derelict shed with no heating situated about 250 metres from the house. He claimed that after a short while he returned to the bed and got up at 9 a.m. to finish the article.

This new version made absolutely no sense. Bailey left a comfortable house with at least some residual heat to go to the studio, a cold shack, in sub-zero temperatures in the middle of the night with no watch (how convenient) to write an article for a deadline he had no intention of meeting.

If indeed he had finished the article, for what possible reason could he have missed the deadline? He had been contacted by the editor on Monday when he had failed to deliver and given until the following day to finish it, which he did by dictating it over the phone. Nothing about this flimsy excuse for leaving the house had the least semblance of logic about it, not to mind truth. The only value it had was the admission that he had left the house, which he had firmly denied beforehand.

His slightly sleeping partner had no recollection of this, so there was no possibility of corroborating his new story. To say that it was a somewhat convenient and weak invention would be an understatement. But taken at face value, Bailey had admitted that he had left the house, therefore removing another element of an alibi which could not be corroborated.

Bailey predictably denied that he had made admissions to being responsible for the crime and had no explanation for why he might have made the admissions. He admitted to being in Schull on December 21 but said he had not seen the victim. But two witnesses had seen him on the main street in close proximity to Sophie. The idea that everyone in the Courtyard bar on the night after the murder knew that the victim had been killed by a block was absurd.

There remained a lot of damning answers to be analysed which would focus the investigation team. Despite the necessity for Bailey to constantly change his version of events, glaring contradictions and inconsistencies remained, especially when compared to the statements of independent witnesses.

After the legal period of detention had expired, Ian Bailey and Jules Thomas were released without charge. This was the beginning but far from the end of the saga of the brutal murder of Sophie Toscan du Plantier.

The following day in Paris, as a member of the *parties civiles*, Daniel Toscan du Plantier made a statement to French police. He stated that his wife was in the habit of visiting the house he had bought for her in Toormore, West Cork two or three times a year. On December 20, 1996, she took a flight to Ireland with a return ticket for December 24. He said she was planning to make some repairs to the house that she had not been to since the previous Easter.

During her stay there, he said that the couple had spoken many times on the phone, once on the Friday night, twice on Saturday, December 21, twice on Sunday, December 22, and their last conversation taking place at midnight French time (11 p.m. Irish time). His wife was, he said, in bed preparing to go to sleep and during the conversation showed no signs of anxiety and had never mentioned having any kind of problem or difficulty.

Back in West Cork, there would be the necessity for the investigating team to formally tie down the account from the only witness to place Ian Bailey outside his house on the night of the murder. This would involve getting an official interview and a signed statement from Marie Farrell, who detectives already realised had a personal problem about what she herself was doing at the time.

Quite apart from that, there were also other important witnesses to be interviewed. Seven days after the arrests, an ex-British Army soldier who had served in the Northern Ireland conflict but who was now a dreadlocked dropout in West Cork presented himself to members of the investigation and the following day told them that he had had contact with Bailey in a rooming house where he had stayed for two nights after his release from custody.

Martin Graham said that he had heard Bailey say that if the police were right, he might have had a blackout and could have probably committed the crime, and also said that he knew the victim. Bailey told the potential witness that Sophie had died at 2.30 a.m. and had confirmed that he was out that night but contested that he was the man spotted at Kealfadda Bridge.

They had been staying at a house where the owner Russell Barrett rented rooms. In response for contact details for himself, he told investigators that they could reach him through a woman nicknamed Eleanorde Newburrey. Bailey was residing with her for a few days to escape the media attention immediately after the arrests.

While Graham's information contained a certain consistency in relation to the number of admissions that Bailey had already made to other parties for being responsible for the crime, there were several red flags raised for the investigators in subsequent meetings. He offered himself as an undercover agent for the investigators to engage Bailey in conversation and to elicit a more substantial admission about committing the crime. He made some ludicrous suggestions about how he could set Bailey up. Members of the investigation team decided to continue to engage with Graham but with an extra degree of caution.

Russell Barrett and another man, Colin Deady, who was also staying in the house, confirmed some of the statements by Graham in relation to Bailey. Barrett said he had told Bailey to shut up (talking about his part in the murder); he was now beginning to doubt him and felt some compassion for him. Bailey wanted to be hypnotised by a Barrett acquaintance by the name of Irma, to establish what he had done on the night of the murder, but the latter declined to get involved. These conversations were entirely consistent with what he had told Bill Hogan.

On February 19, Garda Kevin Kelleher climbed up the same

type of tree that Ian Bailey had said he scaled on December 22 and performed the same cutting operation. He did not receive any scratches on his hands as witnessed on Ian Bailey's. An experienced forester, John Brennan, when later consulted, shown the tree and informed of the circumstances, concluded that it was highly improbable that anyone could have covered their hands and forearms with scratches when involved in such a simple cutting operation.

It became clear that the investigators would be relying on circumstantial evidence to secure any future conviction, as laboratory examination showed there was no conclusive forensic evidence such as hair or blood at the crime scene to supply a link to or comparison with the killer. There was no trace of semen in or on the victim or her clothes. As a result of the huge bloodletting in the attack, most samples provided a match with the victim. The strands of hair found on the right hand, forearm and wrist were those of the victim.

The area where the body had lain, during which time there had been direct physical contact between the killer and victim when she was pulled away from the bushes, also failed to produce a sustainable sample of foreign blood other than that of the victim's. There were human bloodstains on the brambles, but it was impossible to establish the type. This was obviously as a result of the degrading of the stains due to the extended exposure to the elements before the samples were bagged.

These conclusions, allied to the on-scene preliminary examination and subsequent full autopsy by Dr Harbison, considerably undermine the weight given to the view that the crime scene was not properly protected by the Gardai. While this is partially true, the most unpalatable fact is that long before they arrived, the crime scene had been unprotected for in or around eight hours in the most unfavourable environmental conditions for the preservation of vital forensic evidence which under different circumstances, for example in an indoor setting, could have definitively linked the killer to the crime scene. In addition, there was the late arrival of Dr Harbison.

The same applied to the concrete block, where it was not possible to establish a blood type from the stains on it. The first site of the attack, at the rear door of the house, there were small stains of blood on the external surface of the door. The samples were found to be insufficient to establish a blood type, further evidence of the degradation and contamination of the bloodstains by lengthy exposure to wind, freezing temperatures and sun. Stains on the gate were those of the victim.

There were no foreign fingerprints in the house other than those of the caretaker Josephine Hellen and members of her family, and the victim's. There were no fingerprints on the wine glasses beside the sink and the ones on the unfinished glass of wine also belonged to the victim.

To say the killer got lucky would be an understatement, as the man who had taken the bulk of the incriminating evidence away on his person, clothes and hatchet; nature and the delay had contributed to destroy the blood and trace evidence he had undoubtedly deposited at the crime scene in two vital locations at the rear door and at the briars bushes close to the body.

Having perpetrated a monstrous deception on *Sunday Tribune* news editor Helen Callanan and editorial handlers in the *Star* and other news media, the briefly rejuvenated career in journalism of Ian Bailey was over – incompatible with the role of prime suspect in the murder case.

For the press corps, it must have been something else to contemplate that the prime suspect was one of their own. Ann Mooney was surprised but not shocked: "There were rumours that a local journalist was being looked at as knowing what happened to Sophie, but it was not until he was arrested and taken to Bandon Station that we discovered that it was Ian Bailey. As I did not know him personally, it did not bother me when I learned he was the prime suspect. But he had been doing some small local stories and had not impacted on the national scene until Sophie was murdered, and he began offering stories about the murder to national newspapers."

There was no doubt that he had enjoyed and revelled in the role of the journalist who professed to have the inside track on the crime. It had restored his self-esteem and in any legitimate circumstance would have led to a lot more media work and the limelight that he clearly craved.

He had assumed the role of not only reporter but investigative reporter who wanted to reveal the French connection to the murder and flush out the real killer. The part he chose to play he performed with the typical gusto required and the ruthlessness, disregard for fact, propensity for quote invention, and general tawdriness that may cynically characterise the classical red top hack but in this case made them look like rosy-cheeked choirboys.

Putting the moral compass and the matter of fact aside, Bailey was perceived at the time of his coverage of the crime as doing a good job – as good as any confidence trickster. But there was far more to this scenario than might immediately meet the eye.

His reporting was not limited to an act of treachery to media representatives, it also amounted to a gross violation of the victim. Sophie Toscan du Plantier was portrayed by him as a promiscuous woman slain by a lover she had invited into her house. Casting her in that role, the subtext read that she deserved what had happened to her on that fateful night. Nowhere did the reporter note the wider extent of the tragedy and its impact on her family. Quite the opposite.

When the theory of the phantom lover was thrown aside, a new one emerged implicating her husband. Sophie, the story ran, was divorcing her husband and returning to her first husband, the conjecture being that he would lose half of his considerable estate, so had hired an assassin to kill her. A further violation of the victim, and her husband and ex-husband, with no basis in fact.

Once again, it portrayed Sophie as a ruthless woman of loose morals who brought her fate upon herself.

As if this Machiavellian fiction was not sufficient to despoil the dead, it also had the effect of pouring salt into the wounds of the living, namely the Bouniol family, desecrating the memory of a loved one already desecrated by the savage act that had deprived her of her life. The treatment of the victim in his reporting displayed a nasty brand of heartless malice.

There was now a vacuum in Bailey's life that given the attention-seeking aspect of his character and the adrenalin pump of the news wolf in search of a story would need to be filled. From the time of his career as a young journalist in Gloucester and Cheltenham, and afterwards his arrival in West Cork, Bailey as a pathological narcissist was extremely dependent on what other people thought of him and had always strived to impress them, but lacked the necessary tact to avoid the impression of being overbearing in his efforts, or pursued a path that would be totally opposed to his self-interest.

It is well accepted by psychologists that such behaviour has a basis in insecurity about contradictory needs that dominate a subject's personality. Such a person wants to be accepted as strong, confident and competent, for everybody to approve of what they do and to recognise this fact. But they have doubts about their adequacy and strength and worry that the people they have set out to impress would recognise that, so seek constant affirmation of their preferred self.

The contradictory needs and the conflict they produce most often operate on a subconscious level, and such a person has little understanding of their own behaviour and lack the sophistication to restrain their reaction to negative responses from people whom they are trying to impress. Those people are questioning the individual's authority and ability to control and will be subjected to their anger and bitterness by not accepting their torturously wrought self-portrait.

Ian Bailey would display those traits in abundance at a most inappropriate time, just after he had been nominated by the murder investigation team as the chief and only suspect for a horrendous crime.

Most crime suspects in his position would keep their heads down and attempt to get on with their lives as best as they could.

This is precisely what his solicitor Con Murphy advised, and urged him to behave more discreetly, especially with the media. He was also urged to keep away from witnesses who gave statements to the investigation team that he might perceive as prejudicial to his interests.

He would ignore this good counsel on both counts. He simply could not keep his mouth shut. Detective Superintendent Dermot Dwyer had never come across anything like this in his thirty-year career as a murder investigator.

"He is unusual in that he could not help talking about the murder. It is not normal to talk at length and in great detail to both locals and complete strangers about a brutal murder when you are the chief suspect. He introduced himself to a couple from Northern Ireland as the chief suspect in the case and talked in detail about how he thought it had happened. He had invited members of our team to his house to discuss aspects of the crime and his theories.

"The day before his arrest, I visited him at his house and spent four hours in conversation with him. We got talking about the crime and I asked him what sort of person, in his opinion, committed the murder. We narrowed the possibilities down to four types: a foreigner, a nutcase, a local or someone hired by her husband. Logically, a foreigner or hired killer were ruled out, and this was reduced to a local nutcase. I jokingly remarked that, 'Sure, you are the only one that fits. You and I know who committed the murder.' Ian visibly went white in the face."

It was an odd scenario. A senior detective of the murder investigation discussing the crime in the kitchen of the chief suspect in what seemed to be a casual manner over a cup of tea or two. But there was clearly an underlying tension which caused the blood to drain from the visage of the suspect when he was hit on the chin when the detective delivered the punchline. It was a line that must have echoed in Bailey's ears long after Dwyer had driven away from the Prairie, along with the knowledge that his adversary's affable and relaxed manner had barely disguised a steely resolve.

Ian Bailey would not be the first suspect in the history of murder not simply to maintain his innocence but also in doing so adopt the persona of the man wronged. Such transformation from the suspected perpetrator to victim on the surface seems like a convenient knee-jerk reaction, but in this instance, there was a deeper agenda. It was one rooted in a narcissistic nature of self-entitlement, grandiose illusion and the willingness to apportion blame to anyone else but himself. He decided that rather than avoiding it, to instead court the media to portray himself as an innocent man wronged.

It was a dangerous move given the fact that as a reporter of the crime he had employed the elements that have always given the profession a bad name, namely: defamation of character, false statements of fact and reckless disregard for the truth. Ironically, it would be the same elements he practiced himself that he would later claim he was subjected to and which had ruined his life.

CHAPTER 5
A CRAVING FOR ATTENTION

West Cork – 1997

The difference at this juncture was that the subject of Bailey's nefarious manipulation of the facts was dead, had no voice to protect her or support of the law, as it is impossible to libel the dead. This is a conundrum, as a person's reputation survives death. Nonetheless, the shredding of the victim's reputation plus the perfidious treatment by him of media handlers, and the lack of remorse for both, had positioned Ian Bailey as a target for journalists as opposed to a credible subject. Not for the first time, this and related realities would not get in the way of his manipulative nature.

He was blind to the fact that his bad faith in his reporting of the crime might have consequences and clearly thought that he deserved good faith from the media he had so roundly misled. It was the equivalent of kicking someone in the groin and expressing great surprise and hurt when the physical compliment was returned in kind.

The least he could have exercised was suspicion and extra caution when dealing with the media pool. How could he have anticipated a reward instead of punishment after his transgression? Could he not have anticipated that one betrayal would be repaid by another one, and that because of the first action, journalists would be hard-pushed to deal objectively or kindly with the newly adopted persona of not the man suspected of doing wrong but the man wronged?

But there was another impulse at work, which psychotherapist Otto Kernberg, who developed the concept of borderline personality disorder, defined as the "curious contradiction between an inflated concept of themselves and an inordinate need for tribute from others". Which described the underlying reason for not pursuing his self-interest and protecting himself but doing the opposite and exposing himself instead of letting things calm down.

Of course, despite his arrest and nomination as prime suspect for the crime, Ian Bailey was entitled to the presumption of innocence. The problem was that everything he was saying, doing, reporting and stating in interviews with the investigation team was undermining that presumption. He had in addition made admissions of carrying out the crime to Helen Callanan, Bill Hogan and others, all of whom took him seriously enough to report the incidents to the investigation team.

So, the cards seemed to have stacked up against the prime suspect; he was unable to explain the discrepancies between his narrative in relation to his circumstances surrounding the murder and the testimony of numerous local witnesses. His allegations of fabrication by and conspiracy of those witnesses rang hollow. His position would isolate him from the immediate community in a similar fashion as his duplicity did from the media.

He desperately needed a way back to inspire some understanding and confidence of both those communities. It would be extremely naïve to conclude that his action to achieve this was based on the impulsive nature of his character and behaviour. It was driven by an agenda which if not immediately effective would be sustained with varying degrees of success for many decades to come.

Consistent with his reporting, which was to discredit the victim and to deflect from any connection between him and the crime, the agenda this time was to discredit the murder investigation team for corruptly putting pressure on witnesses to fabricate statements incriminating him in the murder. It was a bold and attacking strategy both against the forces of law and the alleged complicity of the local community in the alleged unlawful practices.

There is nothing new about a prime suspect or indeed a convicted murderer proclaiming innocence in the face of facts to the contrary, but rarely has it been done on the kind of scale or stage that Bailey employed. Perhaps apart from an infamous case in California in the 1970s, in which an American army doctor, Jeffrey MacDonald, was investigated for the murder of his pregnant wife and two children in their home on the military base Fort Bragg, Carolina.

An initial army tribunal had cleared MacDonald for insufficient evidence but on the insistence of relatives of his wife Coleen, a State investigation ensued and nine and a half years later it resulted in him being charged with the murders. The method employed in the murders, with weapons of opportunity from the home, had strong echoes of the psychopathic savagery used in the murder of Sophie Toscan du Plantier.

In MacDonald's case, the Justice Department had procrastinated for years before acting, and in the Bailey case, the DPP would do nothing. In both cases, this stalling had been for the same reason – the opinion that there was insufficient evidence to prosecute. The victims received no consideration in the legal process; they were ghosts, and no one was willing to give them a voice while the rights of the suspected perpetrators were, as always, paramount.

MacDonald also presented a similar narcissistic craving for attention and proclivity for publicity-seeking as Ian Bailey, hoping it would portray him as a decent character and a man wronged by law enforcement officers, his reasoning being that it would exonerate him from any responsibility for the crime.

For this purpose, he engaged best-selling author Joe McGinniss to tell his story, the purpose of which was predicated in the subject's mind to produce a book which would prove his innocence at the best and/or a sympathetic treatment of him at the worst.

They became friends and business partners when a substantial advance was secured from a publisher with a sharing of the advance and future royalties. A problem arose when at the conclusion of a criminal trial, MacDonald was found guilty of the murders. This should have given pause for thought by the subject, but so assured was he by the impressions of support and friendship given by the writer that he expected the published book to reflect that relationship.

Fatal Vision instead portrayed MacDonald as a murdering psychopath, a publicity seeker, womaniser and latent homosexual. The convicted doctor was devastated, felt totally betrayed and instructed his lawyers to sue McGinniss for fraud and breach of contract. Some years afterwards, the action came to court in a civil trial which after a hung jury failed to bring a verdict, so a settlement was made in which MacDonald received $350,000.

The result was perceived as a defeat for the writer; however, he protested that his responsibility was not to the subject but to the book and presumably the truth, which as many true crime writers discover can be as elusive and difficult to pin down as mice at crossroads. McGinniss was subjected to a pitiless and trenchant cross-examination by the plaintiff's counsel Gary Bostwick over four days during which the writer's forty letters to the subject while he was in prison almost singularly exposed the magnitude of the so-called betrayal.

The case exposed a lot of troubling questions about journalistic ethics and the perils of a relationship between a subject and a writer, the former in this instance freely co-operating and giving information based on an understanding and arrangement which the writer had no intention of honouring when the tide turned against the subject after the criminal trial verdict.

The subject was dealt with in a series of articles in *The New Yorker* by staff writer Janet Malcolm and a subsequent book entitled *The Journalist and the Murderer*, the brilliant and controversial opening line enraging the more precious members of the fourth estate and running thus:

"Every journalist who is not too stupid or too full of himself to notice what is going on knows that what he does is morally indefensible."

Although at first glance there might seem to be no direct analogy between this case and the murder in West Cork other than a form of journalistic treachery on a dead person and in the MacDonald instance a walking dead person, the first incarcerated in the grave and the other in a prison, there was a connection with the desire of the accused suspect and the ultimately convicted suspect to go to any lengths with the risks involved to enter the public domain to protest their innocence. But there would be other disturbing parallels in the behaviour and psychology of both men and in the history of the cases.

McGinniss was told that his subject would say anything to anybody, he literally could not keep his mouth shut – or as the author would discover late on in the collaboration, that his subject had given him versions of events that were untrue to suit his self-portrait as an innocent man and could not distinguish fact from fiction. He also discovered that MacDonald had not revealed vital documents to him, such as psychiatric reports which were damning of the doctor.

In West Cork in early 1997, Ian Bailey's reporting on the case had been stopped by the newspapers and was about to be replaced by his desire to be written about, a position which the vast majority of journalists would react against as Dracula would when offered a crucifix. Only a narcissist, his judgement overwhelmed by the desire for the attention and approval of others, would have walked down such a path strewn with opportunities for ambush.

After a military tribunal had cleared him for lack of sufficient evidence (it was never indicated that he was innocent of the crime), Jeffrey MacDonald contacted half a dozen high-profile publications to write about his case instead of keeping his head below the parapet. He told people who cautioned him that he wanted to get his side of the story across and to show them he was an ordinary person, not a monster. He was in fact eager to get the admiration and attention of people and at the same time become a celebrity and a form of hero instead of a villain.

Thriving in the attention and his new public profile, he made the foolish mistake of going on *The Dick Cavett Show*, which would prove to be his downfall. The narcissist has a poor grasp or understanding of his behaviour and is equally inept at disguising the less appealing sides of their character. The attention of the media buoys the belief in their competence and ability to control. MacDonald walked willingly into the lion's den of the media, confident that he would emerge not just unscathed but triumphant.

He was asking his sisters to get everyone they and he knew to watch the show, and any others like the Walter Cronkite-hosted *CBS Evening News* programme, demonstrating that here was a man intoxicated at the prospect of publicity and totally ignorant of the nature of media exposure. There is always an inclination for an inexperienced participant to say too much and the wrong things. There is no self-editing facility or ability to be evasive in a credible fashion. Both MacDonald and Bailey were in love with the sound of their own voices and they could not stop themselves talking.

This problem is magnified in the narcissist, with their pseudo-self-insight, self-centredness and dependence on the goodwill and admiration of in this case the audience meaning that there would be an overplay to the gallery. That might have worked had the main emphasis been on the horrendous impact of the tragedy on the victims, the subject's pregnant wife and children, and had he engaged sympathy by breaking down. But among the many deficits in the psychology of the murdering narcissist is a lack of any empathy with the victim.

There was none of that; the whole emphasis was on Jeffrey MacDonald and what had happened to him. There was little or no empathy for the victims, his own wife and kids; instead, he launched an attack on the Army Criminal Investigation authorities for incompetently handling the investigation of the crime and daring to accuse him. At times, he laughed and joked with the host. It was as if he was using a crime of a nature so brutal that it was almost beyond belief, and which happened at his home and in his presence to establish himself as a national celebrity.

The host did his job as he was supposed to do, asking the relevant questions, but the responses on view of the tape were entirely self-serving. MacDonald was living through a nightmare he claimed was not of his own making, and when asked to give an account of the night of the murders he said he would skim through it, and did by putting emphasis on the wounds and suffering he endured, as opposed to those of the real victims.

It was hard to believe that given the ghastly brutality of the bloody murder of his family, that he could refer briefly to the night without the faintest flicker of emotion, not even a fleeting tear in the eye – even if it had been disguised self-pity, it might have impressed the audience as being something approaching grief.

He then launched into an attack against the army investigation: "There were people in the army who wanted a court martial regardless of any evidence. I knew, I've watched these men. I've seen them testify and I've seen perjury."

When asked was that because they had to find somebody, MacDonald replied: "Yes, that is a very large part of it, I think. Absolutely. They had done nothing really. They had performed very incompetently, and they had realised they had to do something. So, they charged me."

This would be the exact replica of the position adopted by Ian Bailey in relation to the murder investigation team in West Cork. The implication of MacDonald's position was not lost on the viewers or his wife's stepfather Freddie Kassab and mother, previously supporters of his innocence but now convinced of MacDonald's guilt. And in common with the Bouniol family and the case of Bailey, they mounted a protracted campaign to bring MacDonald to justice and succeeded when he was put on trial and convicted of the murders. It would take much longer and another jurisdiction to bring Bailey to justice.

Bailey, who should have known better, made the similar assumption that the journalists and interviewers would do the right thing by *him*. MacDonald had been released by a military tribunal of the savage murders of his wife, unborn child and two children on the grounds of insufficient evidence. Bailey had not been charged for lack of sufficient evidence and the best thing for both was to disappear quietly into the dark night and to carefully await the outcome of events. Also, it is important to point out in both cases that the prime suspects were never at any stage adjudged or considered innocent of the crimes.

Another common purpose as part of their publicity campaigns was to mount attacks, in MacDonald's case against the army and in Bailey's case against the murder investigation team, and both actively and blindly sought high-profile publicity to promote their points of view. They shared hatred and bitterness towards the authorities that had nominated them as prime suspects for the horrendous murders, and were determined to expose them as incompetent, stupid and corrupt. Both had expansive egos, delusions of persecution and firm conviction of omnipotence. The suffering of the victims or their relatives was of no importance to them.

Bailey embarked on a plethora of interviews, including on *The Pat Kenny Show*, the popular mid-morning programme on RTE Radio One, and followed this with others in the print media for Irish, English and French publications, many of whom he invited to the house where he and his partner lived. His demeanour struck reporters as calm and confident. A French journalist captured his mood succinctly: "*Smooth and charming, the suspect had no hesitation for the camera. He was at home playing at family photographs, around the kitchen table or standing in the garden, shovel in hand.*"

Bailey was joined by his partner Jules Thomas on *The Pat Kenny Show*, which was broadcast on February 14, 1997. He did not take long to begin lying to his host. When pitching for work with media outlets, he told editors and reporters, including among them Helen Callanan of the *Sunday Tribune*, Paul Webster of *The Guardian* and the RTE *Crimeline* crew that he knew Sophie.

PK: *And had you any previous knowledge of this woman, had you met her before, were you acquainted with her, had you seen her before?*

IB: *I had never met her. I had never been introduced to her and had never spoken to her. I had knowledge of her in as much that two years ago in the spring I was nearby with a neighbour of hers who pointed her out to me.*

PK: *But other than that, no contact of any kind?*

IB: *That is correct.*

After some relatively innocuous exchanges, Pat Kenny came to the nub of the matter that despite his arrest, Bailey and the media outing him – as the host pointed out – was normal journalistic practice for anyone who was arrested in relation to a crime. In addition, he was actually touting for publicity.

PK: *Your reaction to the publicity then? I mean, you have embraced it in the sense that you have ...*

IB: *Well, I took advice from my solicitor Con Murphy of Bandon when it had become known that my identity had been released and it was certain that* The Sun *mentioned the name that eh ...*

PK: *You took advice?*

IB: *I took advice from Con Murphy.*

PK: *And did he clarify matters?*

IB: *He decided we should issue a statement.*

PK: *Reading this morning's* Examiner, *it seems that you have ...*

IB: *I haven't seen that.*

PK: *Okay, but it seems that you have given them some quotes and you have talked to them.*

IB: *Yesterday, we had at our door what seemed to be the entire world's press and I talked to Eamon Timmins.*

PK: Yeah, *the kind of media attention you have had and some details about your personal life have been revealed.*

IB: *They have, haven't they?*

PK: *That there was some complaint to the Gardai that there was a domestic row.*

IB: *Look, where did that information come from, Pat?*

PK: *This is in* The Cork Examiner, *or* The Examiner *as they call it now.*

IB: *Right, de paper.*

PK: *De Paper and something about your former wife having some claims against you.*

IB: *Where ... I don't know where these ... who is releasing these facts to the media? I am not releasing them.*

PK: *So, you would regard this as a gross intrusion on your person?*

IB: *Absolutely.*

The real facts about the so-called intrusion on his personal life were the opposite of what he told Pat Kenny. His solicitor Con Murphy had advised him not to interact with the media. Bailey had given an interview to Eamon Timmins, published on the morning of the programme, but a far more revealing one with Senan Molony published the previous day in the *Star*, which Pat's researchers may have passed or the show's producer judged too contentious.

Eamon Timmins, in his piece for *The Examiner*, described the surroundings of the house:

"From the outside, the white-washed dormer cottage looks like a little patch of paradise. The path leads down along a large vegetable patch to a greenhouse at the side of the house and past a fishing net which keeps the chickens and ducks in the back garden. At the end of the road, a panoramic view of Dunmanus Bay opens out."

The journalist noted that from reporting on the investigation, Ian Bailey had become part of it and quoted him as saying, *"It has become one long day and night, very strained, strange and surreal."*

What was equally surreal was that despite being the prime and only suspect for the crime, that he should be engaging on such a wide level with the media, and predictably he used the opportunity in this and other interviews to criticise the investigation team and to repeat the mantra: "I am not a killer, I am an innocent man." Also, he insisted that he had not known nor ever met Sophie Toscan du Plantier, despite already informing at least four senior journalists that he had known her.

A lengthy interview with the *Star* published on February 13, 1997 was accompanied by a half-page photograph showing Bailey at his kitchen table, leaning over and pouring a cup of tea for the newspaper's crime reporter Senan Molony, who head down was concentrating on his note-taking, a task that any good journalist should be engaged in.

But the lack of eye contact between the reporter and subject told its own story. Jim Walpole's beautifully composed shot portrayed Bailey as a man at ease with himself, which seemed at odds with his circumstances of the time, but nothing to the contrary came across. Perhaps he thought that inviting journalists to his home might somehow disarm them of potentially perfidious practices in relation to himself while allowing him to disseminate his propaganda untrammelled. But the stark reality was that he was being interviewed by an ex-colleague in his new role as the prime suspect for a brutal murder.

The interview also again demonstrated one motive behind his publicity campaign, which was to discredit the members of the murder investigation team. Bailey said:

"The Gardai said they had checked into me in Britain where I had a very acrimonious divorce from my wife. They were clutching at straws all the time. They kept suggesting different motives. I want to make it clear that I never met Sophie and I never spoke to her. I knew that she was French and I had seen her once two years ago.

"When I arrived at Bandon Garda Station there were photographers waiting. Someone had tipped them off and it all became very public. The Gardai could have brought us in very quietly and asked us to come in. I know they were under pressure but they trampled ... like they trampled all over the murder scene. There is a forensic saying: the victim dies once but the murder scene dies a thousand times. It was not properly preserved.

"I saw all this. I was rung up by a press photographer on December 23 and told about the killing and I went up to the site to see for myself. When I was questioned, they took all my clothes away. Someone then went out and bought me what I call the typical guard's off-duty uniform – black shoes, jeans, a check shirt and a very fine jacket. I still have them but the guards have all my coats and quite a few bits and pieces.

"I think the publicity over what has happened has put me in a very prejudiced position not only in relation to my career as a journalist but also should I be charged in relation to a fair trial."

The last line of that quote is incredibly revealing. He is on the face of it complaining about the publicity surrounding his arrest. Yet he is exposing himself to publicity that might add to that alleged prejudice in a calculated and deliberate manner, prompting any rational observer to conclude that this was a part of his agenda that as a result he would never get a fair trial. But without a clear memory, weaving such a web of deceit is a perilous act.

He then referred to other stories he said were based on rumours, including that he committed the murder because he wanted to reinvent his reporting career, killed Sophie and then had written stories which pointed to someone coming over from France to commit the crime. All was coming across as an extended whinge tinged with a large dollop of self-pity. Again, as with MacDonald, there was no mention or empathy displayed towards the victim or her family. Bailey, as with his American counterpart MacDonald, was seeking an easy ride from the media.

All of that might have seemed well and good, but on the following page of the newspaper there was first of all a far less flattering portrait of Bailey by a former boss – John Hawkins, the editor of the *Gloucester News* – and a compendium of his reports for the newspaper on the crime, which clearly as presented cast a large doubt on their authenticity and the motive for writing them.

As for the fair main piece by crime reporter Senan Molony, Bailey not for the first or last time, in his proclamations about the crime, got basic facts wrong and made assertions without the evidence to back them up, such as if he was charged, he would never get a fair trial. He said he got a call from a photographer who told him about the killing. It was not a photographer but a reporter, who told him nothing about a killing but rather about a death of which little was known, including the identity of the victim.

He then said without a scintilla of evidence but his mere assertion that the investigation team had trampled all over the murder scene and he had seen this when he visited the site. How he could have possibly seen this without the benefit of forensic examination he did not or could not explain. He had been kept some distance away when he said he first arrived at the crime scene on the afternoon of December 23, 1996.

He accused the investigation team of tipping off the media in advance of his arrest and questioning at Bandon Garda Station, and once again he could not provide evidence to prove the allegation. He was trying to use the media to attack the investigation team and promote himself in the role of the innocent man. It must be said that despite his incompetent memory and poor grasp of detail, Bailey was fiendishly clever and the myths he created about the incompetence of the investigation became a common perception in the public mind for a long time. His baseless malice was not obvious to everyone.

Senan Molony remembers his exclusive first print interview with his former colleague and now the prime suspect: "There was intense competition to be the first to have a print interview with Bailey and he granted it to me because of our previous interaction while he was working for the *Star*. During the interview, which was conducted in the kitchen of the home in Liscaha, he emphasised the point that he had never met or spoken to Sophie Toscan du Plantier. He said he only had seen her two years before.

"However, I recall doubting that because Bailey had originally told me that the murder victim was 'French' and had in fact referred to her by her maiden name Bouniol. I also found it incredible that as a curious journalist he did not know her. He confirmed that he was the prime suspect and had been threatened by the Gardai and warned by one member that he would end up in a ditch with a hole in the back of his head.

"At no time did I attach a shred of credence to these claims, because of my own extensive experience in the area. No arresting officers in a major murder inquiry could conceivably allow such compromising behaviour to arise from such a threat, especially as he claimed arose on the way to Bandon Station where he was being brought for questioning."

Senan Molony was beginning to suspect that Bailey might be responsible for the murder. "He fitted the signature of the killer. He was tall, strong and powerfully built. There were say 200 houses in the area and half of those were holiday homes and unoccupied at that time of the year. He had a history of violence towards his partner. He had no alibi and I realised that he had no sources for his reporting but knew details of the crime scene and injuries to the body of the victim which only someone present could have known.

"He had also lied extensively to me during my interview with him after the arrest. His allegations about how he was intimidated by the officers on the way to Bandon were totally incredible and had all the hallmarks of the fabrication he had used in his reporting. I asked him to explain the scratches on his hands, forearms and forehead. He said he had got them cutting down a Christmas tree. I looked him straight in the eyes and said no one had ever heard of a person putting up a tree in their house just a few days before Christmas Day.

"He went silent and his mouth opened soundlessly like a fish in a bowl and his eyes protruded. I told him his story about the turkeys was equally nonsensical. I decided after I returned to Dublin and before he could be arrested again to travel to Gloucester and Cheltenham and get as much information as possible on his background before he moved to Ireland and have it published quickly so it would not become sub judice in the event that he was charged."

Senan Molony travelled to Gloucester with photographer Jim Walpole to look further into the prime suspect's background. His ex-wife Sarah Limbrick would not co-operate but Senan interviewed an ex-girlfriend, Ellie Carey, former colleagues and Avon police officers.

The police confirmed there was an ongoing investigation into Sarah Limbrick's statement that Bailey had forged her signature on an insurance policy for £250,000 without her knowledge. Also, Molony established from Bailey's former journalist colleagues in Gloucester and Cheltenham about his attention-seeking and love for being the centre of notoriety, of how he was consistently confrontational and loved causing trouble. Character traits he had not left behind when he moved to Ireland.

"A specific instance a colleague related to me was Bailey drinking champagne behind the big front window of a pub so that passers-by could see him quaffing an expensive drink. Also, by at least two sources, of his tall tales about various encounters and how he had pinned up a nude photograph of himself in the newsroom of the Gloucester and County News Agency. Former colleagues and friends told me that while in Cheltenham, Bailey had a penchant for causing fights by being abusive to people, for effect. They also maintained that he had developed a fascination for the murders committed by Fred and Rose West."

Molony's investigation into the background of the prime suspect was carried in the *Star* edition of Saturday, February 22, 1997 with a banner headline on the front-page reading:

BAILEY IN £500,000 DIVORCE ROW

The usual short tabloid front-page introduction revealed that Bailey's first marriage ended in an acrimonious divorce and he claimed that he was owed £250,000 from the last property they had occupied. He also admitted that he had been questioned by Gardai over allegations that he had forged a signature of his wife Sarah for the same amount of money on a life insurance policy in her name. He claimed to know nothing about the matter.

There was substantial coverage over inside pages four and five, containing facts previously undisclosed about Ian Bailey's past which must have enraged him enough to later sue the reporter and the newspaper. The main piece chronicled the marriage to Sarah Limbrick and their move into a large detached red-brick house secluded by trees at Parton Road, Churchdown, Gloucester.

"Foxmoor House was so big that the couple converted part of the premises for the upkeep of old folks. That side-line brought in even more cash for the couple, who were successful local journalists. In 1987, the couple sold the house and moved into a bigger spread in the post-card pretty Forest of Dean."

This property was worth £500,000. When the marriage collapsed, Bailey discovered that the only name on the deeds was that of his wife, who retained the full cash value of the house when it was sold. Sarah Limbrick, who refused to engage with the reporter, accused Bailey of being psychologically threatening during the bitter divorce proceedings. She had also been interviewed by Avon police in relation to the insurance policy.

A side piece on page four described how Bailey had landed a staff job with the *Gloucester Express* and lost it after ten days. He was threatened with the sack after just four days and was handed his cards six days later. His employer Dennis Apperly told Molony that Bailey was lazy, did no work and thought he qualified for payment by just being present:

"He talked a lot about what he was going to do, but never got around it. But you need something to actually put in the paper and Eoin would have his feet up on the desk, talking on the phone."

What was emerging in this tabloid portrait of Bailey was a man of supreme arrogance who was not just immune to the consequences of his behaviour but also convinced of his entitlement to be considered better than the rest of the journalists and in addition of his attraction for the opposite sex. A side piece on page five underlined that facility for the belief that his sexual prowess was a key to his success as a journalist.

This recounted that a full-frontal nude picture of Bailey had been pinned to a notice board in a busy newsroom by himself:

"The wildly extrovert reporter boasted to colleagues that this was what they were up against – raw sex appeal that would always ensure him exclusive interviews, Bailey cheerfully endures comments that the picture must be an enlargement and displayed no modesty or embarrassment about the full-length snap. He even complained when the picture went missing after co-workers took it down."

His former colleague George Henderson said that he was proud of his prowess with women and he hinted that he could pick them up at will. He also added that Bailey could get into strange states of mind and would say that he was a drunk and wallow in self-pity. This observation indicated a form of split personality, one full of inflated confidence accompanied by severe self-doubt.

In an interview with French newspaper *Le Figaro*, Daniel Toscan du Plantier was somewhat shocked by Bailey's efforts to seek public attention, particularly at that time:

"Bailey has chosen to court the media ... and now he has an amazing new profession – I am not the killer of Sophie Toscan du Plantier ... if I were in his place and I were innocent I would have run away and changed my name and my life."

When high-profile feature writer Brighid McLaughlin travelled to Schull to interview Bailey for the *Sunday Independent*, he seemed to retreat from the prospect, telling her that his lawyer had warned him about speaking about the crime. This was a complete contradiction of what he had told Pat Kenny on his show. Staying in the small East End Hotel, she was preparing to return to Dublin without the story when out of the blue Bailey turned up in the foyer and the interview went ahead.

"Bailey," she observed, *"does talk. He simply can't stop."*

She got the distinct impression which he gave of being the expert on the case, discussing theories about the crime but with an air of excitement that would be foreign to a real expert. She was somewhat repulsed by his constant reference to the victim as "Sophie" as opposed to Mme Toscan du Plantier, a familiarity more appropriate to a friend or acquaintance, an acquired intimacy too far for the writer.

He also could not stop writing in his diaries. Once again, he was gripped by hubris; shortly after his meeting with Brighid McLaughlin, he scribbled down his reaction in an entry:

"Back in print again hip, hip, hip hooray."

Apart from a rather juvenile reaction from a middle-aged man, it expressed just how much Ian Bailey craved attention, loved the spotlight and was out of touch with the motives of journalists who were emboldened by the fact that the subject of their interviews was now prime suspect for the murder and the central character in a story which was the biggest in the region since Irish patriot Michael Collins had been assassinated in West Cork by Republican forces in 1922.

Had he read Janet Malcolm's book *The Journalist and the Murderer*, first published in 1990 and reprinted that same year of 1997, Ian Bailey might not have, figuratively speaking, been jumping about with such obvious glee, and rather have found ways of escaping instead of lying on the tracks and leading the media express train to hurtle towards him. In common with MacDonald, what he wanted from a profession trained to be anything but was a sympathetic ear when, given the circumstances, it would far more likely be one of the cauliflower variety.

Ignoring the prime suspect's publicity campaign, the investigation team got on with the job and at last in mid-February got Marie Farrell to deliver a formal statement at Ballydehob Garda Station in the presence of senior officers including Detective Jim Fitzgerald. While it was extremely damaging to the prime suspect, there were inherent difficulties with the situation in which the witness found herself on the night of the murder and ultimately later on her credibility.

On the morning of Sunday, December 22, she travelled to Cork city to work on a street stall and while there met a former boyfriend. On returning to Schull that evening, she told her husband Chris that she was going out later with some friends. She left the family home at 10.30 p.m. and met the same man in a hotel car park. They drove separately to Goleen, she in her van and he in his car. Apparently, she was prepared in the end and would have to face her own domestic fallout from the assignation but was perhaps unwilling to visit the consequences on the family of her male companion of the night.

Bailey was slowly realising that his new role as the subject of media interviews was not working along the lines that he had expected and that asking for a sympathetic or even fair stance on the part of the journalist was not set in stone as far as the writer was concerned, whatever assurances were given in advance. He was upset about an article in the *Star* published about a week after his interview by Senan Molony, especially the depiction of the relationship with his ex-wife and the life insurance policy that he had taken out on her for a considerable sum of money on which she said during divorce proceedings he had forged her signature.

While reporting on the crime, he had assisted Molony and a photographer who had travelled from Dublin to West Cork at his request, citing the reason of the sensitive and emotional atmosphere surrounding the crime at local level, and requesting that his name be left out of any articles that would follow the visit. No doubt he now considered his former colleague an enemy.

He was even less enchanted by the *Sunday Independent* article by Brighid McLaughlin which was later published in the English *Independent on Sunday* in a revised version. He considered the title "The Devil in the Hills" as referring to him but which was in fact a reproduction of Daniel Toscan du Plantier's description of the killer in an interview with a French publication. He was upset by the reporting in the article of a bonfire sometime after the murder which he told the writer contained his clothes, which he claimed were stained by the blood of a turkey he had killed.

In this passage, McLaughlin wrote:

"People were suspicious. Ian Bailey said he was killing turkeys that morning. There were rumours that he was burning clothes on the morning after the murder. He says he was obliged to burn the clothes because they were covered in turkey blood."

The burning took place a couple of days later but no matter.

She further repeated the *Star* story that Bailey had pinned a full-frontal nude picture of himself in a busy newsroom where he worked in England and boasted to colleagues about his sexual prowess. She described a trip she took with Bailey in his car to Schull and back and mentioned that she was afraid in his company.

If indeed it was the blood of an animal that was subjected to his brutal attention then it is hard to see why it was a source of worry to him for the simple reason that a forensic examination of his clothes would go a long way in exonerating him from suspicion on that point and perhaps providing an explanation for the scratches on his arms.

But he knew from what he had described as his coverage of "fish and chips murders" during his English reporting career that if fibres from the victim's clothes were found on his clothes then this would link him to the crime scene at the time of the murder. Linking him to a turkey would prove him to be the innocent man he proclaimed to be.

Further, two neighbours had given statements to the investigation team of witnessing the bonfire on St Stephen's Day and when Bailey was questioned about it, he had replied that there was no bonfire. One of the witnesses, Louise Kennedy, said she noticed smoke coming from Bailey's backyard. She saw an old mattress that was two thirds burnt. There was no one at the fire. However, another neighbour, Ursula Jackson, saw both the fire and Bailey close to it.

Garda Eugene Gilligan had examined the site of the debris and bonfire behind the studio on February 10. He found the carbonised debris of paper, fabric or clothes, a mattress and some shoelaces. Not the sort of items one would want to dispose of after encountering turkey blood.

In that context, he should have avoided any mention of it. It was just another one of myriad contradictions in the prime suspect's account of his part in events surrounding the crime and again demonstrated his propensity to talk about it even if what he said was incriminating.

Brighid McLaughlin was correct in her assessment that once Bailey got talking, he could not stop. He had previously denied the existence of the fire but told the writer that it had in fact occurred. The subject of the interview had been upset because he claimed that his statement had been "*off the record*". But if so, why even mention it in the first place? But if it had the privilege he claimed, the fact remained that he had admitted to having burnt clothes in a bonfire.

It was not either a sympathetic or flattering piece which no doubt the subject expected, but that did not mean that it had been written with malice intended as opposed to the writer's truthful recording of her impressions of the subject, which many people in that part of West Cork would have recognised having known him a lot longer. He could not as a result of his overweening arrogance perceive the possibility that he could be his own worst enemy through the medium of a mouth the width of the gates of hell.

So now the betrayer, while reporting the crime, felt betrayed by former colleague Senan Molony and Brighid McLaughlin among other journalists down the line. In the face of what he perceived as hostility, why would Ian Bailey continue to place himself in the firing line? That is exactly what he did, perhaps from a pathological optimism or as a result of the gambler's grandiose fantasy in which it does not occur that losses will figure on the ultimate balance sheet. Having so flagrantly exposed himself to media attention, mostly with his involvement, the prime suspect would be further disappointed by that focus, and so it transpired.

An article in *The Times* in London by Audrey Magee was published under the headline Ian Bailey Has No Alibi for the Night of the Murder, which was of course true, and reported that Bailey had admitted that he had a history of violence towards women. The plural was not correct at that time, but the singular was true in a horrific manner that had never been reported in any minute detail before or at the time.

Another article in the same newspaper claimed he was believed to have been introduced to the victim by a neighbour, which was true but upset him as he had told Senan Molony that he had never met her. He must have forgotten that he had previously told every other journalist who he was touting work from that he knew Sophie, one of the reasons he was hired. Like all poor liars, Bailey had an equally poor memory.

Bailey's confident demeanour while engaging with interviewers was accompanied by a lack of care for and consistency with the substance of his statements, as once again illustrated by *The Times* article which truthfully recorded the fact that Bailey knew the victim. In advance of this publicity campaign, he had told several media representatives, including news editor Helen Callanan and the *Crimecall* crew, that he knew Sophie Toscan du Plantier while touting for reporting work.

Is it possible that he could have forgotten this or was he becoming tangled in the web of lies and deceit that he had woven himself? Parents have for generations told their children that to speak the truth is easy but to utter lies is much more difficult for it requires a good memory. At both a macro and micro level in the matter of fact, the prime suspect was doing himself no favours.

Toby Harnden, the highly respected Ireland correspondent of *The Daily Telegraph* and author of the brilliant book on South Armagh, *Bandit Country*, wrote an article in March of 1997 which reported that Bailey's proposal to write a documentary about the environment had been rejected by Sophie. This enraged Bailey because he wrongly interpreted the fact on two counts, the first that he had declared he never had any contact with her and second that it suggested a motive for the murder.

Although Harnden did not know it, a local, Leo Bolger, who was acquainted with and did work for Sophie on her house, had witnessed her neighbour Alfie Lyons introducing her to Bailey while the latter was doing gardening work for the former. Not only that, but Bolger on a separate occasion had also heard Bailey talking about giving a manuscript to Sophie, which not only corroborated the story but also the statement of a French witness who was present when Bailey rang her at her production office in Paris.

The first problem for the subject coming face to face with the interviewer is to maintain the latter's interest by providing information of a compelling enough substance to achieve that end. In some cases, Ian Bailey rehashed material he had reported – the wine glasses at the sink, the chairs pushed together and a new one, a champagne bottle on the floor of the kitchen, placed against a wall. His knowledge of the interior of the house of course aroused further suspicion on behalf of the investigation team.

But to keep the media on the hook, he was forced to give information he could not have obtained during his brief period of reporting, such as telling a local journalist that one of the victim's fingers was almost severed. Only members of the investigation team and the pathologist were privy to the existence of that defensive wound sustained during the savage attack, hidden from the family under a bandage in the mortuary and never released in public.

In other interviews, he returned to his old practice of fabrication. He told French journalist Pascale Gerin of *Le Parisien* that he was the victim of a conspiracy between members of the investigation team and local witnesses:

"They are lying. Better than that, they came to see me in my house recently and apologised, even though I never asked them to. They said the police had forced them to make and sign statements incriminating me. The woman who said she had seen me at 4 a.m. cleaning my boots even told me that they had shown her an amateur film I'd made for Christmas so that she could see me and would be able to describe me in a statement. Some of my friends were even offered money by the cops so that they would testify against me. Not one accepted the deal."

This was pure fiction; not one witness had approached him and said anything of the sort, particularly at that stage the woman who had spotted him at Kealfadda Bridge. That was Marie Farrell and she had never made a statement about cleaning boots. He was, according to her account, staggering along the road, which was well distant from the stream, the only place where one could clean boots. The prime suspect had made another slip of the tongue and revealed that he was in fact cleaning his boots.

Now why would a man abroad near the crime scene on a clear moonlit night in freezing temperatures and on rock-hard ground where mud would turn to concrete be attempting to clean his boots just kilometres from the blood-soaked corpse of a murdered woman? And why would Ian Bailey mention the exercise and put it into the mouth of a witness who had never said anything about it?

Bailey, who was so used to changing his version of events surrounding the crime, was getting confused about to whom he had told what. He had in fact after his release from custody told Yvonne Ungerer, who he might have considered a friend, that there was some unaccounted time for the early hours of December 23. He had left his bed to work on an article and then he left the house.

"That must have been the time they saw me at the causeway" (near Kealfadda Bridge). Yvonne enquired about what he was doing at the causeway. "I suppose I was washing the blood off my clothes." She was surprised by the reply and asked what he was doing at the causeway in his car. "No, no, there was no car." What struck her forcibly was that he did not deny being in the area where he had been seen by Marie Farrell.

Bailey was embittered and disappointed by the post-arrest media coverage. His objective of casting himself in a hero role of an innocent man hunted down by a corrupt murder investigation team who were allegedly putting pressure on local witnesses to make false statements implicating him in the crime had backfired. Instead, he was still stuck in the zero role of prime suspect. He had also been deprived of exercising in his own mind his great investigative powers as a reporter.

The journalists whose approval he had sought and who he had assumed would help his cause had failed to deliver and had in his opinion reinforced his connection with the crime. Further, the members of the media in his view were responsible for depriving him of a living and had ruined his reputation. He had to stop them writing about him and the only way he could do that would be to sue for libel for portraying an innocent man as the murderer. He began to plan that very action and would follow it up with his legal adviser Con Murphy.

PART TWO

CHAPTER 6
THE PLOT THICKENS

West Cork – 1997–99

Detective Superintendent Dermot Dwyer, who had responsibility for Cork city and county, had been on the investigation team since the day of the post-mortem, and in June 1997 – having been promoted to Chief Superintendent at Bandon – took over the role of head of the investigation into the murder. A handsome, affable and charismatic man with a wry sense of humour, he was originally from Kerry and had joined the force in Cork city over two decades previously. He was hugely experienced in the areas of serious crime, fraud and murder.

Soon after the investigation began, he was in Schull at a time when the list of suspects was wide and no one person had been nominated, and was told that he might be interested in talking to a man by the name of Brian Scott McCarthy, who had a holiday home there. He was a businessman in the gift market aimed at tourists and operated from Kinsale, but he also had a qualification in psychotherapy. He called to the house, was invited in and introduced himself to Brian.

A conversation ensued about the murder and Brian questioned him in detail about the crime scene and the injuries to the body of the victim. Both agreed that the level of violence employed went far beyond the necessity to commit the crime. The perpetrator had serious psychological problems which the psychotherapist said would be magnified by a full moon. Some people with underlying mental challenges can be badly affected by the pull of the moon.

McCarthy posited that the man would walk around with what is called a thinking stick and would be easily focused on because he would be inclined to talk about the murder and tell people he was responsible for the crime. He would come across in the community as an eccentric character and would stand out.

He also advised the detective that if the man was arrested, he should be questioned in a conversational manner as he would be convinced that he had a superior intellect and was cleverer than the interrogators, and by avoiding confrontation the suspect would let his guard down.

It was agreed that Dwyer would produce a report or profile of the type of character who might commit such a brutal crime which would be included in the first investigation file. After the meeting, Dwyer called into Schull Station and told one of the officers about his encounter, and he immediately said that fitted a local man called Ian Bailey. The detective had never heard his name before that point. Ironically, during a casual conversation with the detective later, the prime suspect admitted to becoming edgy, tense and agitated when there was a full moon. He described it like a nerve-stricken actor before a performance. It reminded Dwyer of McCarthy's assessment of a possible suspect at a time when the psychotherapist had also never known of the existence of Ian Bailey.

The detective had a particular interest in interrogation techniques, which he had studied and put to good use when questioning Ian Bailey. During his arrest the previous February, Dwyer had elicited from the detainee the fact that he had left the main house on the night of the murder. It was an admission that Bailey regretted making and would hold a grudge against Dwyer bordering on a bitter hatred, blaming the detective for putting him in the position of having no alibi for most of the night of the murder.

The prime suspect was now aware that he faced an accomplished adversary who would leave no stone or detail unturned in hunting down the killer of Sophie Toscan du Plantier. Bailey had got a big charge out of trying to make the investigators look stupid, but he would have a hard time in doing that to a man with as sharp an intellect as the new chief superintendent at Bandon.

Ian Bailey had been told by his solicitor Con Murphy to avoid contact with local witnesses but once again he ignored his legal representative's advice, as he did in the matter of engaging with the media. He had no inhibitions in either matter and in the second instance interfered with a witness in a murder investigation in which he was the prime suspect and thus perverted the course of justice.

He had already begun a sustained campaign to intimidate Marie Farrell into withdrawing her statement that placed him at Kealfadda Bridge and to explain this action by saying she had been put under pressure by members of the Garda investigation team to implicate him in the murder by making a false statement.

Marie Farrell informed Gardai that two days previously, on June 8, 1997, Jules Thomas had visited her shop and invited her to come to her house to make a recording in which she would state how the police had pressurised her to say that she saw Bailey on Monday morning, December 30, instead of Sunday, December 22, 1996. When she refused on the basis that the police had never asked her to say anything, Thomas said that another witness had accepted to do it and alleged that Detective Jim Fitzgerald had provided the witness with illicit substances to get information from Bailey.

This was a reference to Martin Graham, who had offered to get information from Bailey but whom the Garda members handling him had begun to suspect was in fact an ally of Bailey engaged in a sting, and from late May they recorded conversations with him without his knowledge. He had been given modest expenses but never any illicit substances. It was evidence of the lengths that Bailey was prepared to go to in order to discredit the Gardai in the hope that if they slipped up by corrupt behaviour, he could ensure that this would be proof positive that he could never get a fair trial.

Part of his plan included having a photographer from one of the main tabloids on hand, tipped off by Graham in advance, to catch the moment that the hash was being handed over. The architect of this scenario believed that the investigators were not just corrupt but dunces. Mr Bailey could be fiendishly clever at times but equally stupid at others.

Marie Farrell made a comprehensive statement about the incident, as did her shop assistant Geraldine O'Brien who was also present and witnessed what had occurred in the shop.

In the statement, she recounted that she and her husband were in the Galley pub in Schull on June 22 and in conversation with Jules Thomas about babysitting that Thomas's daughter Fenella had done for them when Bailey approached her and briefly took her aside. He told her that there was something he needed her to do but they could not talk about it in the pub. He wanted her to make a statement recorded on tape by him withdrawing her identification of him being at Kealfadda Bridge on the night of the murder.

He also added that by the time he was finished with them, detectives Fitzgerald and Leahy's retirements would be in jeopardy. This was another reference to the role of Martin Graham, who was conspiring with Bailey to have the officers discredited by asking them for drugs in return for information on the prime suspect. What he did not know was that the officers were wise to his ruse.

The following morning, he called into her shop in Schull and told her, "I will see you later." On June 25, Fenella rang her on behalf of Ian to say he would come and see her during the week. The next day, she rang back and said that Ian would come into the shop on Saturday, June 28 when her husband would not be there. Marie Farrell became fearful and agitated at the prospect of Bailey's presence and rang officer Fitzgerald and asked for a tape recorder, which was delivered, and she installed the machine. She was also told that there would be a Garda presence on the main street in Schull.

Bailey, reeking of alcohol with a tape recorder on his belt, arrived at the shop on the Saturday morning at 11.45 a.m. and asked her, "Can I assume this place is clean?" She inquired what he meant by that and he replied, "Bugs and things." He then stood up on a chair and did a hand sweep of the top of the jukebox and then entered the toilets for the same purpose. He came back and talked about the police, who he alleged were harassing Saffie (Saffron Thomas).

He then sat down on a chair and asked for a coffee and cigarettes, and she replied that she had none and realised that he had been drinking. She took the shop assistant Geraldine O'Brien aside and asked her to go out and purchase the cigarettes and inform the Gardai. She rang Detective Fitzgerald and told him about the situation and that Marie could not get the recorder to function. He told her to return to the shop and listen to the conversation.

Bailey produced two notebooks and showed her a page on which he had written the address of her former residence in London and her husband's business address. He asked her if she thought that the investigators would love to know more about her.

When she asked him where he had obtained the information, he replied that he was an investigative reporter. He then produced the business card of his solicitor Con Murphy and said, "I know that you are the one that saw me at Kealfadda Bridge but I did not kill her and you are going to call my lawyer and tell him that you made a false statement about me." He also threatened her: "If you ever do anything behind my back, you will pay the price and the inspectors will never find you."

This strange encounter with the "investigative reporter", obviously under the influence of alcohol and strapped for cash, got more bizarre when he asked the shopkeeper for money for the jukebox. She supplied it, and while dealing with a customer, the under-the-weather Bailey turned up the volume on the jukebox. He then produced a cheque from his pocket for £20 from *The*

Examiner and asked her to cash it, while remarking, "That is all the murder meant to me in the end, I billed them for thirty, but they only sent me twenty."

Geraldine O'Brien could not hear the conversation because of the volume of the jukebox but saw him producing the notebooks. Afterwards, Marie Farrell told her assistant that she could not take any more, that Ian Bailey terrified her, and he had mentioned details of her private life. The young shop assistant would be privy to other incidents of her employer being subjected to more incidents of harassment in an effort by Bailey to get a withdrawal of her sighting of him at Kealfadda Bridge on the night of the murder.

Two days later, investigators called to Ian Bailey at his home and informed him that Marie Farrell did not want to see him again in her shop and wanted to be left in peace. He replied that, "I understand, I did not realise, I will comply." He appeared to be nervous during this exchange, but he would continue harassing Marie Farrell.

Marie Farrell would make further complaints totalling seventeen in all to the officers in relation to intimidation by the prime suspect and all which were followed up and conveyed to Bailey. She claimed he had made menacing gestures towards her by running his hand across his throat and approached her one day and told her, "I am disappointed you didn't do what I asked. I will have to work out what my next move will be." Jules Thomas told her on a street near her home, "Your day will come."

On another occasion, she was again confronted by Bailey near her home and asked, "There is just one thing I need you to do for me. If you do this for me, I will never ask you to do anything else. Just go on tape. Say the detectives made you make a false statement about me."

Marie Farrell replied, "Ian, will you ever fuck off?"

Bailey, then obviously frustrated by the lack of co-operation, roared at her, "There was no blood on me that night, you saw no blood on me."

Well, here was another admission on the prime suspect's part, namely that he had been where the witness saw him on the night of the murder but protesting that she had not seen any blood on him. The implication was clear that there was blood on him, but Marie Farrell could not have seen it.

The most pressing question of course was for what possible reason would the prime suspect of a murder threaten and attempt to force a principal witness to change the statement she had made to senior members of the investigation team? Here was a man who claimed to be innocent taking criminal action to frighten a witness whose evidence had contradicted his statement that he never left his house on the night of the murder. There was only one possible conclusion to be drawn from his obvious desperation.

There was also now incontrovertible evidence that Ian Bailey had harassed, intimidated and attempted to blackmail a principal witness in attempts to make her change her statement, and had also threatened her life. Despite an assurance to officers involved in the investigation that he would desist, he continued the campaign of intimidation. It appeared inconceivable that the man who carried out these acts and who had a history of violence against his partner, who had scratches and wounds on his person consistent with the commission of the murder incompatible with his explanation for them both in time and manner, would not simply be arrested again but also charged with the crime.

A lot of evidential water had flowed under the bridge since Bailey's first arrest in February 1997 so the superior officers in the investigation thought it was about time that he was brought in for further questioning. This time it was decided that there would be a change in the interrogation strategy. It would be less confrontational, concentrate on the facts and deal with Bailey in a more conversational manner, to note any inconsistencies and contradictions in the latest version of his story. He had more serious questions to answer in addition to his previous unsatisfactory and constantly changing versions.

It was a strategy that involved some risk as this would be the last opportunity to arrest and question the prime suspect. If there was to be another time, he would have to be charged. The team were already experiencing a torrid time with the office of the DPP, the body responsible for approving the charging of a suspect. The first investigation file containing a 327-page report was completed and sent to the DPP in September 1997. It recommended that Bailey be charged with the murder.

There followed a train of correspondence from the DPP over the following months, including requests for the investigation team to provide more information and documentation. The team then re-interviewed many witnesses to ascertain whether there was any better recollection or information they may have forgotten since their original statements.

It was the impression of the leading members of the investigation team that the civil servant handling the report for the DPP was going far beyond his remit by attempting to direct the investigation rather than casting a cold legal eye over its progression. And curiously, the DPP took little or no interest in the fact that the prime suspect had been engaging in a campaign of threats to the principal witness, which was a criminal offence. That was quite apart from the fact that a simple question would establish the motive for why the prime suspect for the crime was engaging in such behaviour.

In a statement in early 1997, Bill Fuller – who knew Bailey and had hired him to work on a garden – said that at around 11 a.m. on the morning of December 23, he had seen Jules Thomas driving near Riley's place and drove behind her car for a while until she did a right turn and he took a different direction. She was alone in the car. He also recounted a conversation with Bailey on December 24 in which he made an admission of stalking the victim on the previous Saturday and of being involved in the murder, all of which was spoken in the third person. Bailey also revealed the fact that he had gone to the victim's house looking for sex and had been rejected.

In May 1997, Richard Leftwick, a local gardener, told

investigators that on December 23, 1996, Bailey had rung him between 12 p.m. and 2 p.m. and said that he could not come over and collect some garlic he had ordered. Caroline Leftwick said that the call had been made between 11.30 a.m. and 12.30 p.m. and that Bailey was excited and said, "There has been a murder in Toormore, a French lady on vacation."

Investigators were aware that the body of the victim had not been formally identified until 12.36 p.m., and so if Caroline Leftwick was correct in her timing, Ian Bailey had had advance knowledge of the murder and nationality of the victim despite stating that he first knew of it as a result of the Cassidy phone call at 1.40 p.m.

Among many areas the investigators reviewed in preparation for the arrest was the interaction between Bailey and other journalists on December 23, 1996, during which time the prime suspect was particularly active in resurrecting his reporting career before and after the phone call from Eddie Cassidy.

One of the most intriguing aspects of this was Bailey's initial concentration on offering photographs of the crime scene to journalists as opposed to providing reporting services. Statements by those journalists were examined closely and among other things revealed an extraordinary level of co-operation and communication between reporters working for opposing newspapers, no doubt inspired by the unique character of the case, which matched nothing in their previous experience in the region.

Michael McSweeney of the Provision photographic agency in a statement of February 18, 1997, said he had been contacted by a source in Cork about an incident in the Schull area and sent a photographer, Nick Brown, there to check it out. At 2 p.m., the photographic editor of the *Irish Independent* Padraig Beirne called him to suggest that he send a photographer to West Cork and McSweeney replied there was one already on the way.

About ten minutes later, Beirne rang him again to say that he had been contacted by Ian Bailey, who said that he had photographs of the crime scene.

In a second interview conducted on April 22, 1997, McSweeney said that he had tried to contact Ian Bailey on a number given to him by Beirne but failed to get through. Bailey then contacted him and said that the photographs had been taken by Jules Thomas at 11 a.m. on December 23 on the site.

Padraig Beirne stated in his interview given on May 21, 1997 that he had received a call from Ian Bailey at 1.55 p.m. on December 23 telling him that the body of a French woman had been found in West Cork and that he had a photograph of the victim taken by himself and also some photographs of the crime scene. He told Bailey that he was not interested in the photographs as Michael McSweeney was looking after that aspect.

He suggested that Bailey contact Michael McSweeney and passed on his contact number. Beirne then rang McSweeney at 2 p.m. to advise him of the contact by Bailey.

In a statement given to investigators on December 22, 1997, *Irish Times* journalist Dick Cross stated that he had received a call from Eddie Cassidy at 1.30 p.m. on December 23 informing him that a woman had been killed in Toormore. Cross replied that he would get to the scene as soon as possible. Twenty minutes later, he got a call from Ian Bailey, who told him that he could supply some photographs and write an article on the subject.

Cross declined the offer of the article but suggested that Bailey contact the newspaper's photographic department. He said that Bailey specifically told him that the photographs he was offering were taken before the police secured the crime scene and made the corpse less accessible. The implication of that offer by Bailey was disturbing to say the least and would eventually lead to a far more damning conclusion. For the moment, there would be enough food for thought by the investigators.

What was clear to investigators was that Ian Bailey, the prime suspect for the crime, had immediately in the aftermath attempted to profit from the murder, most obviously by trying to peddle photographs that in the timeline of events he described could never have been taken. Could they have been taken before the body was discovered and the investigation began? The history of murder has long proved that anything, even the most bizarre acts, is possible.

Investigators continued to interview and re-interview local people, a process that would usually result in new information to place another piece in the complex jigsaw of murder investigation. Bailey's arrogance, publicity-seeking, intimidating behaviour and general pushy demeanour had also loosened tongues. Many people in the community were further angered by the negative effects of the event in their home region, which was magnified by the prime suspect's unwillingness to keep quiet and get on with his life.

In early October 1997, Mark McCarthy, a friend of Jules Thomas's daughters Jennifer (Jenny) and Saffron (Saffie), related seeing Ian Bailey talking with a woman he later recognised as Sophie Bouniol during a story-telling festival that took place on the first week of September 1995 on the jetty of Cape Clear island.

McCarthy further added that at Christmas 1996, the Thomas girls Jenny and Saffie told him what they had done for the Christmas tree and decorations because of Ian Bailey's laziness. They insisted that they had had to trim the Christmas tree. He saw a few little stings on their hands but not scratches. He saw Bailey and Jules Thomas in the pub on the evening of December 22 and they were still there when he left at about ten o'clock.

He saw Bailey and Thomas at the 1996 Christmas swim in Schull. He noticed a scratch on Bailey's right temple. Regarding Bailey's violence, Jenny had confided in him that he had hit Jules many times in the face and the ears while driving the car. He himself saw several wounds on her face in June 1996.

In a later interview, McCarthy said that during one of his visits to Schull he was at the home of Michael Oliver (the former partner of Jules Thomas and father of Saffron and Virginia) in early 1997, where Saffron Thomas showed her hands to her father and explained that the little scratches on them came from the cutting down of the Christmas tree and said that it was she that had cut it down and if Ian Bailey claimed to have done it, it was a lie.

In a statement later on, Michael Oliver said that on the Saturday before Christmas in 1996 Saffron had told him that Ian Bailey was a "lazy bastard" and that he did not want to get them a Christmas tree and so she had to cut down the tree. He was a lazy man and they had to do everything, including the killing of the turkeys.

None of this surprised the detectives and was consistent with Bailey's indolent nature, spending his time playing the bodhran, reading poems and occasionally playing another role – that of the inefficient gardener. On top of that, he was an alcoholic, drug taker and domestic abuser of the worst order.

Bailey was arrested again at 8.16 a.m. on January 27, 1998 at his home in Liscaha. The arrest order had been obtained from Bandon District Court on January 26 and issued by the court judge. This was shown to Bailey and read out to him.

The new information sworn before the court grounding the warrant application was based on several facts drawn up by Detective Superintendent Ted Murphy. There were alleged confessions made by Bailey to witnesses since his first arrest concerning his involvement in the murder and his motive.

There were apparent discrepancies in the nature of the information that Bailey had allegedly had in his possession that would not have been widely known at that time, along with the questionable level of detail concerning the murder that Bailey had allegedly disclosed to other parties.

Then there were the alleged attempts by Bailey to threaten and intimidate a person considered by the Gardai to be a key witness in the murder investigation at the time.

He was taken to Bandon Garda Station, where he arrived at 9.15 a.m. He was read his rights, confirmed he understood and given immediate access to a solicitor who was at the station. At 2 p.m., the superintendent authorised the detention period for another six hours. He was released without charge at 8.08 p.m., made no complaints about his detention or interrogation and signed the custody record to that effect. He was given the usual refreshments, rest breaks, access when requested to his solicitor and cigarettes.

During the interviews, Ian Bailey stuck to his script of events, which was not surprisingly at variance almost in full with statements of other witnesses, which he should have been reliant upon to corroborate his story such was the level of interaction he had with them in the hours leading up to and after the crime.

He recounted the call from Eddie Cassidy, who told him the body of a foreign woman had been found in Toormore, which the former stated he had said nothing of the sort, as he did not know anything of the nationality of the victim. He admitted contacting the *Irish Independent* to propose a complete photo service and also Dick Cross to offer his services on the story and to inform him of photographs he had of the crime scene, which he qualified by saying that he anticipated the possibility of acquiring them.

This contradicted the versions of events from Padraig Beirne, who said Bailey had told him he already had photos of the crime scene, from Michael McSweeney, who said Bailey told him that Jules Thomas had taken them at 11 a.m., and from Dick Cross, who said Bailey had told him that they had been taken before the crime scene had been secured. This could only have happened before 10 a.m., when the body was discovered by Shirley Foster.

There was little doubt in the mind of a principal investigator involved in the interview that Bailey had been involved in taking photographs at the crime scene but much earlier than any of the times he had mentioned. Nothing else could explain his efforts to supply photographs as opposed to copy to the media outlets. He gave the unequivocal impression (despite his qualification) that he already had the photographs in his possession.

The wider implication of Bailey's interaction with the journalists was more damning, as the timeline he had applied to the taking of the photographs showed that he had knowledge of not only the crime itself but also the crime scene long in advance of the phone call from Eddie Cassidy which he stated had first alerted him to the event. This was corroborated by the statements of other local witnesses, including the Camiers and the Leftwicks.

Bailey remembered driving to the scene of the crime with Jules Thomas and offered no explanation for the cancellation of the meeting with the Leftwicks. On the way they encountered Shirley Foster, who was driving in the opposite direction, and she informed them that the police had cordoned off the crime scene. They parked the car and Bailey approached the scene on foot but was stopped by Gardai, who told him that he could go no further and refused to give him any information. Jules Thomas, he said, took some photographs on a long lens.

They then drove to the local post office, where with the help of staff they established that the name of the victim was in the post office telephone directory under Bouniol. The purpose of this exercise struck investigators as one of covering tracks and of Bailey distancing himself from the victim. He already knew her maiden name, as did many people in Schull. In his usual fashion, Bailey contested versions of his actions and movements by other witnesses, relying on bald denial without offering any credible alternative.

He denied being at Kealfadda Bridge, saying that he was at home in bed but got up at some stage to write an article for the *Sunday Tribune*, went back to bed and got up at 9 a.m. to finish it. He claimed that between 10 a.m. and 10.30 a.m., the business editor Richard Curran had extended the deadline to the following day. This was true; the deadline had been extended only because it had not been met as agreed and Bailey had in fact dictated the article later to a copytaker at the newspaper long after it should have been delivered.

Contrary to all the evidence of his intimidation of witness Marie Farrell, he came up with the extraordinary explanation that she had confided in him in July 1997 that she was under pressure to make false declarations against him. He denied having pressured and threatened Marie Farrell to get her to withdraw her statement and said he had never talked to her after that meeting. This statement was totally at odds with the events of the intimidation which had been witnessed by both murder investigators, the injured party Marie Farrell and her shop assistant Geraldine O'Brien.

Regarding the night of the murder, when pressed for detail, he said he had gone to bed between 1.30 a.m. and 2 a.m., woke up at 4 a.m. and did some writing, and returned to bed some thirty-five minutes later, waking back up at 9 a.m. to finish the article. When confronted with Jules Thomas's statement about the night in question which left him without an alibi for most of the time, he said that he had never left the house. He also contradicted her when he denied ever saying that he was going to Alfie's house that night and predictably denied making admissions to Malachi Reed and Bill Fuller.

He admitted going to the house of the victim after the Gardai had left and looking into the windows for detail that he passed onto the *Sunday Tribune*. This was another covering up action, like he said about going to the post office to find the name of the victim which he had already known. Anyone who was at the crime scene would know perfectly well that nothing of any value could be seen by looking through the windows.

He said that Marie Farrell disclosed to him that the police had obliged her to make a statement in which she had said that she had seen him at Kealfadda Bridge on December 23, 1996 and they had shown her a video in which he appeared before asking her to identify him.

Once again, the investigation team observed all the rules and regulations and followed them meticulously, all the more so having been given plenty of experience of the toxic attitude towards its members during Bailey's disastrous publicity campaign and knowing well his capacity for twisting the truth of anything and everything to benefit himself.

After the statutory period of detention, Ian Bailey was released without charge. Nothing about Ian Bailey's version of events displayed any credibility and his statements were riddled not just with contradictions but downright lies exposed by the statements of journalists and local witnesses, none of whom had any axe to grind with the prime suspect. He had also made admissions of participating in the crime, which literally caused the hairs on the necks of those who he told to rise.

These indisputable and incriminating facts would have prompted any properly functioning prosecution service anywhere to have the prime suspect arrested and brought to trial. Not in Ireland, where the DPP's office under the direction of Eamon Barnes was busy criticising the Garda file on the murder and expressing prejudice against the conduct of the investigation while assiduously ignoring the contradictions and lies in the statements of the prime suspect.

The office's approach could be described by Jean-Jacques Rousseau's slightly altered phrase: "To deny that which is to explain that which is not."

On the same day as the arrest, investigators had conducted a search of the house at Liscaha during which they had seized Bailey's handwritten diaries and some audio tapes.

In advance of his first arrest, he had given a friend the diaries which contained damning material about his appetite for sex, drugs, alcohol and violent nature, as he did not want police investigators to read them. The filth that he translated from his mind to the page should have been of little interest to anyone unless the contents had some relevance to the crime, which of course they did, providing the reason for Bailey to have them hidden. The diaries would figure largely in a future court setting.

The audio tapes, which would not figure in the case, provided an insight into another side of the sleazy, lecherous mind of Bailey. Some of the content was transcribed by Detective Garda Jim Fitzgerald. Bailey acknowledged in the presence of his solicitor Con Murphy that they were his property. Detective Sergeant Maurice Walsh confirmed that the voice on the tapes was that of Ian Bailey.

In the course of listening to the tapes, the officers became aware that Bailey was describing the stalking of unknown females. A section in the recording went like this:

"I'd say about forty-five yards from the other side of the rivulet sits a woman, a female with a red-caped peak she wears and smothers her skin in Amber Solar [sic], and my desire is to make love with her."

In another section, Bailey speaks into the recorder as he watches a teenage girl:

"There is a little girl... I've seen her about and she is nineteen, maybe twenty, dark pretty hair and I have taken to feel very much to make love to her and I have had a couple of fantasies which have been absolutely wonderful. Lovely little girl and I would love to get to know her a little better and I think we could be good and enjoyable for each other and some time I could teach her the art of realisation and love."

The flesh of the officers must have crawled listening to the unfolding of the narrative of this talking Peeping Tom, providing himself with masturbation material while watching women and girls from afar, unknowing trophies and objects for the depraved stalker to soil himself with during his "wonderful" sexual fantasies.

Fenella Thomas was interviewed in the presence of her mother. She told them that on the night of December 22, 1996 that she went to bed between 11 p.m. and midnight and had gone to the toilet between 2 a.m. and 2.30 a.m. but could not be sure of the exact time and had heard Ian Bailey snoring.

She had done some babysitting for Marie Farrell before and one day Farrell had told her over the phone that she wanted to meet Ian Bailey to discuss something important with him.

Bailey had told her that he would meet Marie Farrell at 11 a.m. that morning and she relayed that information by phone to Farrell, who had mentioned before that she wanted to inform Bailey that four detectives were inciting her to make false statements.

It appeared far more obvious to investigators in the context of the well-proven intimidation by Bailey of Farrell and her statements in that regard that he was in fact using a young and vulnerable teenage girl in his campaign to get the witness to withdraw her statement and provided further evidence of his ruthless use of manipulation within the household. The "lazy bastard", as Saffron Thomas described him, was dragging in totally innocent people to do his dirty work in an environment in which they had been exposed to his brutal behaviour towards their mother.

Meanwhile in Paris, Daniel Toscan du Plantier had married a twenty-nine-year-old immigrant from Eastern Europe, Melita Nikolic, and they had two children, Tosca and Maxime. The daughter Tosca was three months old at the time. It might have seemed to be indecent haste after the death of Sophie just two years or less after the awful event, but it might have also been viewed consistent with his previous history with relationships with women. In an interview, he offered his explanation:

"You have to respond to death with life. It doesn't mean that you don't love the marks left within you by the woman who has been taken from you. It doesn't lessen the misfortune. The memory and the suffering remain. Death by murder is a double death because there was a human will behind it. You say to yourself that somewhere on Earth is the person that did it and there is a devil somewhere in the hills of Southern Ireland."

In West Cork, inquiries and interviews continued. Malachi Reed stated in an interview in early February 1999 that three weeks earlier, while he was in a bar in Schull, he was approached by Bailey, who said, "I didn't have a chance to tell you about the time I brought you home by car two years ago … I only told you what police told me." The teenager replied, "If you did it, I don't regret telling the police."

Bailey became nervous, placed his hands over his head and whined. Another time, he followed Malachi intending to talk to him, but the young man quickened his pace, avoided contact and later decided with his mother to contact the investigation team.

The enduring subject of the photographs Bailey had been trying to sell to newspapers was raised in another interview some days later with Michael McSweeney, who recalled the phone call he had received from Bailey on December 23, 1996 at 2 p.m., when he mentioned having negatives of the murder scene taken that morning at 10.30 a.m. The negatives given to photographer Mike Brown, who he had sent to the scene, were not usable as they were blurred.

He later stated that there were police visible in the photographs, which meant they were taken later than 10.30 a.m., probably after 2 p.m. when Bailey and Jules Thomas had travelled to the crime scene.

Arianna Boarina, a friend of Jennifer Thomas, was interviewed at Clontarf Garda Station, Dublin, in April 1999 by a member of the murder investigation team. She stated that while sharing a house in Dún Laoghaire in south county Dublin she had got to know Jennifer, who in 1996 invited her to stay in her house in Schull over the Christmas of that year. On Sunday, December 22, she travelled to Cork city and stayed overnight. The following day, she went on to Schull by bus and recalled hearing on the bus radio that there had been a murder.

She had been collected by Jules Thomas and when arriving at the house in Liscaha she met Ian Bailey and immediately noticed the scratches on his hands. She described them as numerous and extending to his forearms, and they were fresh in appearance. He appeared agitated and was drinking heavily.

She was told by either Ian or Jules that the wounds had come from either cutting the Christmas tree or killing turkeys. She found this explanation surprising, as she thought they might have been more likely to have been sustained by contact with thorns. She also noted the wound on his forehead. While using the bathroom, she noticed dark clothing soaking in the bath. Bailey had appeared anxious and was continuing to drink heavily. When she went to the bathroom later, she noticed that the clothes were no longer in the bath. She stated that Ian and Jules were arguing a lot.

CHAPTER 7
THE "POET" IS NAILED
TO A LITERARY CROSS

West Cork – 2000–01

July was a busy month for the investigators and early in the month they heard statements from a local married couple that Bailey in dramatic circumstances had made an admission to of his part in the murder. It happened on New Year's Eve 1998, when Bailey invited the couple back to his house. Richie Shelley worked in a bakery. Rosie's father was a director of a fish factory and mother – a one-time local rector. They were a quiet and gentle couple and held in high esteem in the community.

Bailey was "tired and emotional" as he went through a file he had kept about the murder. In his statement of July 2, 1999, Richie Shelley said that he and his wife Rosie had after meeting Ian Bailey and Jules Thomas in a pub in Schull on that night been invited to the couple's home for drinks.

After they had some beer, the subject of conversation turned to the murder and Bailey asked Richie several times if he thought that Bailey was responsible for the murder. He produced a file of newspaper clippings on the crime and asked the couple again if they thought that he was responsible for the murder, to which Richie Shelley replied that he did not think that. Bailey had continued to talk about the crime. At some stage later, Bailey became emotional and started to cry, seeming deeply troubled. Richie found it strange to see a man of his stature crying.

He put his arms around Richie Shelley and repeated four or five times, "I did it." When Richie Shelley asked him what he was talking about, Bailey did not answer but said, "I went too far, I went too far." He then left the room. The witness was convinced that Bailey had been talking about the murder, particularly in the context that the previous conversation had been dominated by the crime. Frightened by this admission, he and his wife were prompted to leave the house immediately.

The following day, the couple again bumped by chance into Bailey and Thomas in a pub in Schull and Richie Shelley told Bailey that he was now convinced that he was guilty of the murder. Bailey said nothing.

Interviewed by officers three days later, Rosie Shelley confirmed that she had heard the conversation between her husband and Ian Bailey. She could not remember the exact words of the exchange but said that she understood that Bailey had admitted to being guilty of the murder and that he had wrapped his arms around her husband and cried. She was frightened and left the house to be joined shortly after by her husband. She also confirmed the meeting in the pub the following day and that Jules Thomas was protective of her partner, and suggested that they leave the pub.

On July 8, officers met with Fenella Thomas in the presence of her father Christopher to question her about her previous statements and contact she may have had with Marie Farrell. She became angry during the interview and locked herself in the bathroom of the hotel where it was taking place. Her father urged them to leave her alone and said that he would keep in touch.

Twenty days later, officers interviewed Saffron Thomas in the presence of her father Michael, and she said that she was with Bailey when the Christmas tree was cut on December 22, 1996, and that they took turns cutting it. She said she had no scratches, but Bailey might have had, but she was not certain of the fact. She and her sister Jennifer appeared to be worried about their mother and needed more time to consider the matter. Officers felt that this was reasonable and merely made an official report of the meeting.

This attitude was more than fair even in the context of her previous statement that Bailey was a "lazy bastard" and that she had to do all the work in the cutting, and also taking into account her and her sister's concern for her mother given his history of violence towards Jules and his manipulative influence in the household. Protecting or exposing a violent and abusive drunk put Thomas's daughters in an invidious position in such a toxic domestic environment. These young girls, as any in an environment of domestic abuse, were also victims and subject to his manipulation.

All the daughters were by all accounts great kids and it was their misfortune to be exposed to not just what happened within the house but also to the unfolding events, as of course was their mother. The blame for all lay with the interloper in the house, Ian Bailey, whose record in terms of domestic behaviour going back to his marriage in England was abysmal.

There is little doubt that his old mentor John Montague's article on the case in *The New Yorker*, published in January 2000 under the title of "A Devil in the Hills" (which the author chronicled in detail to me in an interview with him and his then partner and later wife Elisabeth Wassell in 2002), enraged Bailey, who as a subject had co-operated with and encouraged the author and as always had expected a flattering portrait, and it might well have tipped the scales in relation to him taking action to stop the media writing about him.

The subject might have wondered how a renowned poet would translate his skill to a true crime writer with his former gardener in a central role, and he got his answer in spades, so to speak. He might well have imagined that the writer would, because of their history, cast him in his favourite role as the lone and tortured innocent – the victim of a conspiracy between the corrupt police and the local people. A biblical-like figure wandering the winding boreens and country roads, the streets and markets of the villages and towns in West Cork, proclaiming his innocence in the face of a vile persecution.

He had initially, when Montague and Elisabeth – who also worked on the piece – told him about the intention to write about the murder, been helpful and encouraging – his ego boosted by being written about in a prestigious American publication, as well as expecting a good hearing from someone whom he considered a friend as well as a poetic guru.

It was anything but flattering and went far further than any of the other newspapers in connecting him to the crime, leaving little doubt in the mind of the reader who was responsible for the crime. In one paragraph, Montague recalls giving Bailey a typewriter and wondering if he had lent it to Raskolnikov (the central character in Dostoevsky's novel *Crime and Punishment* who bludgeons his two female victims to death with an axe).

The writer had as he told me also included some scant details supplied by Bailey about the assaults on his partner Jules Thomas, which had been given to him well in advance of the publication of the article and which he might have supposed were given in confidence and most certainly not for publication, and the details of which were known to neighbours but not in the public domain.

The article also provided a most unflattering but entirely accurate portrait of Bailey's character, including accounts of meetings with him, employing him as a gardener and having dinner in the house at Liscaha – things that the host might also have considered as possessing some element of privacy but with which Montague obviously differed and being grist for the mill of journalistic practice.

In one passage, Montague recounted a dinner in the house attended by himself and Elisabeth, Bailey, Jules and her three daughters. One of the daughters was warm and courteous but the poet sensed unease between her and Bailey. Another daughter complained that the Christmas tree had not been brought in but when Bailey ignored the remark she did not let up and he suddenly left the table and the house, eventually returning with a large tree and scattering the pine needles across the floor. A picture of domestic harmony it was not.

There was worse to come when the writer revealed the contents of a letter to him from Bailey describing with scant detail an assault on his partner which he said was not his intention but had been as a result of drink, after which one of her daughters had called the Gardai, and he said that he still loved her. Like a good journalist, Montague was not content to leave it at that and supplied the missing detail that Jules had been taken to hospital for treatment for appalling injuries, including according to a neighbour, "her eye hanging out".

At every turn in the piece, apart from the bald comparison to Raskolnikov, there were more subtle but telling references to the subject's links to the crime. Bailey had asked his poetic hero about lines from Robert Graves's "The White Goddess" which he quoted:

"The holly, dark green
Made a resolute stand;
He is armed with many spear-points
Wounding the hand."

The image reminded Montague of the Christmas tree Bailey had said caused the scratches on his hands and face on "the night of the murder" [sic].

Bailey, of course, had stated to all that those wounds had been sustained the day before. This was just one of a hundred cuts that Bailey would be subjected to during the narrative of the article.

It was by a long stretch the best article ever written up to that point and possibly since on the case, with insights and analysis that no other journalist could have possibly gained at that time. But as with MacDonald and McGinness, the writer had skewered the subject with no obvious animus, in fact with a certain regard for the man but to devastating effect.

On any cursory reading, the article nailed Bailey to a painful literary cross and skirted close to if didn't cross legal lines certainly in terms of inference. It was clear that the writer was interested in the truth of the matter and was not guided or inhibited by any possible legal consequence, a position that at this stage of the whole matter was admirable whatever the outcome.

Inevitably, after the publication John and Elisabeth, as they told me, were rewarded by threatening phone calls, the provenance of which they had not the slightest doubt about and which had already proved to be utterly consistent as a modus operandi of the person of whom they suspected of making them.

Montague wondered towards the end of the article how it would all end, as he knew well that it was early days, but like all great writers – even without the privilege of time – his instinct was prescient.

"Perhaps there will be no real conclusion, and the cloud that settled over West Cork in the aftermath of the murder will gradually dissipate, leaving only the faint impressions of fear and foreboding it brought to a place that had not been sullied for decades. Yet there is something too distilled and concentrated about this story for it to disappear quickly. It seems to be part of a particularly European drama – for which West Cork is only one of many stages."

On May 17, 2000, Ceri Williams, partner of Peter Bielecki, stated that the couple had been friends of Ian Bailey and Jules Thomas, and had often visited the house in Liscaha. During one of their conversations, Bailey recounted an incident with his former wife in England, Sarah Limbrick, in which he had become enraged with her and had a temper tantrum, during which he had lost all notion of time and when he had recovered realised he had lost all control and taken her by the neck and tried to strangle her, ceasing only when he realised the gravity of his action.

Peter Bielecki made a statement on May 25, 2000 in relation to the incident. He confirmed that he and his partner were friendly with Bailey and Thomas but after the latter had been badly beaten by the former in mid-1996 he had nothing more to do with Bailey. Before that, he had told him about being kicked out of the house in England and how his name had been deleted from the deeds of the house. He was angry and during one of the quarrels with his wife Sarah he had tried to strangle her and caught her by the throat to finish her before coming to his senses at the last minute.

Sarah Limbrick had also related this incident to a female Avon police constable, who was interviewing her about Bailey forging her signature on a life insurance policy on her without her knowledge. She told the officer that she thought she was going to die and was so scared of Bailey that she could not bear to be in his company and would not be able to testify against him in a court.

Colette Gallagher related how in 1993, while sleeping in a house on the land of Jules Thomas, she felt a hand resting on her leg and awoke to find Ian Bailey had slipped into the bed. Jules Thomas then entered the room and she and Bailey began to quarrel while she ran to the main house with her clothes to get dressed. Jules Thomas apologised to her for her partner's behaviour while he shouted and whined outside. Thomas told her he did worse things than that and lifted her skirt and T-shirt, showing bruises covering her legs and sides.

On September 22, Jules Thomas was arrested for the second time, as well as her daughter Fenella Thomas for the first and only time. Jules was under investigation for allegedly assisting an offender while Fenella was under investigation for alleged perjury and witness tampering.

They were taken to Bandon Garda Station, arriving at 10.20 a.m., where the detentions were authorised by the Garda member in charge under the relevant act of 1984. They were informed of their rights and signed the custody record to this effect. Extensions to the periods of custody were authorised.

Investigators put it to Jules that Marie Farrell had testified to seeing Bailey at Kealfadda Bridge at around 3 a.m. on the morning of December 23, 1996. She replied, "I know this information is important. I cannot say it is true or not if he got out of bed. I cannot say anything more." She related that on that morning, while Bailey was working on his article, at around 11 a.m. she drove to near the crime scene and took some photographs of the water before going to Goleen, where she had a conversation with James Camier.

Asked about the visit of the Shelley couple to her house on New Year's Eve 1998, she recalled the conversation about the murder. She was present when Bailey discussed the murder with them. When he began to discuss the subject, she told him to shut up. She accepted in the interview that the Shelleys were telling the truth in their statement and was present: "When Ian told Richie he did the murder, I heard him say he went too far."

Jules told the officers that the couple left, "Because they heard Ian confessing to the murder of the French woman. They left because they had heard enough. It looked like he was admitting the killing of Sophie."

She explained that he was drunk and troubled, was crying, had cowered behind the couch and had then placed his arms around Richie. After that, the couple left the house.

The next day, they were in the pub and Bailey went over to Richie and Rosie, who were also present. Before leaving for Schull, she told Bailey to "shut up about the murder", which she meant in a general sense.

Fenella denied being involved in communications with Marie Farrell, whom she claimed had rung the house looking to speak with Ian Bailey. On the night of December 22–23, 1996 she said she had heard someone snoring in the house in the early hours, but in contradiction with her previous statement clarified that it was not Ian Bailey she had heard snoring.

She heard some loud snoring but could not tell from whom it came. She did not know where Ian Bailey went that night and the following morning, and only remembered taking a phone call from a man looking for Bailey. After coming to the phone, he said, "You won't believe what has happened," before saying that a murder had taken place somewhere.

Then he and her mother left the house and drove away. She

remembered taking a call from Marie Farrell but could not remember relaying any message from her back to Bailey.

Fenella said that she did not love Bailey because he had taken the place of her father. She added that she would be happy if Bailey was not in the house anymore. She had a vague memory of her mother and Bailey going to Goleen to do some shopping on the morning of December 23 before the telephone call from the man. When challenged about her answer in a questionnaire saying she had heard Bailey snoring, she denied saying that and claimed it was not him snoring.

She remembered marks on Bailey's nose. It was her mother who had been snoring, she said, and she declared that she would never lie for Ian Bailey. She vaguely recalled her mother and Bailey going to Goleen around nine or ten on the morning of December 23 and returning one or two hours later.

She then seemed to be upset, and asked if she was afraid of Bailey, she said she was not as she could take care of herself; she had told the investigators everything she knew and could not explain why she had said it was Bailey snoring when she did not know. On her solicitor's advice, she refused to sign the official report but agreed it was an accurate reflection of her statement. They were released from custody at 8.53 p.m. that evening without charge.

Earlier in the year, on May 24, 2000, the investigators received an anonymous phone call informing them that a man had asked him to develop negatives from a roll of thirty-six photographic exposures given to him. When trawling through the negatives, he saw that the photographs showed a body lying beside a wall and a closed gate. His customer had been accompanied by a young woman by the name of Jenny. The informant recognised that he knew only one girl of that name who lived with her mother and the prime suspect for the crime outside Schull.

Further evidence that Ian Bailey had foreknowledge of the murder was obtained by investigation officers in an interview conducted with local teacher Paul O'Colmain on October 18,

2000, who stated that Bailey had told him that he had decided to revive his career as a journalist in November–December 1996. On the day of the murder, the witness recounted having received a phone call from Bailey between 11 a.m. and 11.30 a.m., and he sounded excited.

Bailey told him that a murder had taken place not far from his house, that the victim was a French woman and that he hoped to get work reporting on the crime. This of course was entirely consistent with the prime suspect's inability to keep his mouth shut even if his talk was highly incriminating. The statement was significant as it had been made by a friend and confidante of the prime suspect who had no axe to grind with him.

The anonymous informant about the photographs which showed a body came forward and was interviewed by Detective Garda John Moore of the investigation team. On November 4, 2000, Patrick Lowney, a garage owner in Clonakilty, a keen amateur photographer who had a dark room where he developed negatives as a sideline, said that around the first week in the previous May he had received a phone call from a man who inquired if he developed photographs and if he had already worked for Jenny. He replied that he had done so and the man asked him if he would accept work from him discreetly developing some negatives for him.

He agreed and the man arrived forty-five minutes later and gave him a roll with thirty-six exposures. They entered the dark room together while Lowney developed the negatives. Lowney stated that the first seven or eight negatives were of family scenes, but the others revealed the body of a woman lying on the ground inside a place that might have been a farmyard. The road was stony with grass on both sides and in the background, there was a gate with a sign on it.

The photographs, according to Lowney, seemed to have been taken at night because the lighting did not seem to come from behind the gate. The woman looked completely dressed. Some of the shots appeared to have been taken right above the body of the woman and showed the shoes or boots of the taker.

On the grass beside the woman, he could see some brambles or a hedge, and a wall made of raw stones. In other photographs he noticed a sign or a dress thrown over the barred gate. While examining them, the man became anxious and even while the photographs were wet, he took them from Lowney's hands, risking damage, and then agreed to let them hang to dry.

Once the negatives were dry, the man took them, and saying he would return to have them saved on a disc, he left the room. He left the house and joined the person who was waiting for him outside. Two weeks later, the man came back.

Later, Detective Garda Gerry McCarthy showed Patrick Lowney some photographs from which he identified Ian Bailey as the man who had given him the roll of negatives. On the same day, detectives McCarthy and Moore brought him to the crime scene, which he confirmed closely resembled the site in the negatives. At the bottom of the frames of some of the negatives, a pair of boots was clearly visible. The witness in his professional judgement and experience concluded that the photographs had been taken in the dark with the use of a flash.

Less than forty-eight hours after the shortest day of the year, it would have been dark up to eight o'clock, so the photographer could have taken the shots up to half an hour beforehand.

Despite a volume of strong incriminating circumstantial evidence being accumulated by the investigation team against Ian Bailey, which in any jurisdiction would have led to charges being made against the prime suspect, the DPP remained unmoved. The efforts of the investigation team were simply met by more and more demands for further inquiries and constantly failing to consider the massive contradictions in Bailey's version of events, his intimidation of a prime witness and the entirely credible statements of independent witnesses. The DPP obviously had his snout down a deep hole from which there was no retreat – in his view.

The Gardai carried out a full re-examination of the first investigation file and as a result submitted another file to the DPP in

March 2001. The DPP, however, could not be satisfied and on November 7, 2001 produced an unsigned report saying there was insufficient evidence to charge Bailey.

The State solicitor for West Cork, Malachi Boohig, received the report and a covering letter from Robert Sheehan, the DPP legal officer, in early November 2001. The letter stated that it had been decided that a prosecution of Ian Bailey for the crime could on the evidence in the case not be properly sustainable and the memorandum was enclosed to send on to the Gardai, who received it on November 14 from Boohig. The memorandum contained no signature. Astounding? No signature signifying personal responsibility for this opinion. Certainly astounding.

The covering letter from an officer of the DPP means nothing but an exercise of bureaucracy. The only thing that matters is the signature of the DPP and there was none.

The Gardai immediately got to work on what was in effect a critical analysis of the DPP's justification for not charging Bailey, which was debated in depth with argument of fact rebutting the analysis of evidence by the DPP. These included:

"The injuries to Bailey's hands, arms and face received between 12.30 a.m. and 9 a.m. on December 23, 1996.

The sighting of Bailey at Kealfadda Bridge at 3.15 a.m. on the morning of December 23, 1996.

Ian Bailey's ability to drive straight to the scene of the crime unaided.

Jules Thomas's statement that Ian Bailey left their bedroom at approximately 2.30 a.m. on the morning of December 23, 1996.

Ian Bailey's admission that he left the house in the early hours of darkness.

Ian Bailey's ability to communicate precise information about the murder to Paul O'Colmain and Caroline Leftwich prior to receiving the phone call from Eddie Cassidy.

Ian Bailey's persistent intimidation of Marie Farrell.

Ian Bailey's personal knowledge of Sophie Toscan du Plantier – he had been introduced to her, he had been in Schull the same day as her on Saturday, December 21, 1996 and was seen near to where she was by two witnesses.

Ian Bailey's persistent lies about his movements during the period Saturday, December 21–Sunday, December 22 and Monday, December 23, 1996.

Ian Bailey's lies about how he had sustained the injuries and the date when the turkeys had been killed.

Ian Bailey's confession and admission to the Shelleys that he had killed the victim raised a presumption so strong that there could be no doubt as to his guilt."

Of course, all of his confessions were entirely credible in fact and evidentially for admissions for his responsibility for the murder of Sophie, and taken as such by the witnesses to whom Bailey had talked, none more so than Richie Shelley, witnessed by his wife Rosie while Bailey was in a highly emotional state and was crying as he unburdened himself of his guilt to the unsuspecting couple who, shocked, got out of the house as quickly as possible.

The Garda response pointed out in conclusion that the intimidation of Marie Farrell had not been considered in making the decision not to prosecute and it was difficult to understand how the integrity of some witnesses was being questioned in the report.

The DPP analysis it went on was negative and more credibility was being placed on the statements of Jules Thomas and Ian Bailey than most of the witnesses. The Gardai maintained their position that Ian Bailey should be charged with the murder of Sophie Toscan du Plantier. The Garda response document was then sent to the office of the DPP in Dublin.

This was a powerful case with all the evidence admissible in a criminal court. There had been persistent media reports that the confessions would not be admissible. This was incorrect – confessions had been admitted in several Irish murder cases in which convictions were successful, including the DPP vs O'Brien, the DPP vs Nevin and the DPP vs Gillane.

In the case of a Tralee case, a statement made by the accused, O'Brien, to his friend Darren O'Shea during which he confessed to killing the victim was admitted in evidence by Judge Kinlan. O'Shea, who was a convicted criminal, was in a pub drinking with O'Brien when the latter told him of his responsibility for the crime. The accused O'Brien denied he had made the admission but was convicted by the jury.

As far back as 1925, the psychoanalyst Theodor Reik, who had studied with Freud, wrote a book about the criminal's impulse to confess his crime to ordinary people. This impulse grows more and more intense to the point that it tempts the criminal to shout of their responsibility to people on the street or confess to at least one person to relieve them of the burden of the secret that is gnawing away at their brain. The author could have been writing about Ian Bailey.

Hardened criminals often make admissions to friends or even casual acquaintances having steadfastly denied them in police interrogations, and can be subsequently convicted as a result of their informal confessions.

There had been an internal dispute in the DPP's office in the same year of 2001. The solicitor handling the communications with Gardai and the report, Robert Sheehan, engaged in a case against the DPP under the Employment Equality Act 1998 on the basis that he was discriminated against on the grounds of gender and age in a competition for appointment to position of Solicitor to the DPP. It had begun in April 2001 and a hearing was held in March 2002, in which the Equality Officer, Anne-Marie Lynch, heard submissions from the legal firms representing the two sides.

Sheehan complained that he had explained to the Deputy DPP why he objected to his presence on the interview board. He said his objection was based on what he described as a close friendship between the Deputy and another intended applicant and also because he felt that the Deputy harboured an "unjustified personal grievance against him".

He had been invited to discuss this with the DPP and told

him that he felt the DPP would vote in accordance with the wishes of the Deputy DPP, thus ensuring he would not get the job. Despite this, Sheehan still attended the interview believing no other candidate could match his qualifications and experience.

During the interview, an observation was made by a board member that she had known him for a long time and believed he had a "very short fuse".

Sheehan alleged that she had known the Deputy DPP for many years and her observation was deliberate, measured and intended, and the only result would have been to sabotage his prospects of being appointed to the post. The assertion, he said, was that he was a hothead incapable of controlling himself, and the comment was designed to cause irreparable harm in front of other members of the board. He was informed on November 14, 2001 by the DPP that he had been unsuccessful, but it had been close (310–305) against the successful candidate, who was a thirty-four-year-old female.

Sheehan claimed that his reputation and future career had been severely damaged by the unlawful manner he had been treated in the course of the selection process and by his non-selection for the post. This was a serious allegation; the senior official was accusing his boss of treating him unlawfully.

The DPP denied all the allegations and stated that his office had complied fully with all aspects of the investigation by the Equality Officer. The selection process was rigorously fair; neither age nor gender was a factor and the result was based on the marks each candidate was awarded under a rating scheme. The complainant was the leading candidate at the end of the first day, but the successful candidate had performed excellently at her interview.

On October 30 of the following year, Sheehan lost the case when the Equality Officer ruled against him. The Equality Officer concluded that the selection process and the awarding of the position to the successful candidate had been fair and rejected the complainant's claims. Anne-Marie Lynch's decision was: "Based on the foregoing, I find that the Director of Public Prosecutions did not discriminate against Robert Sheehan on the grounds of age or gender, contrary to the provisions of the Employment Equality Act 1998, when he was unsuccessful in a competition for appointment to the position of Solicitor to the DPP."

CHAPTER 8
THE PSYCHOLOGY
OF EVIL

Dublin/West Cork – 2001–03

There was additional evidence in the investigation file from eyewitnesses to Ian Bailey's bizarre and unbalanced personality and behaviour. Several people, including Betty Johnson, saw him at night walking along the road shouting in the rain clad only in his undergarments and a hat. Maurice Walsh saw him go out one night, look up to the sky howling like a wolf before throwing his things in all directions again in the rain. Steven Farthing remembered seeing him cover himself with excrement explaining it was "good for the skin" and Ceri Williams believed that one night of a full moon in late February 1997 she had heard him screaming "no" and "sorry".

Another friend recounted how after the summer of 1998, Bailey was drinking more and more, losing control of his emotions and becoming obsessed with the dark forces of the Earth and the moon. He was aware of the negative effects of whiskey on his control but continued to imbibe it to allow free rein to do things he might be inhibited to do when sober, including being violent towards his partner. By all accounts, in the year of 1996 and long before and afterwards, Ian Bailey was a suitable case for treatment.

The Garda investigation file had a report from a psychotherapist which sketched many character traits that matched Bailey's behaviour which could only be described as dangerously dysfunctional, displaying a strong inclination to extreme violence against his partner while liberated from inhibition by both alcohol and drugs, and magnified by the lunar pull under a full moon. All these conditions were in place on the night of December 23, 1996.

Meanwhile, coverage of the case had all but disappeared from the newspapers as a result of Ian Bailey taking a libel case against seven publications, effectively shutting down mention of the prime suspect in relation to the murder until such time that the trial of the issues could be heard in Cork Circuit Court whenever a slot could be found. I had little knowledge of the case, having been occupied as a journalist at the *Sunday Independent* with the aftermath of the assassination of the newspaper's crime reporter Veronica Guerin, with whom I had been working on a screenplay and a film project on the subject, which became the film *When the Sky Falls*, as well as covering the trials of the drugs gang responsible for four years after her death.

So, when I made a proposal to cover the West Cork case to mark the fifth anniversary of the murder coming up in December 2001, I was informed by the news editor Wille Kealy that the subject was out of bounds because Bailey had sued the newspaper over an article on the case and the prime suspect by Brighid McLaughlin. The next day, I suggested that the article would be a combination of a reconstruction of the crime and a psychological profile of the type of killer who would carry out a crime involving such horrendous violence to the victim, and I got the green light.

This profile would be assembled with the help of a forensic psychiatrist, a forensic pathologist, a murder investigator and my research, and would be objectively based on the physical facts of the crime and the crime scene. The participants in the exercise had no inside knowledge of the crime or of the prime suspect, so would be bringing a fresh and unbiased approach.

In fact, it is a rule of thumb among practitioners never to make the profile fit any suspect. I was aware that given the prime suspect's litigious character I would have to be careful. Still, I welcomed the opportunity in breaking Bailey's embargo on the media and putting the spotlight back on the case. Even more so when the psychiatrist suggested that from detail of the modus operandi of the murder and the ferocious nature of the attack, it was the work of a sadistic psychopath, possibly in the wake of sexual advances being rejected. Therefore, it should be categorised as a sexual murder.

Just a century before the West Cork murder, the first scientific study of sexual murder, *Psychopathis Sexualis*, by German psychiatrist Richard von Krafft-Ebing, Professor of Psychiatry in the University of Vienna, was published in 1886. The case studies provided a sample of varieties of sexual homicide, including some committed by an Italian peasant, Vincenz Verzini. The young man had attempted several attacks on women including his own sister but had run away or escaped before realising his perverted sexual homicidal fantasies.

His first victim was Giovanna Motta, a fourteen-year-old girl whom he strangled and disfigured with savage wounds, removing her intestines and biting and sucking blood from her right calf, which he cut away afterwards with the intention of cooking and eating it. The author gave an account of his second murder:

"On August 28, 1871, a married woman, Elisabetta Frigeni, aged twenty-eight, set out in the fields early in the morning. As she had not returned by eight o'clock that evening, her husband started out to fetch her. He found her corpse lying naked in the field with the mark of a thong on her neck, with which she had been strangled and with numerous wounds on her body. The abdomen had been ripped open and the intestines were hanging out."

To illustrate the impulsive nature of the perpetrator, the following day at noon, nineteen-year-old Maria Previtali was stalked by her cousin Verzeni. He dragged her into a field of grain, threw her to the ground and began to choke her. He let her go for a moment as he thought he heard a passer-by; she got up and begged to be released, and he acceded to her request.

The perpetrator was arrested, tried and convicted. He was first incarcerated in a prison and later in a lunatic asylum. Verzeni was interviewed by famous Italian criminalist Cesar Lombroso, who also recorded his confessions and published them in a book in 1873, a considerable aid to Krafft-Ebing in his own study. The psychopathic killer told Lombroso:

"I had an insatiable delight in strangling women, experiencing during the act erections and real sexual pleasure. It was even pleasurable to smell female clothing. The feeling of pleasure while strangling them was much greater than I experienced while masturbating."

He recounted that he felt an enormous strength during the attacks and said that the act of squeezing the throat and the mutilation of the bodies and sucking of blood gave him a paroxysm of sensual pleasures, during which he achieved erection and ejaculated.

"At last my mother came to suspect me because she noticed spots of semen on my shirt after each murder or attempt at one. In the moment of strangling my victims, I saw nothing else. During the strangling and after it I pressed myself on the entire body. I took the clothing and intestines because of the pleasure it gave to smell and touch them."

Verzeni first experienced sexual pleasure at twelve years of age while he was choking chickens on the small family holding and later achieved orgasm through strangulation of fowl. In common with many psychopathic sex killers of future generations, he would move from the slaughter of animals to humans and keep trophies of his killings.

Krafft-Ebing found, as did Lombroso, a complete absence of empathy, inhibition and remorse on behalf of Verzeni and other subjects of case studies for the victims of their appalling acts. It appears that these acts could be shoved away into some convenient psychological drawer, the key thrown away, and could be forgotten. The German psychiatrist examined several other cases illustrating the connection between lust and cruelty, thoughts of blood stimulating sexual excitement.

Traditional forms of detection were challenged as far back as the infamous unsolved murders in the Whitechapel area of London by Jack the Ripper in the late nineteenth century. Police surgeon Dr George Phillips attempted to reconstruct the murders and analyse the horrible wounds sustained by the victims to gain an insight into the psychology of the killer.

Phillips believed that such an approach could provide clues about the behaviour and personality of the serial killer. The surgeon was certainly on the right track and was before his time, but lacked the resources to properly develop his theory, which was an early manifestation of the work of a crime profiler.

Profiling in its most modern form was developed by the FBI at their headquarters in Quantico, Virginia, and familiar to readers of Thomas Harris's best-selling novel *The Silence of the Lambs* and the successful film adaptation starring Anthony Hopkins as the jailed serial killer Dr Hannibal Lecter and Jodie Foster as Clarice Starling – the FBI agent interviewing him to get information about another serial killer on the loose. Agent Crawford, Starling's boss, was based on FBI agent John Douglas.

The origin of this approach was in concrete terms the establishment in 1970 of the Behavioural Science Unit in Quantico and involving Roy Hazelwood, John Douglas and a team of nine investigators called the "Mind Hunters". The profiling involves deductive analysis of the crime scene to establish the characteristics of the unknown suspect and relied on experience, reasoning, insight and intuition to narrow and focus on a suspect search.

Hazelwood and Douglas wrote a paper in 1980, the subject of which concentrated on homicidal sadistic and lust murders, which they divided into two main categories of killers under the titles of organised and disorganised characteristics. The organised types took pride in their crimes, involving elements of fantasy, sexual acts with the victims in advance of death while exercising a great degree of control.

The disorganised counterparts acted in a more spontaneous manner with a frenzied and impulsive modus operandi, leaving weapons at the scene, positioning and depersonalising the body.

That was also characterised by a staging of the crime scene, and the authors wrote that the profiler must have a deep understanding of the criminal mind in addition to a basic grasp of human psychology. They pointed to a profiling approach that encouraged a subjective perspective on the part of the investigator.

The crime scene is the first and main focus, as well as the physical method of the killing, as the state of both can provide a wealth of information about the murderer and his state of mind before and at the time of the crime. For example, whether it was a crime of passion, a dispassionate and coldly executed act or one of revenge or sudden rage when the motive was frustrated. The scene and the body can also indicate if the killer fitted the major category of organised or disorganised perpetrator or as in some cases a combination of both and elucidate the motive for the crime.

The use of profiling had long been successfully utilised in the investigation methods of police in the U.S. Using the services provided by the FBI was and still is virtually unknown in the Irish jurisdiction but becoming more important in other European countries such as France both in the initial investigation and the judicial processes.

Despite years of development and especially with the aid of empirical research carried out by academic medical professionals such as psychiatrists and psychologists, profiling cannot be considered an exact science, but it is still a highly valuable aid to murder investigation.

It is particularly effective in crimes where there are no witnesses and no direct connection between the perpetrator and the victim, such as being in the category of family, workplace or a relationship, and in crimes with no apparent motive. These circumstances certainly seemed to fit the murder of Sophie Toscan du Plantier.

The motive in this case was not immediately apparent; it appeared that the killer called to the door without a prior plan of the crime but looking for something, most likely sex. Some interaction transformed the lack of intent into a full-blooded and bloody homicide, as expressed by the exceptional brutality used in the commission of the killing, which had all the appearance of being a result of a sudden onset of uncontrolled rage followed by a cold, dispassionate and merciless despatching of the victim.

Another empirical study revealed that in general, psychopathic sexual sadists prefer direct contact killing of the victims, utilising strangulation, mutilation and bludgeoning, the last of which was entirely apposite to the murder of Sophie Toscan du Plantier.

The professional profiler has access to a lot of information from primary sources, including police files, autopsy reports and photographs of the crime scene. All these help in the reconstruction of the sequence of events during the carrying out of the crime, including the acts committed by the perpetrator and the reaction of the victim interpreted by defensive injuries. Such detail was of course beyond bounds for us but did not preclude a reasonably educated assessment of what had happened in Toormore and provided a portrait of the mentality of the killer.

While we had at that time an outline of post-mortem details, there was also sufficient evidence from reporting and my contacts that there were about forty wounds on the body, plus the considerable blunt force trauma, and that the killer had got access to the victim without forced entry to the house, which indicated that Sophie was familiar with the visitor.

What was strikingly obvious was that the victim was subjected to violence of such savagery that went far beyond the necessity to achieve her death. For example, strangulation could have been used to get a result much more quickly, but the killer was not interested in a more merciful means to the end. Rather, the means employed was to inflict a massive destruction of a human being with maximum physical injury and maximum fear for the victim.

These facts once again demonstrated the act of a sadistic

sexual psychopath, as found in international studies, with the main criteria focused on evidence of beating, torture, mutilation or overkill, and the use of multiple weapons from the crime scene with multiple incidents during the commission of the crime.

In relation to the crime scene, given the explosive character of the violence, it fitted the description of a disorganised perpetrator and as such was not thought out in advance or pre-planned, and was spread out over at least three locations outside the house. The use of weapons found on the scene and left there by the attacker was a further qualification for the category which provided clues about the nature and personality of the killer through the characteristics of the violence, a better understanding of the motivation of the killer which could lead to a narrowing focus on the suspect list.

The factors at play in such circumstances, according to Hazelwood and Douglas, are:

DISORGANISED SCENE
Spontaneous Offence
Victim/Location Known
Depersonalises Victim
Minimal Conversation
Crime Scene Random and Sloppy
Minimal Use of Restraints
Sudden Violence to Victim
Sexual Acts after Death
Body Left in View
Weapon/Evidence Often Present
Body Left at Death Scene

In 1985, the FBI at Quantico in concentrating on the behaviour and psychology of the offender developed the characteristics of an organised perpetrator, which did not mean that he was not capable of leaving the crime scene in a disorganised state. It was about his character, background, intellect, domestic situation and other important factors which in total seemed to fit the Toormore killer.

ORGANISED CHARACTER
Average to Above Average Intelligence
Socially Competent
High Birth Order Status
Father's Work Stable
Sexually Competent
Controlled Mood During Crime
Use of Alcohol With Crime
Precipitating Situational Stress
Living With Partner
Mobility (Car in Good Condition)
Follows Crime in News Media
May Change Job and leave Town

In the opinion of the forensic psychiatrist, the murder was the work of a sadistic sexual psychopath, as no other category of criminal activity could explain the gratuitous violence utilised by the killer, characterised by acts that went way beyond the necessity to simply achieve the death of the victim as, for example, to eliminate her as a witness to the initial attack.

In addition, the use of a concrete block to literally destroy and disfigure the face was an act of depersonalisation to rob the victim of her beauty and identity. This was a classic act of a psychopath. The killer, the forensic psychiatrist judged, had a history of predatory sexual behaviour and violence towards a female or females in which violence was concentrated on the head and face.

He provided a lengthy insight into the mind and behaviour of such a predator, who possessing a combination of psychopathy and sexual aggression is highly dangerous, manipulative, domineering and likely to indulge in deviant sexual activities to exercise power and control. Impulsive, egocentric, deceitful and thrill-seeking. Emotional and physical abuse towards sexual partners would be part of his agenda and history of his relationships.

In the psychiatrist's practical experience and findings of international studies, psychopaths who offend sexually are significantly dangerous in relation to the physical and emotional abuse they inflict on their victims. They lack inhibition and remorse, and spurred on by thrill-seeking, they display no constraints or appreciation of the possible consequences when it comes to acting on their sexual impulses, in which physical punishment plays a big role.

They are excited by the suffering and helplessness of the victims, and sadism is a dominant feature of their sexual arousal patterns. Fully aware of the criminality of the act, the psychopath takes pride in his ability to thwart the police investigation of the crime. In several American cases, the killers visited bars frequented by the murder investigators and in some instances engaged the investigators in conversation. The psychiatrist felt that this type of behaviour might be applicable to a killer in such a small community even as a method of deflecting attention from his involvement in the crime.

So, in relation to a motive not easily to be established at this stage, what might be the parameters, I asked. He suggested that the killer may have – from the information about the victim, who was successful, beautiful and rich – considered her a threat unless he could exercise some intimate control over her to diminish the failures in his own life. He would not tolerate rejection of his sexual advances and would react with violence.

If she was inclined to resist and fight back, that would prompt him to resort to even greater brutality. He had no doubt that the killer had some contact with the victim beforehand and had stalked her in advance of the act. This may have been to establish that she was alone in the house but was also a part of his obsessive focus on the beautiful, stylish woman who in stark contrast to him was successful and wealthy.

In a social sense, this man constantly sought to be the centre of attention to disguise feelings of worthlessness and low self-esteem. In the matter of wrongdoing or bad behaviour, he was subject to convenient amnesia with what he would like to erase from his consciousness and placed the blame on anything and anybody other than himself.

The forensic psychiatrist had told me that while he might not have been a man of religion but of faith, that in his experience the psychopaths that he had dealt with were simply not amenable to treatment; their mentality was set and could not be changed. They were incapable of being cured and had little or no insight into the nature of their crimes, which meant they were likely to repeat them.

An author of an academic paper I accessed agreed on many points with his Irish counterpart on such basic facts as the psychopathic mentality was not just unresponsive to treatment but was more dangerous than other criminals and habitually engaged in predatory violence no matter what was presented to them in terms of clinical or moral assessment of their behaviour.

Associate Professor of Psychiatry at the University of California, San Diego, John Reid Meloy contributed an article to the September 1997 publication *Psychiatric Annals* entitled "The Psychology of Wickedness: Psychopathy and Sadism", which proved apposite to the case and revealing in relation to the mental profile of the killer of Sophie Toscan du Plantier. In his introduction, he wrote that these are people we must study and understand, yet fear.

He referred to the classic work of Cleckley on the subject, and carefully and empirically defined by Hare as a constellation of traits and behaviour characterised by two factors: the first a callous and remorseless disregard for the feelings of others, and the second a pattern of chronic anti-social behaviour.

"Some of the psychodynamics of the psychopath bring us closer to what we see as their evil, or their wish to destroy goodness. Psychopaths are

aggressively narcissistic ... and this aspect of their character pathology is often expressed behaviourally by the repetitive devaluation of others, not predominantly in fantasy as we see in narcissistic personality disorder but in reality.

"Psychopaths generally do this for two reasons. First to maintain grandiosity, or their sense of being larger than life, and second to repair perceived insults or emotional wounds by retaliating against those they held responsible."

The devaluation of others, ranging from verbal insults to homicide, is attributable to envy, the wish to possess the "goodness" perceived in others. If the "good object" cannot be possessed, it should be destroyed or damaged until it is not worth having. In this case, the victim would be seen precisely through that mental prism, being a woman, beautiful, sophisticated, successful in a media career and owning property and having material wealth.

The second psychodynamic that contributes to the psychopath's propensity to commit evil acts according to Professor Meloy is a chronic emotional detachment from others, and relationships are defined by power gradients and not emotional or affectionate ties. This deficit can be inherited or acquired, and the main focus is to dominate and control partners and lovers. But as well as stimulating grandiosity, the behaviour diminishes the possibility of empathy and inhibition of aggressive impulse.

The third psychodynamic of wickedness involves the deception of others. According to clinical experience and research, the psychopath is given to persistent and pathological lying.

"The psychopath lies for many reasons, the most common of which is to experience the feeling of contemptuous delight when a deception is successfully carried out and makes him feel smarter than most."

The forensic psychiatrist agreed completely about mendacity, pointing out that whether the man is interviewed by a policeman, a psychologist or a journalist, he will consistently and persistently continue to lie through his teeth. It is such an embedded element in his mental make-up that it is a total waste of time attempting to get him to tell the truth.

This encourages more lying, as the sense of grandiosity increases, fuelling a misguided belief in self-authority and a hatred towards any other authority that might contradict that belief.

Meloy summed up:

"These three aspects of the psychopathic personality-behavioural devaluation of others, chronic emotional detachment and mendacity are the catalysing agents of his wickedness. The historical trail of the psychopath's life is often marked by the wounded and angry people he or she leaves behind, sometimes unwittingly stripped of their own capacity for goodness."

What became abundantly obvious from the conclusions of all sources was that the psychopathic killer was not simply unamenable to treatment but also likely to reoffend at any given opportunity. Therefore, investigators in any community, whether urban or rural, would be justifiably correct to warn inhabitants to be on their guard with every manner or means, including locking their doors and reporting any suspicious activity by any individual day or night.

This was a well-established practice for decades in all international jurisdictions and murder investigators would be found wanting in their duty not to issue such warnings, and that had been done at an early stage in the investigation of the murder of Sophie Toscan du Plantier.

I had between all sources a voluminous amount of research in relation to the profile of the killer which, but a tiny proportion would be included in the article. I later travelled to Schull for further on-site research and managed through the good grace of Val Duffy, the manager of the East End Hotel, where I stayed to get an introduction to and interview with Jules Thomas. This was assisted by the fact that her partner Ian Bailey, after an assault against her and conviction for it, had been barred by the court from the area.

I knew little or nothing at the time of the details of the attacks on her. She struck me as a decent woman but incredibly vulnerable from the history she recounted of her previous relationships. My impression was of a woman possessed of talent and a propensity for hard work who deserved a lot more from what life had thrown at her. But a victim of considerable manipulation and control by her partner.

To say I felt sorry for her might have seemed patronising, but I did as one would for any person exposed to extreme acts of physical and psychological abuse.

She was most reluctant to discuss anything in relation to the murder but we did get around to it and she repeated fallacious theories such as the responsibility of the killing to Daniel Toscan du Plantier, who she said had hired an assassin to commit the crime as he was splitting up with his wife and she would take away a lot of his wealth.

My suspicion was that her partner had influenced such a view. The interview was conducted in the studio of their house and was relaxed. She was a practiced artist and her work and industry was abundantly obvious in the surroundings. I found nothing in the atmosphere of the house to suggest anything untoward. It was situated in an attractive location, which it should have been, especially for an artist – a source of contentment and inspiration, a modern West Cork version of the little house on the prairie.

I had no agenda with the interview as I was blissfully ignorant of anything of real importance about the case other than a general suspicion. There had been one thing that slightly bothered me. The night before the interview, myself and Jules had gone to Hackett's pub in Schull for a few drinks and a meal. At one point in our conversation, I had asked her if she had any contact with Ian.

She looked down at the table, looked up and replied that she had not. When I returned to the hotel, I rang one of my police contacts and he informed me that she had been observed meeting him several times. The significance of that I put down to undue influence, but some weeks later, in advance of the publication of the first article in late December 2001, Jules phoned me and requested that she would prefer that the interview should not be published.

I instantly recognised that this request was prompted by her partner's intervention and whatever her misgivings, which she could not really explain, I said that I was not going to accede. He had successfully to this point shut down the media and this was a further effort to stop any mention of the case. I politely refused the request, saying that it was in the printing works and could not be pulled at that stage. That was probably a bit of nonsense, but I was not going to be bested by an alternative voice with an agenda that I would only come to know more clearly as the years rolled on.

The articles were published in the *Sunday Independent* in late December 2001 and early January 2002, and had an immediate impact, not least because I had broken the libel action embargo, bringing the case back into the public consciousness through the medium of the country's highest-circulating Sunday newspaper. The psychological profile was particularly effective as it provided a perfect mental fit for Bailey's character and as an unintended consequence, he was run out of the town he was staying in at the time.

The articles also produced a commission for a book on the case published later in 2002, entitled *Death in December*, which became a best-seller and not only frustrated the elimination of publicity about the case but opened it up again. All of which appeared to be a big deal then, but in the passage of time proved otherwise, yet for me forged an enduring relationship with the Bouniol family and the case that would last for decades of pain, suffering, frustration and a long period during which the prime suspect would add salt to their bleeding wounds. I now intended to open a few more veins of their tormentor.

I had consciously become the hunter and haunter of the West Cork killer who was never going to face justice in the Irish jurisdiction. I would do everything in my power to shed light into the darkness of his mind and frustrate his Machiavellian and evil plans to enrich himself by his libel attack on the media and his slandering of members of the investigation team and the people of Schull and its surrounds. Much of my mind up to that point had been occupied by the victim and the injustice to her and her relatives.

At the house in Toormore, I had witnessed the tears of Sophie's parents Georges and Marguerite, and of her favourite aunt Marie Madeleine as they recalled the fate that had decreed that she had travelled to the house in West Cork alone for the first time and how one intervention in their own lives by acceding to her request to go along with her would have saved her life. From the living room window, you could see the spot now marked by a memorial Celtic cross bearing her name where she took her last breaths.

In Paris, I had seen her bedroom, a silent witness to her past, and had been in the magnificent living room of the Bouniol house which housed the photographs that chronicled the precious stages of her life with her family, her presence beautiful in adulthood, beatific in her childhood – *la jeune femme fatale*. The tender grace that will never return, her voice silenced forever.

Earlier, as we had gathered in front of the Celtic cross in brief silence, tears had slipped down my face, sadness soon replaced by anger as I imagined her body there, her beauty stolen by the building block that rested on a part of her clothing, a halo of blood around her crushed head. A mangled crushed corpse – the handiwork of a bloodthirsty maniac.

I thought of the ghost's words to Hamlet that inspired the prince's revenge:

"O horrible! O horrible! Most horrible!
If thou hast nature in thee, bear it not."

On many occasions, as the dawn crept through the bedroom window, I had awakened from a recurring nightmare in which the terrifying last minutes of Sophie were replayed as my semi-conscious watched on helpless and frozen in the same fashion we all experience when being chased in a dream by someone determined to inflict serious injury. A soundscape of shouts and screams accompanied the ghastly visual representation played out in the choreographed fashion of silent cinema, building to a crescendo of one single ascending scream which catapulted me upright into the silence of the bedroom.

Daniel Toscan du Plantier had once asked me while we were talking in the UniFrance offices in Paris whether I was in love with Sophie. It was a strange question, but I half understood why he might ask. I replied that had I known her when alive, I might well have been, as I imagined that it would have been easy to fall in love with such a beautiful, intelligent and cultured woman who was such a force of nature.

But now she was more in my mind than in my heart, though her presence had certainly grown. A sort of romantic notion to be in love with a dead woman, I posited.

Daniel said that there was someone who was in love with her or even the idea of her. Yes, I said, I can imagine. I wished I had met her when she was alive, yet now she lies in a grave. I thought of the last lines of poetry Sophie would ever read at the end of the Yeats poem "A Dream of Death":

"*And left her to the indifferent stars above*
Until I carved these words:
She was more beautiful than thy first love,
But now lies under boards."

I tried to bring her alive in *Death in December* because too often in cases I had covered, the victim got lost in the narrative, and in this instance through the good graces of Sophie's family and friends the public got to know what an extraordinary person had been so cruelly lost to the world.

Although she has never faded from my memory, I carried a picture of her just in case. It was that portrait of enigmatic beauty that graced the cover of *Death in December* and of which I spoke many times along the paths of defeat and glory that dogged and elevated the case over the decades.

Another person had entered the frame, the monster who was responsible for that loss. One who for all the wrong reasons had forced himself on the public consciousness but whose true evil nature I was determined to expose. Call it an obsession, yes, but the territorial imperative of the true crime writer no more or no less than Joe McGinniss with Jeffrey MacDonald in *Fatal Vision* or Michelle McNamara in *I'll Be Gone in the Dark* with the Golden State serial killer. Two books that inspired me along the journey, as well as Janet Malcolm's *The Journalist and the Murderer*.

As McGinniss observed on his journey: "It affected my dream life and not for the better. I did not think that I would get emotionally involved." I was now in that same position. In some cases that is inevitable.

I was aware already from knowledge of some contents of his diaries that Bailey had a twisted mind, but with manipulative powers that could not allow him to be underestimated as an enemy of the truth, which as a masterful liar he could twist and turn to his own advantage. His lack of empathy for the victim and her friends and family would make a saint's blood boil.

Sophie's good friend Catherine Clement wrote in rage that she would like to spill his blood:

"Without justice, spilled blood calls for revenge. Yes, I would like to take revenge. I would like to avenge Sophie by spilling blood. I imagine I am not alone."

In January 2002, a review team was appointed by the Commissioner Pat Byrne following the critical analysis of the DPP. The outcome in December 2002 concluded that while there was no further evidence gathered, Ian Bailey remained the prime suspect.

This implication of the conclusion simply underlined the gap between the views of the investigation team and Garda authorities, and the DPP, who demonstrated in the face of any amount of inquiries and revisions of the case file an unwillingness to shift from what in many respects was an untenable position.

The Bouniol family were now convinced that a criminal prosecution would never be taken in Ireland against the prime suspect. To give him a few sleepless weeks, to rattle his Liscaha cage and further frustrate his attempt to shut down media coverage of him and the case, I came up with a plan.

I suggested that the family consider taking a civil action for damages against Bailey, the reverse action of the O.J. Simpson case, which would continue the pressure on him and his legal team, and further break the embargo on publicity about the case. I consulted two top-class barristers Jim O'Callaghan, Frank Callanan, and solicitor Robert Dore and they agreed to take the case pro bono.

As the statute of limitations of six years would run out on December 23, 2002, the papers were drawn up quickly and a plenary summons lodged in the High Court in Dublin on December 19, 2002. The plaintiffs were Sophie Toscan du Plantier's parents, Georges and Marguerite Bouniol, and her former and present husbands, Pierre Louis Baudey and Daniel Toscan du Plantier.

They claimed damages against the defendant Ian Bailey for her wrongful death; for loss and emotional upset; intentional infliction of mental distress and financial loss as a result of the alleged action of Ian Bailey.

Although Daniel had remarried in 1998 and fathered two children with his spouse Melita Nikolic, he still maintained contacts and influence at the highest levels of the French Government and thus was an important ally for the Bouniol family in their fight for justice. This ended tragically with his sudden and unexpected death in early February 2003 while attending the Berlin Film Festival. He suffered a heart attack as he left a screening of a film directed by Claude Chabrol.

He was only sixty-two years of age and he had died just one month to the day after director Maurice Pialat, his and Sophie's neighbour near their country home in Ambax. All three were now gone, with Pialat the only one to reach what could be described as real old age.

President Jacques Chirac described Daniel as "one of the most talented servants of French cinema and one of its most determined advocates". He was buried in the famous Père Lachaise Cemetery in Paris, established by Napoleon and among whose notable occupants are Oscar Wilde; rock star Jim Morrison, lead singer with The Doors; Frédéric Chopin, Marcel Proust and Édith Piaf.

The obituaries, while acknowledging his value as a producer who had worked with such classic cinematic directors as Fellini, Bergman and Pialat, reminded readers that he had almost bankrupted French cinema giant Gaumont and was an unrepentant snob, claiming to have been descended from the Chevalier de Bayard, a sixteenth-century knight.

Obituarists (and journalists) have long ignored the recommendation of avoiding the Latin aphorism of respecting and not speaking ill of the dead, and much was also made of Daniel's fondness for the opposite sex, as if it was a rare French vice or somehow not a favourite pastime of film producers the world over.

More could have been made of how he shepherded Ingmar Bergman's classic and my favourite film *Fanny and Alexander* to post-production and completion, and ultimately four Academy Awards, which demonstrated as in other risky films his commitment to realising the dreams of cinematic artistes, a rare quality in a film producer.

Clearly there was a perception that he lacked a popular touch and was absent of humility. I found during two meetings to interview him, one in central Paris and the other at his UniFrance office, a personable and honest man, especially about his relationship with Sophie, and with a wry and entertaining sense of humour. Larger than life and impressive in an occasionally brusque way?

Wearing the mantle of power as of a right? Certainly. But that he was a loss as an advocate in the search for justice for his murdered wife was indisputable.

The details of the plenary summons against Bailey entered the public domain at the end of the same month and received widespread publicity in the national newspapers, many of them only too glad to be able to associate Bailey (under legal privilege) – who was suing them – with the facts and in particular the charge of "unlawful killing and death", and consequently going much further than simply nominating him as they were entitled to as the "prime suspect".

So, while he was holding a tranche of newspapers to ransom by his libel action, Bailey was now outed and accused of committing the crime without a whit of a possibility of redress. It was the least he deserved because as matters stood, he was literally getting away with murder and milking this undeserved immunity by slandering everyone in sight: the investigators, the people of the region and the newspapers, accusing all of lying, making false statements and ruining his life and career.

Rich coming from the biggest slanderer of all, the master of falsehood, the professor of mendacity, and – as his diaries revealed – a violent alcoholic and drug taker obsessed with sex. The public and the media did not know these details of the true nature of the man. I knew some of them but for legal reasons could not bring them into the public domain. I did not know it then, but the opportunity would arise soon.

In early August 2003, I travelled to Cork and met with a summons server who was employed by the family legal team to personally deliver the plenary summons document to Bailey at the house in Liscaha, and I would report the event as arranged exclusively for *The Sunday Times*. We travelled to Schull and on to Liscaha, where I witnessed the documents being handed to Bailey at the gateway to the house by the summons server and a colleague, recorded by a photographer.

Whatever path this civil action would take, it had already had an unintended consequence of a value that no one involved at the time could have possibly predicted. It would involve me trespassing in a territory once a foreign land for a journalist but now becoming both familiar and somewhat satisfying as the initial inhibition had been set aside.

One year later to the month, the critical analysis of the DPP in relation to insufficient evidence for the charging of Ian Bailey would be tested to devastating effect in a court setting. Bailey had decided to get his own back against the media by issuing defamation proceedings against eight newspapers claiming among other things that they had nominated him as the murderer and had ruined his life and career. If he had succeeded in his action, he could have walked away by his own financial standards a rich man and at the same time have engineered a situation where the media would not be able to report any more on the case and particularly his connection with the crime.

It was entirely consistent with his narcissistic traits that Bailey would look forward to the trial, and particularly the publicity that would surround it would satisfy his craving for attention and grandiose illusions no matter what the outcome. Once the spotlight was on him, he was satisfied, but at the same time was blind to the inherent danger, as demonstrated by his interaction with the media after his first arrest.

But typical of Ian Bailey in his dealings with anyone, he could not imagine that he would not win because his arrogance would not tolerate that possibility. He should have been reluctant to push his case to the courtroom in the wake of the mauling he was subjected to after his first arrest when attempting to get the media on his side in search of an imagined sense of fair play, which none of the journalists had been vaguely interested in subscribing to given his status at the time. Now, like a rejected lover, instead of moving on, Bailey was seeking revenge.

Publicity, as crime investigators and indeed relatives of victims know, is the lifeblood of maintaining interest, particularly in relation to long-term, so-called unsolved and cold-case murders.

Many of those murders are "unsolved" on technical points but investigators and indeed the communities in which the crimes took place can know well the identities of the killers. The prime suspect of a murder was now on the cusp of squeezing the lifeblood of publicity from the case. The date for the trial was listed to open at the Circuit Court in Cork on December 8, 2003, and to last for at least a week.

On numerous occasions, I had been asked over the duration of my involvement in the case why I had not sought to interview Bailey. The answer was simple: I had no intention of being a stenographer to a pathological liar. Most if not all interviews with him by journalists then and into the future, with the notable exception of Senan Molony's, had given the prime suspect an easy ride and never contained the normal ammunition of any self-respecting writer of vigorous confrontation about the facts.

That act would be reserved, for obvious reasons, for police interrogators and legal counsel in court settings.

CHAPTER 9
THE "MURDER" TRIAL SENSATION

Dublin/Cork – December 2003

Some weeks before the trial was about to begin, I was contacted by a senior member of the combined newspapers defence team. She wondered, with my background in writing about the crime, if I could help. Of what nature, I enquired. "Any" was the reply and I remarked that this communicated a sense of desperation. She admitted that she was even at that late stage somewhat pessimistic about the outcome. The defence was pleading justification for the paper's description of Ian Bailey as the prime suspect.

That meant proving as a matter of probability, she said, that the plaintiff could commit the murder. It seemed that this trial would go far beyond the claims of libel and defamation. If certain defence evidence to prove justification was judged inadmissible by the court, then the plaintiff would most likely win the case. The lawyer anticipated that the plaintiff's team and the Director of Public Prosecutions would vigorously oppose a defence motion to have it included and seek to have it withheld.

While of course there was an abundance of evidence against Bailey, there was, according to the solicitor at that time, little enough that the defence, with any legal barrier, could produce in court.

The stakes were high; the plaintiff was a man of straw with no money or property, so win or lose, the defence would be left holding a huge bill. The Circuit Court had a limit of individual damages of £38,000 and if Bailey was to succeed, he could walk away with well over £250,000. The defendants would then be faced with this bill in addition to their own and the plaintiff's costs, which would add up to close to a million euros. Needless to remark, the media after such an outcome would not be writing about Ian Bailey again, which would be disastrous in terms of further pursuit of the case.

With the considerable benefit of such a potential success behind him, there was little doubt that he would turn his litigious aim at the next target with even greater possibility of further enrichment – the State and the Garda authorities – on the basis of his allegations of the corrupt practices of the murder investigation team. So, the defence needed a document that would assist in the inclusion of the evidence, without which, even with the best efforts of counsel, the case could possibly be lost.

The prospect of a man who I was becoming increasingly convinced was guilty of the crime becoming a rich man on the back of the savage murder and sinking the case for all time with no possibility of justice for the victim or her family was more than enough reason for agreeing to help the defence. I neither sought nor would have accepted financial reward because that was not the point of the exercise on my behalf. I had already stepped over the line from writer on the subject to being facilitator when I suggested to the Bouniol family and Daniel Toscan du Plantier to take the civil action for unlawful killing against Bailey. That action would have an unpredictable and important influence on the outcome of the libel trial.

Libel, of course, is the bête noire of the practicing journalist, capable of ruining or at the very least damaging his or her professional reputation, souring the relationship with the newspaper, a consequence of financial loss and loss of trust in the capabilities of the reporter who has been successfully sued. The reporter's loss is aggravated by a negative impact on confidence and self-esteem.

The lawyer checking copy at the *Sunday Independent* while I worked there estimated that in the financial scenario of libel that damages represented one third of the liability while costs accounted for two thirds.

So, while journalists may play fast and loose with the facts, they do so at their own peril and they know as well and better than most that a court case – particularly one with high stakes – is an experience not to be recommended, a source of great stress, fear and loathing. It is little wonder that judges in civil cases consistently remind opposing parties that mediation is a far better alternative than fighting an issue in the courtroom setting and in addition cost effective.

The reality is that too many litigants see a pot of gold at the end of the legal rainbow and like gamblers they are far too willing to risk everything to get their hands rummaging through a pile of glorious currency. There was little doubt in my mind that Ian Bailey had a similar perception of the outcome of his action. For my part, I had a basic grasp of libel law, the sort that most journalists have, which is not in great detail. I needed to know a little more about the plea of justification. My research, as limited as it was, provided some clarity.

Defamation cases are different from any other case. When a claim is filed, it is incumbent on the defendant to prove the defence right from the first filing. If there is a failure to sustain the plea of justification, this may be considered by a judge or jury as an aggravating factor in estimating damages where there is no reasonable evidence to support it. The plea must be made in good faith under the honest belief in the truth of the matter published and with reasonable grounds for such a belief. If the plea fails, then all other additional pleas must fail as they would express malice.

With the plea of justification, the rules of evidence apply to the defendant and must be strictly proved at trial. When a plaintiff's character is at issue (on a plea of justification), proof must be established of what that general character is or is not. In such cases, particular incidents are also admissible prior and subsequent to the publication of the alleged libel. That struck a bell with this case as it was a matter of court record that Ian Bailey had assaulted his partner Jules Thomas both before and after the publication of the articles which were the subject of his complaints.

On September 17, 2001, he had received a three-month suspended sentence for a vicious assault on his partner and was banished by court order from the house and area for three months. In the following month, he received a fine for public intoxication. He had two previous convictions for being drunk in charge of a motor vehicle in 1994 and 1998.

While the details of the assaults were not in the public domain, I assumed that the defence would have gathered them as part of evidence of his proclivity for violence towards a female. I had also discovered as part of my general research the existence and some of the contents of Bailey's diaries which had been seized by members of the investigation team during the operation coinciding with his second arrest. These diaries provided a stunning insight into the dark aspects of Bailey's character.

I made more assumptions as I did not want to become a de facto researcher for the defence team by consistently ringing the lawyer to answer any of my queries. Clearly such evidence would be vital to the success of the plea of justification and would naturally be contested by Bailey's counsel and a submission made to be declared inadmissible by the court. But on what grounds would the Director of Public Prosecutions be objecting to the evidence being ventilated in court?

The most obvious reason would be to block evidence ventilated in a civil action that might have a prejudicial effect on a subsequent criminal trial. This I remembered had been a subject of discussion with the Irish lawyers representing the Bouniol family in the civil action against Bailey for unlawful killing. The opinion was that a civil action could proceed without prejudice to a future criminal trial. The lawyers for the family wrote to the Director of Public Prosecutions to ascertain his intention regarding bringing anyone to trial for the crime.

This prompted me to search the small file I had made on matters concerning the civil action, which included cuttings of news reports including my own on the subject. After I had conducted the search, I came across a document that I felt might be helpful, but with no idea if it might have any influence whatsoever on the outcome of the libel proceedings. I had some misgivings about the process and the path I was undertaking. It was all very well to be adopting the role of nemesis of the prime suspect of the murder, but it certainly compromised the so-called objectivity of the position of a writer on the case.

On the other hand, the prospect of Ian Bailey defeating the right of newspapers to cover the case in the future and in the process enriching himself was anathema to me, so I rang the lawyer and arranged to hand over the document which she told me would be helpful. But as the start date of the trial got closer, I experienced the same sense of trepidation that accompanies the prospect any such event; journalists, police officers and lawyers will say that it is almost impossible to accurately predict the outcome of any legal action.

The case was listed in the Cork Circuit Court to start on the morning of Monday, December 8, 2003 and the proceedings it was indicated would take at least a week before Justice Patrick J. Moran. The plaintiff was Ian Bailey and the defendants were the *Sunday Independent*, the *Independent on Sunday*, *The Times*, *The Sunday Times*, *The Daily Telegraph*, *the Irish Daily Mirror*, the *Irish Star* and the *Irish Sun*.

The magnificent old courthouse on Washington Street in the heart of Cork city was being refurbished, so the court was in a makeshift premises on Camden Quay, which had the distinct look and feel of the warehouse it had once been. Given the huge interest in the case, Court Number One was allocated for the hearing and with a touch of supreme irony, a large section of the media army was accommodated in the jury box along with three rows at the back of the spacious room.

From early morning on the opening day, the pathway outside the court occupied a large gathering of still photographers, reporters and camera crews all awaiting the arrival of the plaintiff, who sprang into action when a taxi pulled up and Ian Bailey – wearing a sober grey suit, shirt and tie – got out followed by his partner Jules Thomas. He had aged, put on weight and his once lush dark locks had thinned out and were streaked with grey, and she was stick-thin, strained-looking and clutched his arm as they entered the court.

Inside, they took their seats near their legal team on the upper left-hand side of the court in an almost direct sight line with the jury box bursting at the seams with members of the fourth estate, including some of his alleged persecutors. As the clock crept towards 10 a.m., the tension mounted as it might before the curtain rises in the opera house just across the River Lee on the opposite quay.

Just close to 10 a.m., Judge Moran entered and the whole room rose and then resumed seats after the judge was seated at the bench. A sensational trial which would have more in common with a murder trial than defamation proceedings began. Bailey was represented by his long-time solicitor Con Murphy, a small, rotund, florid-faced man with a pleasant demeanour, and Jim Duggan, a leading barrister in Cork, a thin man with a lined face whose spare frame belied his ability to make his presence felt in a courtroom setting.

Four firms of solicitors represented the defendant newspapers and the team was led by senior counsel Paul Gallagher, a small, powerfully built man with a shallow beard who was not only one of the top counsels in the Law Library but had a fierce reputation as a highly skilled and aggressive advocate. He was assisted by David Holland S.C., able if less experienced than his leader.

The morning was predictably taken up with legal submissions and argument on the contentious matter of the evidence the defence needed to prove the plea of justification and the plaintiff's team and counsel for the DPP wanted to be declared inadmissible. The latter was a notice party not directly involved in the case, whose counsel objected to the inclusion of members of the investigation as witnesses and material collected and seized utilised as evidence or exhibits.

Counsel for the DPP James McCarthy in his submission said the State was concerned that if ten to twelve of the Garda witnesses were called, it might prejudice a future criminal prosecution, if one were to be undertaken. He added that the State's concern was that a proper and fair prosecution could well be prejudiced if evidence given by these officers was revealed in the civil case.

Jim Duggan B.L. for Bailey referred to the horrific murder of Ms Du Plantier and said he did not want the statements of the officers to go into this civil trial. "They [the defendants] are now going to use material they could not have known at the time to justify their handiwork in defaming my client." While the statement was true in relation to the time of the knowledge, counsel was skipping over the legal fact that material related to incidents prior and subsequent to publication was admissible.

Nonetheless, as he stood up from the defence table, Paul Gallagher S.C. had a mountain to climb in his argument. If the submissions were accepted by the court, then the newspapers' defence team might as well have booked the next train out of Cork. Counsel pointed out that the defence would say that Mr Bailey was the main and only suspect for the murder when the articles were published, that he was a violent man and that he courted publicity concerning the murder.

With lengthy reference to case law, Mr Gallagher cogently and persuasively argued that evidence ventilated in a civil case that preceded a criminal trial can be used in the former without proving prejudicial to the latter. One thing was established at this early stage – whatever the decision on the submissions, Paul Gallagher had a powerful and charismatic presence in the court.

In normal circumstances, I would have been figuratively reaching for the prayer book to support the right decision not just for the newspapers and my journalistic colleagues but also the Bouniol family, but I just hoped that the document would prove the effective remedy and noted that counsel must have been keeping it as an ace up his sleeve. My pulse rate still jumped when

Paul Gallagher concluded his legal argument and asked that a document be handed to the bench.

Judge Moran perused it carefully and referring to the contents said it was crystal clear from the document that the Director of Public Prosecutions stated that he had no intention of proceeding to a criminal trial, so he was ruling that the evidence requested by the defence was admissible. The statement of the DPP had been made in an official response the previous March to the letter sent to him by the family's lawyers in the civil action taken against Bailey for unlawful killing, a copy of which I had found in my file and provided to my defence contact.

Nobody, not even the most seasoned of court reporters, could have possibly predicted the impact of the decision on both the course and the nature of the proceedings, and the horrendous character of evidence that would be ventilated with regard to events, incidents surrounding the crime and providing a dramatic insight into a savage murder in a relatively small and peace-loving community.

It was now midday and Jim Duggan rose to make the opening speech on behalf of the plaintiff. He proved to be of the declaratory school of adversaries sawing the air with his arms for emphasis accompanied at times by a form of vocal exaggeration which was quite effective at times but offering total contrast to his court adversary on the defence side.

He chronicled how his client's life had been affected by "these monstrous articles" and how he had been forced into a living nightmare. He told the court that Bailey's nightmare began when he was contacted by *Examiner* journalist Eddie Cassidy to check out a story that a woman had been murdered at Toormore. The body had been found about 3 miles from where he lived with his partner Jules Thomas.

"To this day, the crime is unsolved, despite the fact that the greatest resources were put at the disposal of the Gardai to try and find the perpetrator of this horrific case. The murder shocked and numbed not just the people of West Cork but everyone nationally and internationally. She [Sophie] was the wife of an influential film producer who himself was a very well-known figure and a personal friend of the French president Jacques Chirac."

His client did not know the murder victim and yet had been put on trial by the media. There were hordes of media outside his house on a twenty-four-hour basis after his first arrest in February 1997. He said that Bailey, his partner Jules Thomas and her three daughters had been made prisoners in their own home, the Prairie, Schull. He had been persecuted and the slanted and biased articles had resulted in his client being shunned by society, and he was referred to within his own community as "the murderer".

He had not brought the case for financial gain but in the hope that he could clear his good name and find some method of showing ordinary people that he did not kill Sophie Toscan du Plantier. If he was doing it for money, then he might have brought his case to the High Court rather than the Circuit Court. "I don't know whether Ian Bailey committed this murder or not. He says he did not, and I accept it."

He accused the defendants of a character assassination and demonisation of his client, who was in addition persecuted and victimised. The grossly defamatory nature of the articles complained of had given him no option but to resort to legal action to clear his name. Here was classic courtroom rhetoric which had assiduously avoided the fact that his client had actively courted the media in the wake of his first arrest and had missed the opportunity of explaining the reason for this, for example that it was a first effort to clear his name which through, as he might have put it, a reasonable action of his client which had gone disastrously wrong.

Opening speeches in a trial provide an outline of the evidence which will be relied on by the opposing sides during the proceedings; the battle lines are being drawn by the adversaries and being the first impression of sword crossing by the eminent counsels can have a lasting effect especially to a jury.

But they are also important in the presence, as in this instance, of a judge, however cold he casts his eye on the subject and presentation of the arguments of the barristers. Judge Patrick Moran, an upper-middle-aged man with a well-trimmed beard, at first glance seemed to have a benign aura but to be belied with an eagle eye and meticulous attention to detail.

Paul Gallagher had made a profound impression during his long case law submission to have the vital evidence for the defence allowed and had scored what in sporting parlance was a winning goal with a crucial assist from the document I had provided. Jim Duggan knew that he would have to do his best for his client in the wake of that setback.

After lunch, he began a trawl of the content of the newspapers which he claimed were grossly defamatory. He repeated the headlines over the offending articles, which struck observers as both predictable and somewhat innocuous.

"Investigating with the Prime Suspect" appeared over Brighid McLaughlin's *Sunday Independent* piece and "Devil in the Hills" on her reworded version in the *Independent on Sunday*. The first certainly reflected the theme of the content and it was hard to see any element of libel, while the second one was capable of an interpretation that Bailey was the devil. However, in common with the other headlines and articles punctiliously examined by counsel to demonstrate animus towards his client, not one described Bailey as other than the prime suspect; nowhere was he described as the murderer.

But counsel ploughed on, painting a portrait of the vitriol displayed to his client by the media. He said that an unprecedented number of police and journalists descended on the small West Cork community after Sophie Toscan du Plantier's murder, and Bailey was one of the journalists working on the story. "He had worked for Irish and French papers, but the matter took an entirely different turn of events two weeks later.

"On February 10, 1997, three detectives arrived at his home and, to his horror, arrested him for the murder of Sophie Toscan du Plantier. They did not inform him that his partner Jules

Thomas would be arrested half an hour later. He was taken to Bandon Garda Station where there were twenty or thirty journalists waiting and one TV crew. The gate was conveniently left open for photographers to get a shot of him." From then on, there was no anonymity for his client and after respective periods of twelve hours' detention, Bailey and Thomas were released without charge.

He then described the siege of the house in Liscaha by journalists after Bailey and Thomas had been released, virtually rendering them prisoners in their own home. The little house at the Prairie was not a happy place for its occupants. "Various journalists tried to ingratiate themselves with him so they could write articles that were sympathetic to him. He fell for this on a number of occasions and he was deceived as horror stories were written about him and his partner."

Mr Duggan was in full flight and claimed the newspapers had robbed him of his career and livelihood after his arrest and printed his name liberally, resulting in him becoming known in the community as "the murderer". Even though the DPP did not recommend that he be charged with the murder, the fourth estate was not satisfied and continued at every turn to demonise him.

He believed there had never been a more thorough murder investigation in the State. His client had been arrested and interviewed on two separate occasions. The file had been reviewed by the DPP three times. The case had been reviewed two years ago by a new set of Garda personnel investigating.

This reference, entirely accurate, was meant to convey the message that after all this investigative effort, his client had never been charged. That decision rested entirely in the remit of the DPP and was a source of great disappointment to the Garda authorities and the investigation team.

But the most curious aspect naturally not referred to by counsel was that the DPP had attempted to persuade the court to block vital evidence, knowing full well that there was no intention of prosecuting Ian Bailey.

Counsel delivered his next line with an uncommon flourish and appropriate emphasis and some effect: "He is not the murderer and he did not murder Sophie Toscan du Plantier."

Now this statement reverberated around the courtroom with strange and dissonant effect. Counsel had strayed far from his script of the matter in hand, the defamation of his client, and was issuing a bald challenge to the defence to contest the case in a manner foreign to a trial for libel and never experienced in any court in the land. Or perhaps and more likely, Jim Duggan was heralding the defence, introducing the necessary proof of justification that his client was capable of the crime while never having been referred to as the murderer by the defendants and was making his point in advance.

When he finished his address to the court, he called Bailey to the stand, who under oath swore to tell the truth, something he had found virtually impossible to do up to this point in time, and nobody was expecting him to depart from his narrative of his movements preceding, during and following the murder. He looked calm, collected and assured while being examined by his own counsel, which of course was the easy part. He said he was not taking the case for financial gain, believing that it was the only way to clear his name.

He told the court that he had married another journalist in England and the marriage had lasted five years. They were both young and he said that he gave too much time to his job and not enough to the relationship.

He recounted coming to Ireland and to Schull, where he worked in a fish factory, met and fell in love with Jules Thomas and eventually moved in with her and her three daughters from previous relationships. He tried to get work in journalism and supplied stories on an irregular basis to newspapers but had taken up gardening work.

After the harmless preamble, his counsel had to get to the nitty gritty and asked him about getting involved in the reporting of the crime. Then he reprised his contentious version of the phone call he had received from Eddie Cassidy of *The Examiner* to check out the death of a person in the Toormore area, and his insistence that he had never met the victim but that she had been pointed out to him outside her holiday home through the window of her neighbour's house.

His statements about these matters, and of course the killing of the turkeys and the contact with the Christmas tree, were only too familiar to the journalists covering the court case, as he attempted to explain away the scratches that had been on his arms without ever alluding to the wound to his forehead.

His counsel asked him what he was doing on the morning of the murder. "I received a phone call from Eddie Cassidy shortly before lunch. I was asked if I could maybe find out about the incident. He said there had been a murder and that it had involved a foreign national. It was thought that the person may have been French."

Replying to what he had been doing before the call, he said that he had been preparing turkeys for Christmas Day; he and his partner used to rear free-range turkeys and the idea on this occasion was to kill two and sell one, which would cover the cost of their own. "The turkeys were being prepared for the table. I had to kill them. But I got one small scratch from a talon as I did the job. I used a knife. But it's not a job I enjoy, and we don't do it anymore."

He then repeated the story of the Christmas tree that he had already told to members of the investigation team to account for other injuries. He picked a tall fir tree and was accompanied by Saffron, one of Thomas's daughters. It was 20 feet high and he scaled it to cut the top off and during this action he said that he had got scratches on his arms.

In relation to his movements after the phone call from Eddie Cassidy, he and Jules Thomas travelled by car to the lane leading to the crime scene. "I went to the lane and I could see Gardai and a lot of activity on the hillside. A little later, a few Gardai came up to me and I explained I was there for *The Cork Examiner*. They told me to contact the Garda press office."

Jules Thomas, he said after they retreated a bit, took photographs of the scene from a long-lensed camera. Bailey was the first reporter at the scene of the crime, from which he had travelled directly from his house. In response to further questions from his counsel, Bailey provided a story which struck reporters who had covered the crime strange. He said that he eventually discovered the name of the victim which the local community knew very well indeed without any resort to investigation.

He said that he and Jules Thomas had gone to the local post office to seek information about what had happened. "The word was spreading that a terrible thing had happened, and I was trying to find out a name." He eventually found out it was Sophie Toscan du Plantier, as he was confused by the fact as he claimed that she was known locally by her family name Bouniol. A confusing narrative it certainly appeared, with no qualification about what the trip to the post office could have possibly provided.

His investigative skills were not immediately recognised as his first two filings on the murder to the *Examiner* and the *Irish Independent* were not published, but as he informed the court, he would subsequently go on to work on the story of the murder for the *Sunday Tribune*, the *Irish Star* and French publication *Paris Match*. At this juncture, Mr Justice Moran terminated the day's proceedings at 5 p.m.

On the morning of the second day, Tuesday, December 9, his counsel Jim Duggan took Bailey through his first arrest on February 10, 1997, and he described his shock, which would have been a natural reaction from anyone who had been handcuffed at their house, an action which he would have realised would spell the end of his reporting on the crime for newspapers who had previously employed him and would certainly have shared his shock when the news of the arrest broke.

He conceded that the arresting officers had behaved in a friendly manner at first. Bailey, as it had been well established, was a sympathy seeker as well as a publicity seeker, and had he been more constrained in his description of the event, he might have received some. His penchant for talking and embellishment might have been considered ill-conceived in the outside world, but in a court, it was asking for trouble – a setting he chose to sue the media.

His next section of evidence was an attack on the arresting officers whom he alleged to have a Jekyll and Hyde transformation once he was placed in the car and proceeded on the drive to Bandon.

"Shortly after we were on the road, the atmosphere towards me changed to what I can only describe as one of great hostility. I was bombarded with verbal claims and allegations." He accused the officers of carrying out an orchestrated and premeditated routine, and he alleged he was told by one that he would be found dead in a ditch with a bullet in the back of his head.

The credibility of a witness is paramount in court proceedings and the plaintiff under the friendly examination of his own counsel had already succeeded in putting a large question mark over the truthfulness of his account of the arrest.

The arresting officers were experienced and reputable, and it was highly unlikely that they would have exposed such naked prejudice in advance of an arrest and subsequent interrogation, which they and of course the prisoner knew full well would make national and international headlines. This was no "fish and chips" murder beloved of his English journalistic beat, but a high-profile killing with international dimension and unsurpassed savagery.

But in the witness box, Bailey was relating how he had become the victim of the savagery of the media and was sick to the stomach by reading one article which the reporter had promised would be sympathetic to the subject and had only given the interview as a result of that promise. He claimed the impact of the articles on his life were devastating.

"I was stripped of my presumption of innocence. I used to go out when I wanted to. I don't do that anymore. I'd go to Bantry or Skibbereen. I don't do that anymore. Life has been a struggle. It feels like I have been eaten alive. I have been battered." He felt that a campaign had been waged against him.

As far as battering was concerned, his counsel were aware that what would be examined by the opposing counsel were Bailey's actions towards his partner Jules Thomas on a number of occasions, which had caused him to be arrested in 1996 and 2001 in the wake of the violent domestic incidents. Obviously, his counsel would attempt to skate over the details, which the defence would spend some time examining. Bailey would follow suit and play down the implications for his character.

"It is to my eternal regret that during our thirteen years together we have had three fights. But I accept full responsibility for what happened. I hurt her and I admitted it." He tried to shift the blame for the battering in 2001 on the pressure he had been living under, the source of which he described as external forces, presumably as he did not define what they were – the aftermath of his arrests in 1997 and 1998 in relation to the murder and the media attention.

"We had been under the most extraordinary pressure for five years, but I am not going to defend what I did. Over a period of time, we made it up. But I am not proud of what happened."

What was missing from the exchange on the matter with his counsel was the nature and narrative of the assaults; all the court heard was the bare fact that the incidents had occurred. It was a deficit that Paul Gallagher, now on the cusp of cross-examination, would immediately address when in the mid-afternoon Jim Duggan completed the examination of his client.

The defence counsel from his first questions set out his stall like a gentle boot by comparison of what was to come. Bailey now had to face the looming reality of the details. There was an assault on Jules Thomas earlier in the same year as the murder, 1996. Mr Gallagher recounted an incident when the couple were returning from a party when the plaintiff launched an assault on his partner, causing injuries which comprised of bite marks, a wound on the mouth of the victim which required eight stitches, clumps of her hair being pulled out and bruises to her eyes.

Bailey looked rattled but tried to maintain his composure.

Counsel paused and then asked: "How would you describe the person who did that?"

"Not very nice, it is appalling."

Counsel asked whether appalling was as far as he was prepared to go. "Would you think it was animal-like?"

"No."

There was a sense of rapt attention in the courtroom and a degree of shock. Nobody, including the reporters, had heard anything of these details before.

Bailey, instead of taking on the facts which were apparently indisputable, attempted to somewhat deflect from his responsibility for this atrocious behaviour as it dawned on him that the attacks made on him as he alleged by the media might well be minor by comparison. He claimed that his partner had a scalp condition that explained the removal of the clumps of her hair. As if she had thin hair unrooted to her scalp and the act of pulling it out was some sense of mitigation. Jules Thomas, sitting in the court, had a full head of hair stretching to her shoulders. Counsel let him continue to explain this unlikely scenario.

"I am not a violent man; this was not a premeditated attack. All the violence between us occurred with drink. I did not intend to hurt her."

So, the plaintiff claimed in the face of evidence and fact to the contrary that he was not a violent man, blamed the reason for the attack on the consumption of alcohol but went further and said his partner was responsible for instigating the row.

"If she had not started to go at my face this would not have happened. I am not a violent person. When we both drink violence occurs. I believe there is a difference."

On that astounding note, the day's proceedings finished. It was just the beginning of a cross-examination from hell for which Bailey, his legal team and the court audience were totally unprepared. But already the plaintiff was showing some unappealing characteristics that his cool demeanour could not disguise. His voice was flat, somewhat boring and monotonous. He came across as unfeeling when the subject of his assaults on his partner was broached. He displayed no understanding of his violent behaviour and no empathy with the victim. His answers were matter-of-fact, with no hint of human frailty or trace of remorse.

Such things occur when a few drinks too many are on board. It was obvious that here was a man who did not express his feelings, and the reality of his actions was beyond his reach. It is natural and understandable to defend oneself and not accept blame when innocent of a charge, but what was happening here was an admission of the charge but no acceptance of personal blame.

It is difficult for a person who displays no empathy to expect or get sympathy, especially when being nudged towards and led into a legal trap, which was exactly the fate shortly to befall the plaintiff, who was totally unaware, as was any member of the full house in the court.

Trials, especially those involving murder, are akin to theatrical dramas or films composed of a series of moments, which can include shock, horror, revelation, surprise, sorrow and emotion in an evolving script, a lot of the content already written and the rest fashioned on an improvisational basis. There are the moments that veteran observers of such courtroom drama recognise as the turning point in a trial, not necessarily recognised at the time but certainly so in retrospect.

Under the legal scalpel of Paul Gallagher S.C., the third day, Wednesday, December 10, would be packed with the kind of moments described above and applied with pitiless and merciless surgical precision. He opened his cross-examination *medias res* but the intent of questioning would lurk under the surface for a short while.

He began by referring to two violent assaults carried out by Bailey on his partner Jules Thomas in May 1996 and in August 2001. During one of them, he had attacked her with a crutch that he had been using while his leg was in plaster.

Regarding the latter incident, counsel for the defence took the plaintiff through a list of the injuries he had inflicted on his partner:

Paul Gallagher: "She sustained a black eye?"
Ian Bailey: "Yes."
Paul Gallagher: "A swollen cheek?"
Ian Bailey: "I won't dispute that."
Paul Gallagher: "Bruised lips?"
Ian Bailey: "If that's …"
Paul Gallagher: "A cut chin?"
Ian Bailey: "I didn't see a cut."
Paul Gallagher: "So this assault was to Ms Thomas's face?"
Ian Bailey: "Well, she pulled the crutch towards her … she started pulling the crutch. I was trying to get it back and she was pulling it and I let go, it struck her."
Paul Gallagher: "But surely Ms Thomas was struck twice with the crutches. Did you use a second crutch to hit her?"
Ian Bailey: "It may have come in contact with her."

This was another extraordinary explanation by the plaintiff for a vicious assault on his partner, which attributed the blame to her for pulling the instrument that wreaked the damage and suggesting that it had had a trajectory of its own which had had nothing to do with him. He further shifted the responsibility away from his brutal tendencies.

Ian Bailey: "I then tried to get past her to get out of the room. But she was in the way, I was immobile. She was hysterical, she had also taken drink. We both had quite … I don't know … we seem to have temperaments …"
Paul Gallagher: "Which gave way to violence?"
Ian Bailey: "On occasions in the past when we have drink [*sic*] have led to violence."
Paul Gallagher: "You are a man with a temper, that when you have drink is violent?"
Ian Bailey: "Just with Jules."
Paul Gallagher: "Just with Jules?"
Ian Bailey: "I have a temper, which as I said alcohol does not suit me. I now completely abstain from it."
Paul Gallagher: "Just with Jules, you're sure of that? You said,

'I'm here to prove my innocence', so think carefully about that, Mr Bailey."

Ian Bailey: "Am I here to prove my innocence?"

Paul Gallagher: "That is what was described on the first day."

Indeed it had been said on his behalf by his counsel, who told the court his client had not been motivated by money but had brought the case in the hope that he might find a way to show ordinary people that he was not the murderer. Bailey had already forgotten that statement. Bailey in reply said he had not assaulted anyone else. He said that he was totally ashamed of what he had done.

The defence counsel now moved – though it might not have seemed so at that time – subtly towards the jugular. Thus far, the plaintiff had maintained his composure for the moment.

Paul Gallagher: "Would you describe yourself as an animal?"

Ian Bailey: "Certainly not."

Counsel asked him if the abuse that his partner had been subjected to on these two occasions exceeded the abuse he said that he felt after reading the articles about being the prime suspect in the murder. The plaintiff said they were different and the effect of them both being wrongly accused of murder was worse. He failed to hear counsel describing the articles as casting him as prime suspect, which was perfectly legal. He was thus downplaying the horrendous assaults he had carried out on his partner, especially the ferocious one in May 1996 which resulted in Jules Thomas being hospitalised in Cork.

Bailey had not accompanied her to hospital and the court was told by the defence counsel that when they arrived home, he became hysterical and would not give the keys of the car to the victim's daughter Virginia in an attempt to prevent his severely injured partner being taken to hospital.

A neighbour, Peter Bielecki, was forced to intervene and take Jules Thomas to hospital, and while she was being treated moved into the house to provide comfort for her daughters in the wake of the horrendous incident. In court, Bailey accepted that he should have accompanied her to hospital but did not.

Paul Gallagher: "What sort of man are you? What sort of man are you?"

Ian Bailey: "How can I describe that?"

Paul Gallagher: "You took objection to an article that said you had a history of violence with women?"

Ian Bailey: "A history of violence towards women, plural."

Paul Gallagher: "Your objection is that you had a history of violence with women, plural?"

Ian Bailey: "Yes."

Paul Gallagher: "And what do you think readers would have thought of the description you just gave of the assaults on Ms Thomas?"

Ian Bailey: "I don't know."

Paul Gallagher: "Might they be forgiven for thinking you were an animal?"

Ian Bailey: "I don't know … a lot of people have said to me the difference between domestic violence and assault and a murder are hugely different."

Paul Gallagher: "Do you think readers would have been more shocked to read details of these vicious assaults rather than read that you were a suspect in a murder?"

Ian Bailey: "I don't think so."

The real and damning effects of the admissibility of evidence into the proceedings argued against by his counsel and that of the DPP came into play in a later exchange with dramatic impact.

Paul Gallagher: "You'll remember on a number of occasions I asked you would it be correct to describe yourself as an animal and on each occasion, you said 'no' … Can I put it to you that this is the very description of yourself in your books and diaries?"

Ian Bailey: "I don't know."

Paul Gallagher [reading from diary]: "I am an animal on two feet."

Ian Bailey: "Can I explain that when I'm writing in my books I'm writing in a style."

Paul Gallagher: "So it was a poetic way to describe yourself?

[continues reading] "I'm confused and depressed by the way everything is going. I am an animal ..."

Ian Bailey: "It is not a poetic description, not of myself. I write poetry on and off. I put myself into the position of being a lion, a monkey in a tree. What are you supposed to do if you're describing, you're describing a poetic description?"

Paul Gallagher [reading from a diary entry made on May 6, 1996]: "'One act of whiskey-induced madness coupled and cracked and in an act of awful violence I severely damaged you and made you feel death was near.' This was describing the vicious assault on Ms Thomas some days previous?"

Ian Bailey: "That was written in an abstract form."

The proverbial pin could not be heard in a court stunned into absolute silence by the unfolding horror of the evidence of Ian Bailey's violence and his inability to accept full responsibility for his despicable actions instead of throwing away the last scintilla of dignity he could maintain by trying constantly to deflect from his brutal role in the events and as a consequence drawing more damning evidence and increasing the ferocity of the defence counsel's cross-examination. He was now trying to say there was some fictional element in his writing, as if it was an episode in a novel.

Paul Gallagher: "But that was an expression of your regret at what happened?"

Ian Bailey: "Everything I write should not be taken literally ... You can take it whatever way you want."

There was a small exchange about writing and the plaintiff's view of it.

Paul Gallagher: "You said you made her feel death was near?"

Ian Bailey: "Death is always near ... it isn't to be taken literally."

Paul Gallagher [reading]: "And as I lay and write I know there is something badly wrong with me ..."

Ian Bailey: "It says that there and if you ask does this apply to me, I would say, 'Not necessarily.' It might but I am not saying it in relation to the assault."

Paul Gallagher [reading from same passage]: "'Although remorse-filled sentiments and disgust floods me I am afraid for myself, a cowardly fear, for although I have damaged and made grief your life, I have damaged my own destiny and future to the point I can see in destroying you I destroyed me ... and time will tell that I damned to hell.'"

Once again, Bailey in reply to counsel failed to accept the literal meaning of the passage which was unequivocal in the writer's concern for himself above the victim of a vicious assault with more emphasis on the damage done to *himself* as a result of his violence. If he was sorry for the battered partner, he was even more sorry for himself.

It was typical of the plaintiff's response to evidence that he would reject if it did not suit his self-serving narrative. It might have annoyed or frustrated a less patient and skilful adversary than Paul Gallagher, who instead used it quite correctly to push his point further, even more painfully for the now-embattled witness whose only strategy was denial, denial, denial even when it flew in the face of the facts.

After a brief exchange in which Bailey tells counsel he can read this passage his way if he wants it:

Paul Gallagher [reading]: "It is difficult for me to put down what occurred as due to a bottle of whiskey, two pints of porter, a bottle of wine and a number of tequila slammers, I attacked and severely beat Jules to such an extent that she required hospital treatment, when on reaching the house I relived the attack and proceeded to cause further injury on top. I felt a sense of sickness at seeing my own account of that dreadful night I actually tried to kill her.'

"'At present two nights on, she is badly hurt and walking wounded with bruises on her face, lips and body. How could I have perpetrated on someone I both love and owe so much to, I can't properly explain. I have never had a history of violence towards women, and yet of late since Easter I have on a number of occasions struck and abused my lover – the thing I believe is the worst crime a man can commit against one's own mother's sex. I know that each time has been over drink.'"

Counsel put it to the plaintiff in the wake of his own recorded admission to a propensity of brutal violence towards a woman that he actually tried to kill her and asked him if he could tell the court about that occasion.

Ian Bailey: "I can't explain that."

Paul Gallagher: "You are in truth a person who tried to kill your lover ... So, when you came into this court and said through your counsel how devastated and abused you were to be a suspect, you knew yourself to be a person who tried to kill someone?"

Ian Bailey: "No."

Paul Gallagher: "What were you then?"

Ian Bailey: "I don't know."

Paul Gallagher: "So you think the court should award you damages for being called a suspect of a murder even though you are a self-confessed person who tried to kill your lover?"

Ian Bailey: "The reason I am here is because I have nothing to do with the murder of Sophie Toscan du Plantier. I had nothing to do with that."

Paul Gallagher: "What was printed of you is far less damning than what you printed about yourself and I put it to you people have a right to be frightened of you."

Ian Bailey: "I don't think so."

Having left the courtroom stunned and breathless in the elicitation of details of the brutal acts of the plaintiff, the violent nature of his character and his disturbing and bizarre diary accounts, counsel for the defence moved on swiftly to other matters, firstly the admissions by Bailey of his participation in and responsibility for the murder. Indeed, the proceedings were becoming close in nature to a criminal trial, with Paul Gallagher in the role of prosecuting counsel and Bailey as the defendant who the evidence proved had a propensity for instant and explosive rage, which resulted in sickening physical attacks and a desire on one occasion to kill his partner. The inference was that here was a man who was capable psychologically and physically of carrying out a murder like that of Sophie Toscan du Plantier.

What was emerging from his general attitude and response to highly damaging evidence against his character was Bailey's willingness to blame his appalling behaviour on anything but himself and his complete lack of empathy when presented with the bare facts of his brutality and his own written accounts of it. Alcohol was blamed and one assault happened because his partner came at him – she was to blame.

Jules Thomas had sought two barring orders against him following beatings, although they returned to living with each other after a period of time in each instance. He said in evidence that he did not know if the barring orders had been sought because of his partner's fear that she might be assaulted again and then astounded spectators by blaming the Gardai for pressurising her to protect herself. He said that they were delighted when they heard of the assault that followed the murder and sought to use it to their advantage.

When enquiring about his diary recording of actually trying to kill Jules Thomas and telling the court about it, he said he couldn't explain it. Counsel's later remark was a classic comment: "You had forgotten that you had been so frank with yourself," said Mr Gallagher, knowing full well frankness was a rare thing to be displayed by the plaintiff.

The court was told that several witnesses would testify that the plaintiff had confessed to the murder and counsel put the fact to the witness.

Ian Bailey: "Can you be more specific. I heard it being suggested around the place, but I didn't take it seriously."

Paul Gallagher: "Just before I come to the specifics, the unfortunate Ms Du Plantier was a victim of a most brutal attack."

Ian Bailey: "I would have reported on that ..."

Paul Gallagher: "And the assault involved the disfiguring of her face."

Ian Bailey: "There were certain rumours flying around, specifically I don't know."

Paul Gallagher: "And you said that a concrete block had been used to disfigure her face."

Ian Bailey: "In the Courtyard pub on the Monday night, everybody seemed to know that."

The purpose of this small diversion from the main script by the defence counsel was interesting and the purpose of which was at first glance not obvious. The subject of the disfigurement of the face of the murder victim had echoes in one of the assaults on Jules Thomas which left her face a bloody mess and the gory details would emerge in later evidence by a witness. To say the least of it, Bailey's contention that everyone in a bar on the Monday night knew about the concrete block was an impossibility as even members of the investigation team could not have established this as a fact at such an early stage.

Paul Gallagher: "Coming to specifics, you first told Helen Callanan that you had committed the murder."

Ian Bailey: "She said it was being said I was the killer and I said to her I was just in jest. That was right. I didn't think at the time it was of any significance ... I had nothing to do with this. It is hard to take a false allegation seriously."

Paul Gallagher: "That was before any arrest?"

Ian Bailey: "It was prior to my first arrest."

Paul Gallagher: "You told Ms Callanan you were the murderer?"

Ian Bailey: "She said I was, and I jokingly responded yes."

Paul Gallagher [later]: "She was saying to you, 'You are the murderer,' you didn't say, 'That's terrible, it's an outright lie what you said I am'?"

Ian Bailey: "I couldn't take it seriously."

Counsel then upped the ante and the pace of his searing questioning of the witness was like an attacking boxer who had his opponent on the ropes, using a series of punches and taunting him, but holding back on the knock-out blow. The courtroom audience was leaning forward in rapt attention akin to the spectators at a pugilistic encounter, not knowing what was going to happen next.

Paul Gallagher: "Didn't you say it to Yvonne Ungerer?"

Ian Bailey: "I reiterated that conversation [with Ms Callanan] to her. I don't know how she took it, but I didn't think she was taking it seriously. It sounded ridiculous."

Paul Gallagher: "Didn't you tell her about washing your boots, washing the blood off?"

Ian Bailey: "No."

Paul Gallagher: "Didn't you tell Malcolm Reed you were the murderer?"

Ian Bailey: "I told him it was being said I was the murderer."

Paul Gallagher: "Who is Malcolm Reed?"

Ian Bailey: "One evening prior to the arrest I went to Schull. There was a young man from out west who wanted a spin home. I gave him a spin home."

Paul Gallagher: "He was a fourteen-year-old boy and he was in your car alone."

Ian Bailey: "I said to him that it was being said that I was the murderer."

Now what was obvious from Bailey's replies to counsel about the admissions thus far was the consistent position of explaining that in the conversations that third persons – members of the local community – were saying all this and he was merely repeating the local conventional wisdom on the matter. While it would remain to be seen what their versions of the conversations would be, it begged the question that if Bailey's version was true, how could there be any possible contention about the matter, so why should it be brought into evidence in the first instance? The problem that might arise for the plaintiff would be the more forceful consistency of the local witnesses' evidence.

Mr Gallagher continued apace.

Paul Gallagher: "Why would you say that to a fourteen-year-old boy alone in your car?"

Ian Bailey: "I don't know, it came out that evening in Schull. People were starting to point … I didn't know how to react. I gave him a lift. I talked to him about what he was doing."

Paul Gallagher: "You told Malcolm Reid you went up with a rock and bashed her brains in."

Ian Bailey: "What I said to him was the rumours, what was being said around Schull."

Paul Gallagher: "Long before the articles were published, you were saying you were the murderer and you were giving fuel to those rumours."

Ian Bailey: "I wouldn't have thought about it that way, it sounded so unreal, the whole thing seemed so bizarre."

Defence counsel then moved to another occasion when Bailey made a confession which produced a frightening effect on the couple involved. It occurred on New Year's Eve 1998, two years after the murder, when Bailey and Thomas invited a local couple, Richard and Rosie Shelley, to the house for drinks. It was a night to celebrate the coming year but for the couple it was transformed into a nightmare.

A large quantity of drink was consumed by Bailey in particular. He had an album with newspaper cuttings on the murder including his own reports and spent a large part of the night talking about these and his poetry. He invited the couple to stay for the night, but they declined and decided to phone for a taxi. They were directed to a bedroom where there was a phone followed by a drunken Bailey, who seemed to be overcome by emotion, and to the fright and amazement of the couple confessed that he had committed the murder.

Paul Gallagher: "This was 1998, two years after the murder, and you had invited them to your house, discussing poetry and murder. You broke down and sobbed, 'I did it. I did it, I went too far.'"

Ian Bailey: "I said it was being said I went too far."

Paul Gallagher: "This was New Year's Eve and you were telling these people, 'I did it. I did it.'"

Ian Bailey: "That was the phrase used repeatedly by the Gardai. It was a mantra used by two detectives."

Paul Gallagher: "Were you in an emotional state when you said that?"

Ian Bailey: "I was drunk ... Christmas brought it all back, it's quite dreadful. I have dreaded it for seven years and unless something is done, it will keep coming back."

Paul Gallagher: "They left as quick as they could and went home."

Ian Bailey: "What I was saying was a repetition of things I heard, more and more that I had done this. It was quite dreadful."

His narrative that it was being said that he was the murderer was one with which none of the witnesses would concur. If that was so, then there was no reason for his guests on New Year's Eve to be so shocked that they could not wait to get out of the house. Such was the impact of the confession when they later bumped into him in a pub in Schull that Richie Shelley told Bailey he was now convinced that he was responsible for the crime. As one revelation after another came out, so were a lot of spectators in the court.

Another witness would, counsel said, give evidence of a confession relayed to him by Bailey in the second person but talking about himself. He told Bill Fuller: "Yes, you did it, you saw her in Spar, and she turned you on, walking up the aisle with her tight arse. So, you went up there to see what you could get but she wasn't interested. You chased her and it stirred something at the back of your head. You went a lot further than you should have."

This statement provided not only a motive for the murder but a description of the onset of the psychopathic rage that led to the crime and again mirroring the rages that led to the assaults on Jules Thomas, the worst of which was perpetrated in May 1996, the same year as the murder, and motivated by the desire to kill her.

He mentioned in evidence the role of alcohol in those incidents and it was well known that Bailey around the time of the crime was drinking heavily and taking drugs. In his diary he said that he was feeling like a "crazed beast" and that he was beginning to frighten people. If there was a better description of the killer of Sophie Toscan du Plantier, no one else including the journalists had written it.

Mr Gallagher said that witnesses would testify that Bailey talked about the murder, as did Jules Thomas before he received the phone call from Eddie Cassidy around 1.40 p.m. asking him to check out a death in the Toormore area. Bailey, counsel said, told locals Paul O'Colmain and Richard and Caroline Leftwick about the murder hours before the call.

His partner Jules Thomas told Richard and Christine Camier from Goleen that Bailey was "out on a story" when she visited them before lunchtime on the same day.

As usual, Bailey's memory of the event failed him, and he insisted that he had no knowledge of the murder at the time. The list of local witnesses lining up to provide evidence which contradicted the plaintiff's accounts was growing and at the same time diminishing his credibility. What could possibly explain decent ordinary members of the community having sufficient animus towards the man as to collectively invent a narrative which, if he was to be believed, involved giving false testimony under oath?

A most unlikely scenario.

CHAPTER 10
THE PEOPLE VS BAILEY

Cork – December 2003

On the morning of the fourth day, Bailey was clearly showing the strain of the rigours of his cross-examination and his demeanour changed from a sort of forced calmness to irritability and agitation.

Bailey had been run ragged by the defence counsel while in the witness box, which was inducing either a form of paranoia or a Machiavellian strategy to undermine those he perceived to be his enemies. If it was the latter, it was doomed to failure considering the strength of the forces being lined up against him. He next complained about a Garda operation near where he was staying in Cork, which he inferred was targeting him and was unlawful. He failed to provide one scintilla of evidence to back up the charge and no detail of the nature of the "operation".

Mr Gallagher said that two neighbours had noticed a bonfire outside the house occupied by the couple some days after the murder. Mr Jackson, who lived 100 yards from the house in Liscaha, saw smoke from a fire, and one of the Kennedys' other neighbours saw a fire and burning material including a mattress in the blaze.

Paul Gallagher: "Another matter of which you made a complaint in the articles was that you were seen attending a fire on St Stephen's Day and you say that never happened?"

Ian Bailey: "Correct; to this day it is a complete mystery. I read it first in Ms McLaughlin's piece about people saying Bailey was burning clothes and it never occurred."

Paul Gallagher: "Did any fire occur on St Stephen's Day?"

Ian Bailey: "No, not started by me and not started by Jules."

Paul Gallagher: "Two neighbours saw a fire in the distance and another neighbour, Ms Louise Kennedy, not only heard the fire but walked to your studio area and saw the fire, and she saw something being burned. She saw what she thought was a mattress."

Ian Bailey: "I have no knowledge of a fire."

Quite apart from the fact of the incident that was witnessed by neighbours and admitted by the plaintiff during the interview with Brighid McLaughlin of the *Sunday Independent*, the inference was that Ian Bailey was destroying evidence that might link him to the crime scene. It did not impress upon him that his explanation to the reporter that the reason for the fire was to burn clothes damaged by turkey blood might have challenged the inference reasonably. Or simply say that he was burning rubbish.

Why he should have seen the necessity to put a mattress into the fire might well from his point of view pose another question such as why someone would get into bed saturated with animal blood. But to deny it ever happened aroused suspicion and justifiably so. While dealing with counsel's enquiry about another detail, Bailey almost roared the reply: "I know I had nothing to do with this crime, that's all I know."

His counsel Jim Duggan leapt to his feet and asked how far the defence was prepared to go in defending the defamation. Mr Gallagher could have replied to prove his client was capable of murder. He didn't; instead, he said it was never claimed by the defence that it would say that Mr Bailey committed the crime. But as everyone who had watched the proceedings was well aware, they were only marginally different from a criminal trial. The judge had to intervene, but as the phrase goes, the train had already pulled out of the station.

Judge Moran addressed Paul Gallagher: "You are taking on the mantle of a prosecution case and cross-examining the plaintiff as if he were the accused. He is not the accused but is entitled to bring a claim for defamation. We have to be careful that this court does not become an inquiry into the murder of Ms Du Plantier."

He added that the Gardai were the authority to investigate the matter and the outcome of their inquiries were known. Everyone should bear this in mind given nobody had been charged with the murder.

Mr Gallagher, however, would not change his style of trenchant cross-examination as given the extraordinary nature of the trial, he was entitled to do. The defence had to prove the plea of justification and were bound by the very same rules of evidence in a criminal trial. The difference was that the civil trial outcome would be decided on the balance of probabilities as opposed to beyond all reasonable doubt. It also confirmed that both the plaintiff and his counsel had declared on the first day he had come to court to prove his innocence was a big mistake. Ian Bailey was in court for the money, knowing full well that the combined newspapers were a hefty mark for a large sum of financial damages.

The defence counsel changed nothing in his cross-examination strategy and continued to ask the same questions a prosecuting advocate would at a criminal trial. He took Bailey through his movements on the night of the murder and contradictions between his and his partner's accounts. He read a statement to Gardai by Jules Thomas saying that Bailey had left the bed during the night and returned in the morning with a mark on his forehead.

"Is there a polite word for absolute nonsense? Did she say that? I wasn't aware she had made that statement." It was inaccurate anyway, said Bailey, and he and Thomas had expressed concerns about "anomalies" and "distortions" in Garda statements attributed to them, he added. Counsel took him through the changing narrative of his movements on the night of the crime.

He had first stated that he had gone to bed at 12.30 a.m. and did not leave the house all night. He later changed that and said during the night he had got up to write.

Ian Bailey: "I had no reason to tell them [Gardai] that I did get up to write. My honesty on this point has led to this. I was over-honest about it and it seems to have backlashed."

The plaintiff's answers as usual were self-serving. He told the court that in regard to Jules Thomas's statement while under questioning on the occasion of the arrests in February 1997, that this was the first he had heard of it. This was blatantly untrue because it had been put to him during the interrogation in Bandon Station by members of the investigation team. The only reason that he changed his story about being in bed all night was to conform to Jules Thomas's version that he had left and returned in the morning to explain his absence from the bed. It had nothing to do with honesty but an attempt albeit weak to provide a more credible explanation than the lie he had told in the first statement.

The man who had come to court to prove his innocence was then confronted by Mr Gallagher about the campaign of harassment and intimidation he carried out against Marie Farrell, the Schull shopkeeper who saw him at Kealfadda Bridge in the early hours of the morning of the murder and not far from the scene of the crime. Counsel said that Bailey had gone into her shop in Schull and asked her to change a cheque for £25 from *The Cork Examiner* for an article about the murder and told her: "There is no money in knocking people off."

The court was told that Bailey subjected Marie Farrell to threats in order to pressure her into withdrawing a statement she had made to Gardai about seeing him acting suspiciously on the morning of the murder. In the statement she said she saw a man walking along the road swinging his arms. A letter from Ms Farrell's solicitor was read to the court by Mr Gallagher giving details of a "campaign of intimidation and harassment" of his client by Bailey.

Counsel then referred to other incidents, one in which Bailey had drawn his fingers across his throat in front of her, placed his finger against his temple and – parking his car opposite her shop premises – stared at her all as part of a campaign to get her to withdraw her statement to the investigation team. Bailey denied all and counterclaimed that it was Marie Farrell who had approached him saying she had given a false statement to the

Gardai and did not want to see an innocent man blamed for the murder.

He claimed that he had gone in to see her in the shop with a tape recorder in case she wanted to formally withdraw her statement. On another occasion, counsel pointed out he had visited her in the shop and threatened to report her to the Department of Social Services in Britain for some alleged false dealing with them if she would not withdraw her statement. Bailey denied this, saying he knew nothing about her background.

Mr Gallagher responded by saying Bailey told her that he was an investigative reporter and had found out about her husband's business in England, and predictably the plaintiff said he knew nothing about the matter. He admitted he had got visits from the Gardai about the intimidation but claimed that it was bogus. In other words, Marie Farrell and all the other witnesses who would give evidence to the court were liars and fabricators, and by implication slanderers, along with members of the murder investigation team and the journalists who had written articles about him. It followed that he expected the court to accept that he was the only person in the trial who was speaking the truth.

Whether it was a result of exhaustion or the unrelenting probing of the defence counsel, Bailey briefly closed his eyes before fielding another question. By the afternoon, he was yawning regularly and pawing his head like the monkey whose persona he said he might inhabit in his writings. There were a couple of moments of levity on the way. The first related to evidence Bill Fuller – once a work colleague and good friend of the plaintiff – would give about calling into the house in Liscaha to find Bailey wearing a black skirt. The plaintiff laughed loudly and said that it was a kilt which was comfortable.

This produced a good few stifled giggles among spectators, many of whom would know that there is a distinct difference between a skirt and the traditional Scottish kilt which is unmistakeable in make. Fuller said that Bailey offered him cider to drink and pipe to smoke, presumably containing hash, but the plaintiff claimed it was food and tea. Fuller, then, was witness to his cross-dressing host taking out a melon and stabbing it with a large knife.

Fuller felt that Bailey was in a way communicating to him that he was responsible for the murder. Bailey's reply was that everything that came out of the witness's mouth was garbage and then took the court aback by accusing Fuller of intimidating him in the hall at lunchtime, saying, "I've got you now." He also accused witness Peter Bielecki of staring at him in an intense fashion. Judge Moran said that this was a form of intimidation and should not happen.

Bailey's diary entries suggested that it was not tea on the menu in the kitchen the morning that Bill Fuller called over. A red rimmed hardback book contained the lines, an acknowledgement by the author of his degeneracy:

"I'm totally, totally obsessed by sex, I love my drugs and adore alcohol."

As he had quoted Dylan Thomas in relation to his descriptions of his appalling domestic violence, he now said that the bald admission of his voracious and salacious appetites was a play on the lyrics of the late Ian Dury of the Blockheads band. The composer of "Hit Me with Your Rhythm Stick", as with the great Welsh poet, was in no position to complain about such malign influence being attributed to the plaintiff's writings.

His counsel Jim Duggan said he was concerned all this talk of drug taking was further blackening his client's reputation and must be reflected in the damages should he be successful in the case. With a dry sense of humour, the judge warned the counsel that Santa Claus was not coming to town just yet and he should hold off until Santa Claus comes round, a remark that prompted loud laughter in the courtroom, including from the previously tense Jules Thomas. Mr Gallagher joined the lapse in the general serious tone of the proceedings, remarking that the plaintiff's legal team might not even believe in Santa Claus.

In relation to the infamous diaries, Mr Gallagher pointed out the fact that Bailey had removed them from his house and given them to a neighbour, Paul O'Colmain, for "safe keeping". They were subsequently obtained by members of the murder investigation team, who searched the house when Bailey was arrested for a second time in January 1998. The inference was clear that Bailey had, in the first instance, attempted to hide potential evidence, which of course provided additional proof of his extremely violent character.

Paul Gallagher: "And was the reason you had put them away so that the guards could not see them?"

Ian Bailey: "Of course I didn't want them to be revealed ... on the first occasion they took bag loads of stuff, soft toys, the girls' books and most of my best clothes. I have been severely hampered in my preparations for the case by being unable to obtain the diaries that had been taken away by the Gardai."

Paul Gallagher: "The diaries were only made available to our legal team on Monday after Judge Moran ruled that the evidence possessed by Gardai could be used during the hearing."

The brief interlude of laughter had been left behind and there was a return to the serious tone of the proceedings; the battle had recommenced.

During the fifth day of proceedings the following day, Friday, December 12, the plaintiff made a formal complaint to the court in relation to the alleged intimidation in the hallway outside the courtroom by Bill Fuller from Schull, who he alleged told him, "I've got you now."

He said that another witness, Peter Bielecki, had been staring at him in the courtroom "in the most intense fashion". As if that was not enough, he said that things had been moved around in the room in which he and his partner were staying during the trial. He was convinced that Gardai were involved in a "conspiracy" against him.

Judge Moran said that no one should be intimidated while exercising their legal right to make a claim in court and ordered that the two witnesses should not be in the court until it was time for them to give their evidence. "Mr Bailey feels that he is being subjected to something unpleasant and I am of the opinion it would be better that the two witnesses were removed."

He added, "He is entitled to make a claim and is entitled to some respect ... It is not unusual to have people removed from the court."

Defence counsel protested that they should be able to put their side of the case before being removed from the courtroom in relation to the complaints and were entitled to listen to the proceedings. The judge said he would keep an open mind about the complaints and pointed out that the witnesses would be entitled to inspect transcripts of the day's proceedings in any case.

Judge Moran said that while he could not draw any conclusion about the accuracy of the allegations, he could not tolerate any suggestion of intimidation. Without reflecting anything negative about the good name of the witnesses, he ordered that they be excluded from the proceedings until they were called to give evidence. It was a fair compromise but without a hint that he believed in the allegations.

Bailey told the judge in relation to the "conspiracy" matter: "I believe where we have been staying in Cork, things have been altered and moved, and I think something conspiratorial is going on in relation that we are able to bring to court in relation to the initial murder investigation. Something is going on which is not of a legal nature. The place we are staying in Cork there is a Garda operation, I cannot be more specific."

The judge said he could not conduct an inquiry into the matter; all he could say was that if there was any evidence of more intimidation, a contempt of court situation could arise, and Mr Gallagher knew the steps he would have to take.

It was obvious to the press corps that this was an effort by Bailey to discredit the witnesses in advance of being called to the box to give important evidence as they were scheduled to do. I happened to be in the hall at the time Bailey entered on his way to court and saw no sign of any intimidation of the kind described. He was putting the judge in a bind; there was only the plaintiff's word for the allegations and no independent corroboration. But Judge Moran had to address it and did so as fairly as possible and in the context of the punishment that the plaintiff had justifiably been subjected to in the witness box, and was about to step down.

He was on a roll and launched into another attack on the Gardai, this time of the West Cork variety, one of whom he accused of saying to him that he must have acted like a werewolf monster on the night of the murder because there was a full moon. He said he had evidence of attempts to pervert the court of justice. Judge Moran had had enough and warned him that this was a defamation case and no more.

He was replaced in the witness box by his partner Jules Thomas, who began her evidence by attempting to play down the physical attacks she had suffered at the hands of the then drunken and out-of-control Bailey. She provided a total contrast to the sagging hulk of a lover – thin, frail, her lined but once beautiful face showing signs of the passage of troubled times.

Physical and psychological abuse leaves its mark no matter how much the victim might attempt to mitigate the savagery of the perpetrator. Mitigate Ms Thomas did, by describing the injuries she had received in the 1993 beating as being a result of a tussle, and claiming that the extent of the injuries had been exaggerated. She told Jim Duggan: "We were staying in a small bed, we drank too much, a fight ensued and we got into bed. It was over in a minute. It was a moment of alcoholic madness."

Listening to this, I quickly speed-read my notes of Bailey's diary entry about the incident:

August 22, 1993:

"I beat her to such an extent that she required hospital treatment. On reaching the house I relived my assault and proceeded to cause further injury to her. At present, two nights on, she is badly hurt and walking

injured with bruises on her face, lips and body ... I feel a sense of sickness at seeing my account of that dreadful night. I actually tried to kill her."

She said that while she had required hospital treatment, she did not need stitches and Bailey later had expressed "total remorse". They resumed living together several weeks after the incident. The contrast between Bailey and Jules Thomas's accounts is startling to say the least. It appeared she was standing by her man no matter what the facts.

She blamed the "demon drink" for the next beating in May 1996 and said that the fight was over in minutes and that was it. "It's not something that goes on, it's like a temper flash."

Bailey's diary entry:

May 15, 1996:

"I am an animal on two feet ... one act of whiskey-filled madness coupled and cracked in an act of such awful violence, I severely damaged you and made you feel death was near."

The court had heard earlier that after the 1996 assault her lip was severed from her gum, her eye was bruised and the "size of a grapefruit" and that she had clumps of hair missing from her head.

She now told the court that this was exaggerated. "My eye was not the size of a grapefruit ... his finger caught inside my lip ... but my lip was not hanging off. I'm not sure why everything has to be out of proportion."

Nonetheless, she had to admit her injuries required hospital attention and that she had needed eight stitches in her lip. In tandem with her partner, she was attempting to convince the court that brutality which had occurred resulting in appalling wounds was not really that bad despite the evidence of facts to the contrary.

Beryl Thomas, mother of Jules, said that Bailey always seemed like a normal man and described the newspaper headlines in the days following his arrest as a "crushing awful thing". Cross-examined by Paul Gallagher about bringing her daughter to hospital following one of the assaults by Bailey, she said she remembered her daughter appeared to "have wounds and scars" and thought they were a result of actions from her "previous bloke". She said that all men were violent, and that the world would be a much better place if women ruled it.

She was followed into the witness box by her granddaughter Saffron, who told the court that her mother and Mr Bailey "had cried for two years" after the allegation of murder arose. Their lives had been altered forever as a result and many of the locals had stopped speaking to the couple.

"People did not know whether to talk to them or not. They had a lot less contact, they were out less. I don't think they have had any gathering in the house since." When asked by Jim Duggan about the effect of the events on their life at home, Ms Thomas said: "It's like a huge weight on us all the time, it's like a dark cloud that never goes away."

She said that she could not believe the content of the newspapers following Bailey's arrest in 1997. "I was disgusted, sick to the stomach. I just couldn't believe it. The things that were lies were just blatant."

The plaintiff's solicitor Con Murphy told the court that hordes of journalists and cameramen gathered outside his office after his client's second arrest in February 1998. A number of cameramen had climbed a six-foot wall behind the office to capture footage of Bailey. Dealing with the intimidation of Marie Farrell by his client, he said she had got a solicitor to write to Ian Bailey requesting that he desist from this behaviour.

He brought in Ian Bailey to discuss the matter and he denied it, but he advised him under no circumstances to go near her.

Jules Thomas would continue her spell in the witness box on the following Monday after proceedings were adjourned for the weekend after a drama-packed, exhaustive and exhausting exploration of major issues in the trial, and the break provided breathing space from the tension-laden atmosphere of the courtroom for all participants.

The court reconvened for the sixth day on the morning of Monday, December 15, all somewhat refreshed but facing another long haul in these extraordinary proceedings. First up, two West Cork shopkeepers gave evidence on behalf of the plaintiff and said that newspapers had treated him unfairly by suggesting that he had been responsible for the murder. Brendan Houlihan, the owner of a newsagent's shop in Skibbereen, said people had turned against Bailey as a result of the coverage. "People went completely downhill on him. He was branded for a crime that he had not been charged with."

He knew that Bailey had his "domestic troubles" but did not think he was capable of murder. Mr Holland suggested that Mr Bailey's arrest as part of the murder investigation would have been a subject of conversation notwithstanding the newspaper articles, and the witness agreed. The witness made the extraordinary statement that the assaults would not have affected his overall view of the man "that much" and such incidents were almost everyday "occurrences" nowadays.

Thomas Brennan, the owner of a supermarket, a B&B and a restaurant in Schull, said that media coverage had given the impression that Bailey had committed the murder. "If you believed what you read in the newspapers, then you'd more or less say he was convicted." The witness said he found Bailey an "interesting person" given he used to live in England, and read a local paper which Bailey had worked for. He tried to avoid discussing the murder with others and people had an attitude to Bailey "some more negative than others".

Jules Thomas, tense-looking but outwardly composed, once again took the stand. She had stood by the plaintiff resolutely so far and she would not surprisingly continue as she had started, no doubt having been afforded the time to consult with her partner and his lawyers.

She said that remarks in a Garda statement containing her signature regarding a "raw, fresh and bloody" scratch to Bailey's face on the morning of the murder were an "invention" and that the statement had been signed under duress. She added that she was put under pressure by Gardai to seek a barring order against her partner after he had assaulted her two years previously. "I was put under enormous pressure. Two detectives came around to the house. They seemed to be delighted. They were revelling in it. They were saying to me, 'You must charge him, you have got to do the right thing.'"

Little wonder, despite the witness's spin on an incident in which she was severely battered, that instead of her dubious account, police officers might have been more concerned about her safety and welfare, as was well-proven when her partner subsequently pleaded guilty to the assault in court and received a three-month suspended sentence.

A neighbour had also done his duty by driving Jules Thomas to hospital after the most brutal beating, but he would now get no thanks from her. Nor another neighbour in the wake of the incident, who begged her to get rid of Bailey. She was told: "I would rather Ian than no man at all."

With regard to the pressure she alleged she was put under by members of the investigation team to link her partner with the murder and the "invention" of the bloody scratch, there is nothing in the transcript of the interrogation to back up or corroborate her version. Like Bailey himself, Jules Thomas was changing the narrative to suit the court roles they were now playing as victims of the investigation methods.

She told the court that the newspaper articles written about Bailey following his original arrest on February 10, 1997 had sabotaged their lives. Perhaps she forgot that her partner had invited the media into the house they shared at that time.

"These seven years of pain and suffering … have been a million times worse than any beatings. The overall feeling is that our lives have been sabotaged. I don't feel like a free citizen. Some people actually crossed the road so as not to make contact with us. He was someone that somebody couldn't go near. Detectives even told our friends that Ian was guilty. The articles were sensationalist and inaccurate. We were deeply upset by it all." She said her sleep had been disturbed; she could not get a sleep pattern and was beset by nightmares. She could not paint for a long time afterwards as her concentration had gone. "It guts you," she claimed.

She went on to describe the media reaction to the arrests of Bailey and herself in February 1997, when on the way to Bandon Station she had requested a coat to cover her head, and after being released without charge she returned home to be greeted by an army of media.

"The press were absolutely unbelievable. We were actually under siege. It was completely over the top. We were stunned by it all. We had no light in our house for six weeks because we had to keep the curtains drawn. Our lives were completely and utterly disrupted. It would be hard for anyone to put themselves in our position at the time and imagine what it was all like."

It would have been seen as a sterling performance in the witness box and strong support of the plaintiff's case had Jules not omitted the well-established fact not lost on the defence that in the wake of the 1997 arrests, it was her partner who had courted the media attention, going as far as inviting journalists into the very house that the witness was telling the court was under siege. A half-page picture in the *Star* just a short time after the arrests showed Bailey pouring tea at a table in their kitchen for the reporter Senan Molony.

Could it be that this lone star media cowboy had by some extraordinary subterfuge breached the ramparts of the house at Liscaha and persuaded the occupant to give an interview? Jules Thomas had herself participated with Bailey in an interview at the time, with the host of the most popular morning radio show in the country. In light of this and more, her credibility was further undermined by the statement that what the journalists had written was far worse than the savage beatings of her by Bailey and caused more pain and suffering.

I saw a number of female reporters in the court shaking their heads in disbelief listening to this proposition; a newspaper headline would put this aspect of her evidence thus:

Beaten, bloodied and bruised
But still sticking by her man

Her family life had been disrupted by the intrusion of the media and lack of contact with neighbours, whom she said were warned off by Gardai.

David Holland, the second counsel for the defence, then took on the cross-examination of Ms Thomas, who was resolutely living up to the newspaper headline wording in the box. He said that the grievances outlined by her were as a result of Bailey's arrest and Garda activity rather than anything contained in the newspaper articles. She said that the Gardai put her under pressure into agreeing to a signed statement in which she recorded that Bailey returned to the bed after an absence and felt cold on the morning of the murder, that he looked tired that morning.

A document was produced to the court of a complaint by Ms Thomas to the chief State solicitor's office about the accuracy of her signed statement. In it, she said that details such as the raw bloody scratch were "fiction" and it was later in the day of the murder that he had got some scratches after killing a turkey and chopping down a Christmas tree.

As with her partner, when confronted by statements she had previously made, she claimed that she could not remember them, including the substance of those made to investigators when first arrested on February 10, 1997. She had made some replies under questioning which were highly prejudicial of her partner, but when put to her by counsel in court she said that they were invented and included afterwards without her participation in the statement.

She said that she never told them that her partner had a raw, fresh and big bloody cut on his forehead on the morning after the murder, after he had returned from wherever he had been.

Firstly, she was going to have a go at the Gardai, accusing them of not believing what she was saying and claiming that they were putting words in her mouth. She was also unhappy with details of the original statement of her interrogation by Gardai, despite signing off on it as being correct not just once but twice. She then rewrote her original account given under questioning, attempting to create the alibi that Ian Bailey lacked.

She was convinced that he had been writing in her kitchen on the crucial night. "He was not tossing and turning like it says. We curled up together, absolutely, still. But I have no knowledge of what time he may have got up; I was not conscious. I vaguely remember him getting back into bed." She told the court that she had found a large handwritten article on the table, suggesting that he had worked on it during the night.

Predictably, she denied as true the evidence from local witnesses that Bailey had confessed to the murder, sticking like glue to the evidence given by her partner. She claimed that those witnesses had been put under enormous pressure to make the statements by the Gardai as she had. The real fact was that none of those witnesses ever complained of such pressure.

Bailey had not been seen burning clothes three days after the murder and she had not been taking photographs at the crime scene before the murder came into the public domain, she said.

The Shelleys had got it wrong, there was no question of an admission; all Ian had been doing was repeating what the Gardai had said to him. So, what the witness was telling the court was that members of the investigation team told Bailey: "I did it. I did it. I went too far." Little wonder there were a few wry smiles shared among the reporters.

In common with her partner, she played down the vicious incidents of assault, saying the alcohol was a big factor and he didn't drink anymore; he never meant to kill her as written in his diary entries; when he writes he tends to exaggerate the situation.

Luckily for the sake of objectivity if not the truth, there would shortly be in the box one witness to the most damaging beating in terms of injuries sustained, unlike her partner not prone to exaggeration or like her prone to mitigation.

David Holland S.C. said that Ms Thomas was accepting Mr Bailey's version of events to protect him and downplaying the effects of the assaults for the same purpose. "I put it to you that you had to believe him because you need him. I put it to you that you have to believe him because your life would change irrevocably [without him] … and I suggest you are doing everything possible to protect him."

Counsel enquired why her daughter Virginia was not giving evidence, as she was a key witness to many events. She replied that her daughter was travelling in Thailand and admitted under cross-examination that she had departed just the day before. Judge Moran interjected and pointed out that this was understandable, given the trial had originally been expected to last just three days. The court heard that her two previous relationships had featured violence.

When Mr Holland questioned her in relation to the 2001 assault, she described it as a "tussle"; Bailey had a snapped Achilles tendon and was using aluminium crutches. "He was on strong painkillers and he had taken alcohol that night. His resistance was low to anything I would say at the time." She had received a blow to her face from the crutch and had been left with bruising.

Defence counsel suggested that there was a substantial gap between her version and other accounts of the injuries she had received. When asked to describe them, her reply was "not good", adding that "any incident of this nature is appalling". But what was entirely lacking in her testimony was the exact and appalling nature of the beatings to which she was subjected.

However uncomfortable the proceedings had been for the plaintiff up to this point, as the hearing entered the seventh day on Tuesday, December 16, Ian Bailey must have been somewhat dreading this phase, as twenty witnesses – the vast majority from

West Cork – were due to give evidence about encounters with him in and around and after the time of the murder. Without exception, they would give accounts of incidents which would totally contradict the plaintiff's versions and in one instance bring out the horrendous nature of the brutal May 1996 assault, which both Bailey and Thomas had attempted in their evidence to play down.

Thus far, both had identified the media and the officers of the law as hounding them and persecuting them, ruining their lives in a manner of some imagined loose conspiracy, and what now remained to be seen was whether other witnesses and in particular people of West Cork would be joined by the plaintiff to the packs of 'wolves' hunting him down. *How much more,* Ian Bailey might have thought to himself, *is my reputation going to be damaged?* So far, it had been damaged under court privilege far beyond anything that had been printed in the articles which were the subject of the action.

The proceedings received huge media coverage, with acres of space devoted to them in the newspapers, every lurid detail of Bailey's behaviour faithfully reproduced with fresh pictures daily of Bailey and Thomas arriving or departing the court. *The Examiner* had three reporters at times, whose accounts filled a full broadsheet page cross-referenced by a front-page piece. The headlines hardly needed to be screaming to reflect the bloody carnage inside and outside the house on I Prairie.

Already, in spite of his myriad denials, a portrait had emerged through the proceedings of a man who displayed minimal remorse for acts of extreme violence towards a woman and who revisited those crimes in his diaries, admitting in one entry that he had intended to kill his victim.

There emerged a character lacking in empathy with a passion for sex, alcohol and drugs, with eccentric behaviour of poetic ambition without the skill or application to realise it, and who made the bizarre claim that he adopted the persona of animals in his poetic description of extreme violence and licentious fantasies which had a disturbing foundation in reality.

In court, Ian Bailey wore suits, ties, laundered shirts and carried a briefcase, but spectators could be forgiven for having the impression that the clothes could not disguise a nasty and weird person.

His accusations of intimidation by two of the local witnesses had heralded his expectation of tenor and substance of the evidence he faced from the ordinary people who had the sort of close experience of the plaintiff which neither the media nor the members of the murder investigation team could have matched. Dramatic additions of dark colours were about to be added to the portrait of the central character of a trial full of twists, turns, shocks, surprises and revelations.

Continued in Part 2 ...

To contact the author, Michael Sheridan, please email Gadfly Press at gadflypress@outlook.com

If you have enjoyed this book, we would appreciate you leaving a review on Amazon or Goodreads.

ACKNOWLEDGEMENTS

People imagine that the author does all the work – the loneliness of the long-distance writer. In reality, there is a supporting cast, many of whose members would never dream of requesting a credit. The publisher leads the cast, so my gratitude to Shaun Atwood for his faith in the project. Agent Isabel Atherton, who toiled ceaselessly when the time was not right. Sheridan family members Cian, Fionn, Sarah and Geraldine Norton for their tolerance.

Fionnuala Dwyer for her mastery of scanning highly important material, Sam, Freddy and Tommy of Copy Graphics for their trustworthy handling of confidential documents from both jurisdictions. Journalists Ann Mooney and Senan Molony for their constant co-operation and insights, and Sarah Collins and Sharon Gaffney for their assistance at the trial in Paris. Nick Foster for our valuable ruminations on the case mutually beneficial.

John Coleman, the concierge without compare of the Metropole Hotel in Cork, Tricia Daly, Donal Gaffney, Liam le taxi, Jean, Dr Patricia Comer, Alain Spilliaert, Jean-Pierre Gazeau and Jean-Antoine Bloc for their unfailing support and advice and comments on the manuscript. Roisin Moran of the Old Rectory writer's retreat in Westport, Dave, Cecilia, Bea and the staff of the 105 Café for providing a working haven away from home, and for the same of staff members Jodi and Diana of The Natural Bakery in Stillorgan. The muse Fedelma.

The late Danny McCarthy of Mentor Books, who championed me in the early stages of writing true crime books.

The named and unnamed sources without whose participation no book of this nature could be written.

BIBLIOGRAPHY

Books

Cameron, Deborah, *The Lust to Kill*,
New York University Press, 1987

Cleckley, Hervey M., *The Mask of Sanity*,
Mosby Medical Library, 1982

Cros, Julien, Bloc, Jean-Antoine, *Justice Denied*, ASSOPH, 2014

Dostoyevsky, Fyodor, *Crime And Punishment*,
Penguin Books, 1991

Douglas, John; Olshaker, Mark, *Mindhunter*, Arrow Books, 2017

Malcolm, Janet, *The Journalist and the Murderer*, Granta, 1997

Meloy, J. Reid, *The Psychopathic Mind: Origins, Dynamics, Treatment*, Jason Aronson Inc., 1988

Morris, Errol, *A Wilderness of Error*, Penguin Books, 2012

McGinnis, Joe, *Fatal Vision*, Signet Books, 1983

McNamara, Michelle, *I'll Be Gone in the Dark*,
Faber and Faber, 2018

Somerville-Large, Peter, *The Coast of West Cork*,
Appletree Press, 1991

Sheridan, Michael, *Death in December*, O'Brien Press, 2002

Sheridan, *Michael, Frozen Blood: Serial Killers in Ireland*, Mentor Books, 2003

Reports

2000 DPP's Analysis of Evidence in the STP Case: An Opposing Point of View, Jean-Pierre Gazeau, Jean-Antoine Bloc, Daude, Frances Lefevre, ASSOPH, 2012

Annual Report EAW, 2016

Crime Scene Awareness for Non-Forensic Personnel, United Nations, New York, 2009

The Role and Impact of Forensic Evidence in the Criminal Justice Process, Peterson, Joseph; Sommers, Ira; Baskin, Deborah; Johnson, Donald, U.S. Dept of Justice, 2010

Garda Ombudsman's Report, July 2018

Fenelley Commission Report, March 2017

Office of the Director of Equality Investigations

Employment Equality Act 1998, Equality Officer's Decision, Dec-E2002-047

Parties: Sheehan and the DPP

Journals

Meloy, J. Reid, *The Psychology of Wickedness and Sadism*, Psychiatric Annals, September 1997

Vitaco, M.J., *Psychopathy*, The British Journal of Psychiatry, 2007

Woodworth M. and Porter S., *Historical Foundation and Current*

Applications of Criminal Profiling in Violent Crime Investigations, Kluwer Academic Publishers, 2001

Hold, Meloy, Strack, *Sadism and Psychopathy in Violent and Sexually Violent Offenders*, J Am ACAD Psychiatry Law Vol. 27, No. 1, 1999.

Magazines

Montague, J, *A Devil in the Hills*, *New Yorker*, January 10, 2000

Paris Match, various editions

Newspapers

Irish Examiner, Irish Times, Irish Independent, Irish Star, Irish Daily Mirror, The Sunday Times, The Daily Telegraph, Sunday Independent, The Echo, Sunday Tribune, Le Figaro, Le Monde, Le Parisien

OTHER BOOKS BY GADFLY PRESS

By Steve Wraith:

The Krays' Final Years:
My Time with London's Most Iconic Gangsters

By Natalie Welsh:

Escape from Venezuela's Deadliest Prison

By Shaun Attwood:

English Shaun Trilogy
Party Time
Hard Time
Prison Time

War on Drugs Series
Pablo Escobar: Beyond Narcos
American Made: Who Killed Barry Seal? Pablo Escobar
or George HW Bush
The Cali Cartel: Beyond Narcos
Clinton Bush and CIA Conspiracies:
From the Boys on the Tracks to Jeffrey Epstein

Un-Making a Murderer:
The Framing of Steven Avery and Brendan Dassey
The Mafia Philosopher: Two Tonys
Life Lessons
Pablo Escobar's Story (4-book series)

By Steve Wraith:

The Krays' Final Years: My Time with London's Most Iconic Gangsters

Britain's most notorious twins – Ron and Reg Kray – ascended the underworld to become the most feared and legendary gangsters in London. Their escalating mayhem culminated in murder, for which they received life sentences in 1969.

While incarcerated, they received letters from a schoolboy from Tyneside, Steve Wraith, who was mesmerised by their story. Eventually, Steve visited them in prison and a friendship formed. The Twins hired Steve as an unofficial advisor, which brought him into contact with other members of their crime family. At Ron's funeral, Steve was Charlie Kray's right-hand man.

Steve documents Ron's time in Broadmoor – a high-security psychiatric hospital – where he was battling insanity and heavily medicated. Steve details visiting Reg, who served almost 30 years in a variety of prisons, where the gangster was treated with the utmost respect by the staff and the inmates.

By Natalie Welsh:

Escape from Venezuela's Deadliest Prison

After getting arrested at a Venezuelan airport with a suitcase of cocaine, Natalie was clueless about the danger she was facing. Sentenced to 10 years, she arrived at a prison with armed men on the roof, whom she mistakenly believed were the guards, only to find out they were homicidal gang members. Immediately, she was plunged into a world of unimaginable horror and escalating violence, where murder, rape and all-out gang warfare were carried out with the complicity of corrupt guards. Male prisoners often entered the females' housing area, bringing gunfire with them and leaving corpses behind. After 4.5 years, Natalie risked everything to escape and flee through Colombia, with the help of a guard who had fallen deeply in love with her.

By Shaun Attwood:

Pablo Escobar: Beyond Narcos

War on Drugs Series Book 1

The mind-blowing true story of Pablo Escobar and the Medellín Cartel beyond their portrayal on Netflix.

Colombian drug lord Pablo Escobar was a devoted family man and a psychopathic killer; a terrible enemy, yet a wonderful friend. While donating millions to the poor, he bombed and tortured his enemies – some had their eyeballs removed with hot spoons. Through ruthless cunning and America's insatiable appetite for cocaine, he became a multi-billionaire, who lived in a $100-million house with its own zoo.

Pablo Escobar: Beyond Narcos demolishes the standard good versus evil telling of his story. The authorities were not hunting Pablo down to stop his cocaine business. They were taking over it.

American Made: Who Killed Barry Seal?
Pablo Escobar or George HW Bush

War on Drugs Series Book 2

Set in a world where crime and government coexist, *American Made* is the jaw-dropping true story of CIA pilot Barry Seal that the Hollywood movie starring Tom Cruise is afraid to tell.

Barry Seal flew cocaine and weapons worth billions of dollars into and out of America in the 1980s. After he became a government informant, Pablo Escobar's Medellin Cartel offered a million for him alive and half a million dead. But his real trouble began after he threatened to expose the dirty dealings of George HW Bush.

American Made rips the roof off Bush and Clinton's complicity in cocaine trafficking in Mena, Arkansas.

"A conspiracy of the grandest magnitude." Congressman Bill Alexander on the Mena affair.

The Cali Cartel: Beyond Narcos

War on Drugs Series Book 3

An electrifying account of the Cali Cartel beyond its portrayal on Netflix.

From the ashes of Pablo Escobar's empire rose an even bigger and more malevolent cartel. A new breed of sophisticated mobsters became the kings of cocaine. Their leader was Gilberto Rodríguez Orejuela – known as the Chess Player due to his foresight and calculated cunning.

Gilberto and his terrifying brother, Miguel, ran a multi-billion-dollar drug empire like a corporation. They employed a politically astute brand of thuggery and spent $10 million to put a president in power. Although the godfathers from Cali preferred bribery over violence, their many loyal torturers and hit men were never idle.

Clinton Bush and CIA Conspiracies: From the Boys on the Tracks to Jeffrey Epstein

War on Drugs Series Book 4

In the 1980s, George HW Bush imported cocaine to finance an illegal war in Nicaragua. Governor Bill Clinton's Arkansas state police provided security for the drug drops. For assisting the CIA, the Clinton Crime Family was awarded the White House. The #clintonbodycount continues to this day, with the deceased including Jeffrey Epstein.

This book features harrowing true stories that reveal the insanity of the drug war. A mother receives the worst news about her son. A journalist gets a tip that endangers his life. An unemployed man becomes California's biggest crack dealer. A DEA agent in Mexico is sacrificed for going after the big players.

The lives of Linda Ives, Gary Webb, Freeway Rick Ross and Kiki Camarena are shattered by brutal experiences. Not all of them will survive.

Pablo Escobar's Story (4-book series)

"Finally, the definitive book about Escobar, original and up-to-date" – UNILAD

"The most comprehensive account ever written" – True Geordie

Pablo Escobar was a mama's boy who cherished his family and sang in the shower, yet he bombed a passenger plane and formed a death squad that used genital electrocution.

Most Escobar biographies only provide a few pieces of the puzzle, but this action-packed 1000-page book reveals everything about the king of cocaine.

Mostly translated from Spanish, Part 1 contains stories untold in the English-speaking world, including:

The tragic death of his youngest brother Fernando.

The fate of his pregnant mistress.

The shocking details of his affair with a TV celebrity.

The presidential candidate who encouraged him to eliminate their rivals.

The Mafia Philosopher

"A fast-paced true-crime memoir with all of the action of Goodfellas" – UNILAD

"Sopranos v Sons of Anarchy with an Alaskan-snow backdrop" – True Geordie Podcast

Breaking bones, burying bodies and planting bombs became second nature to Two Tonys while working for the Bonanno Crime Family, whose exploits inspired The Godfather.

After a dispute with an outlaw motorcycle club, Two Tonys left a trail of corpses from Arizona to Alaska. On the run, he was pursued by bikers and a neo-Nazi gang blood-thirsty for revenge, while a homicide detective launched a nationwide manhunt.

As the mist from his smoking gun fades, readers are left with an unexpected portrait of a stoic philosopher with a wealth of charm, a glorious turn of phrase and a fanatical devotion to his daughter.

Party Time

An action-packed roller-coaster account of a life spiralling out of control, featuring wild women, gangsters and a mountain of drugs.

Shaun Attwood arrived in Phoenix, Arizona, a penniless business graduate from a small industrial town in England. Within a decade, he became a stock-market millionaire. But he was leading a double life.

After taking his first Ecstasy pill at a rave in Manchester as a shy student, Shaun became intoxicated by the party lifestyle that would change his fortune. Years later, in the Arizona desert, he became submerged in a criminal underworld, throwing parties for thousands of ravers and running an Ecstasy ring in competition with the Mafia mass murderer Sammy 'The Bull' Gravano.

As greed and excess tore through his life, Shaun had eye-watering encounters with Mafia hit men and crystal-meth addicts, enjoyed extravagant debauchery with superstar DJs and glitter girls, and ingested enough drugs to kill a herd of elephants. This is his story.

Hard Time

"Makes the Shawshank Redemption look like a holiday camp" – NOTW

After a SWAT team smashed down stock-market millionaire Shaun Attwood's door, he found himself inside of Arizona's deadliest jail and locked into a brutal struggle for survival.

Shaun's hope of living the American Dream turned into a nightmare of violence and chaos, when he had a run-in with Sammy the Bull Gravano, an Italian Mafia mass murderer.

In jail, Shaun was forced to endure cockroaches crawling in his ears at night, dead rats in the food and the sound of skulls getting cracked against toilets. He meticulously documented the conditions and smuggled out his message.

Join Shaun on a harrowing voyage into the darkest recesses of human existence.

Hard Time provides a revealing glimpse into the tragedy, brutality, dark comedy and eccentricity of prison life.

Featured worldwide on Nat Geo Channel's Locked-Up/Banged-Up Abroad Raving Arizona.

Prison Time

Sentenced to 9½ years in Arizona's state prison for distributing Ecstasy, Shaun finds himself living among gang members, sexual predators and drug-crazed psychopaths. After being attacked by a Californian biker in for stabbing a girlfriend, Shaun writes about the prisoners who befriend, protect and inspire him. They include T-Bone, a massive African American ex-Marine who risks his life saving vulnerable inmates from rape, and Two Tonys, an old-school Mafia murderer who left the corpses of his rivals from Arizona to Alaska. They teach Shaun how to turn incarceration to his advantage, and to learn from his mistakes.

Shaun is no stranger to love and lust in the heterosexual world, but the tables are turned on him inside. Sexual advances come at him from all directions, some cleverly disguised, others more sinister – making Shaun question his sexual identity.

Resigned to living alongside violent, mentally-ill and drug-addicted inmates, Shaun immerses himself in psychology and philosophy to try to make sense of his past behaviour, and begins applying what he learns as he adapts to prison life. Encouraged by Two Tonys to explore fiction as well, Shaun reads over 1000 books which, with support from a brilliant psychotherapist, Dr Owen, speed along his personal development. As his ability to deflect daily threats improves, Shaun begins to look forward to his release with optimism and a new love waiting for him. Yet the words of Aristotle from one of Shaun's books will prove prophetic: "We cannot learn without pain."

Un-Making a Murderer: The Framing of Steven Avery and Brendan Dassey

Innocent people do go to jail. Sometimes mistakes are made. But even more terrifying is when the authorities conspire to frame them. That's what happened to Steven Avery and Brendan Dassey, who were convicted of murder and are serving life sentences.

Un-Making a Murderer is an explosive book which uncovers the illegal, devious and covert tactics used by Wisconsin officials, including:

– Concealing Other Suspects

– Paying Expert Witnesses to Lie

– Planting Evidence

– Jury Tampering

The art of framing innocent people has been in practice for centuries and will continue until the perpetrators are held accountable. Turning conventional assumptions and beliefs in the justice system upside down, *Un-Making a Murderer* takes you on that journey.

Hard Time by Shaun Attwood

Chapter 1

Sleep deprived and scanning for danger, I enter a dark cell on the second floor of the maximum-security Madison Street jail in Phoenix, Arizona, where guards and gang members are murdering prisoners. Behind me, the metal door slams heavily. Light slants into the cell through oblong gaps in the door, illuminating a prisoner cocooned in a white sheet, snoring lightly on the top bunk about two thirds of the way up the back wall. Relieved there is no immediate threat, I place my mattress on the grimy floor. Desperate to rest, I notice movement on the cement-block walls. *Am I hallucinating?* I blink several times. The walls appear to ripple. Stepping closer, I see the walls are alive with insects. I flinch. So many are swarming, I wonder if they're a colony of ants on the move. To get a better look, I put my eyes right up to them. They are mostly the size of almonds and have antennae. American cockroaches. I've seen them in the holding cells downstairs in smaller numbers, but nothing like this. A chill spread over my body. I back away.

Something alive falls from the ceiling and bounces off the base of my neck. I jump. With my night vision improving, I spot cockroaches weaving in and out of the base of the fluorescent strip light. Every so often one drops onto the concrete and resumes crawling. Examining the bottom bunk, I realise why my cellmate is sleeping at a higher elevation: cockroaches are pouring from gaps in the decrepit wall at the level of my bunk. The area is thick with them. Placing my mattress on the bottom bunk scatters them. I walk towards the toilet, crunching a few under my shower sandals. I urinate and grab the toilet roll. A cockroach darts from the centre of the roll onto my hand, tickling my fingers. My arm jerks as if it has a mind of its own, losing the cockroach and the toilet roll. Using a towel, I wipe the bulk of them off the bottom bunk, stopping only to shake the odd one off my hand. I unroll my mattress. They begin to regroup and inhabit my mattress. My adrenaline is pumping so much, I lose my fatigue.

Nauseated, I sit on a tiny metal stool bolted to the wall. *How will I sleep? How's my cellmate sleeping through the infestation and my arrival?* Copying his technique, I cocoon myself in a sheet and lie down, crushing more cockroaches. The only way they can access me now is through the breathing hole I've left in the sheet by the lower half of my face. Inhaling their strange musty odour, I close my eyes. I can't sleep. I feel them crawling on the sheet around my feet. *Am I imagining things?* Frightened of them infiltrating my breathing hole, I keep opening my eyes. Cramps cause me to rotate onto my other side. Facing the wall, I'm repulsed by so many of them just inches away. I return to my original side.

The sheet traps the heat of the Sonoran Desert to my body, soaking me in sweat. Sweat tickles my body, tricking my mind into thinking the cockroaches are infiltrating and crawling on me. The trapped heat aggravates my bleeding skin infections and bedsores. I want to scratch myself, but I know better. The outer layers of my skin have turned soggy from sweating constantly in this concrete oven. Squirming on the bunk fails to stop the relentless itchiness of my skin. Eventually, I scratch myself. Clumps of moist skin detach under my nails. Every now and then I become so uncomfortable, I must open my cocoon to waft the heat out, which allows the cockroaches in. It takes hours to drift to sleep. I only manage a few hours. I awake stuck to the soaked sheet, disgusted by the cockroach carcasses compressed against the mattress.

The cockroaches plague my new home until dawn appears at the dots in the metal grid over a begrimed strip of four-inch-thick bullet-proof glass at the top of the back wall – the cell's only source of outdoor light. They disappear into the cracks in the walls, like vampire mist retreating from sunlight. But not all of them. There were so many on the night shift that even their vastly reduced number is too many to dispose of. And they act like they know it. They roam around my feet with attitude, as if to make it clear that I'm trespassing on their turf.

My next set of challenges will arise not from the insect world, but from my neighbours. I'm the new arrival, subject to scrutiny about my charges just like when I'd run into the Aryan Brotherhood prison gang on my first day at the medium-security Towers jail a year ago. I wish my cellmate would wake up, brief me on the mood of the locals and introduce me to the head of the white gang. No such luck. Chow is announced over a speaker system in a crackly robotic voice, but he doesn't stir.

I emerge into the day room for breakfast. Prisoners in black-and-white bee-striped uniforms gather under the metal-grid stairs and tip dead cockroaches into a trash bin from plastic peanut-butter containers they'd set as traps during the night. All eyes are on me in the chow line. Watching who sits where, I hold my head up, put on a solid stare and pretend to be as at home in this environment as the cockroaches. It's all an act. I'm lonely and afraid. I loathe having to explain myself to the head of the white race, who I assume is the toughest murderer. I've been in jail long enough to know that taking my breakfast to my cell will imply that I have something to hide.

The gang punishes criminals with certain charges. The most serious are sex offenders, who are KOS: Kill On Sight. Other charges are punishable by SOS – Smash On Sight – such as drive-by shootings because women and kids sometimes get killed. It's called convict justice. Gang members are constantly looking for people to beat up because that's how they earn their reputations and tattoos. The most serious acts of violence earn the highest-ranking tattoos. To be a full gang member requires murder. I've observed the body language and techniques inmates trying to integrate employ. An inmate with a spring in his step and an air of confidence is likely to be accepted. A person who avoids eye contact and fails to introduce himself to the gang is likely to be preyed on. Some of the failed attempts I saw ended up with heads getting cracked against toilets, a sound I've grown familiar with. I've seen prisoners being extracted on stretchers who looked dead – one had yellow fluid leaking from his head. The constant violence gives me nightmares, but the reality is that I put myself in here, so I force myself to accept it as a part of my punishment.

It's time to apply my knowledge. With a self-assured stride, I take my breakfast bag to the table of white inmates covered in neo-Nazi tattoos, allowing them to question me.

"Mind if I sit with you guys?" I ask, glad exhaustion has deepened my voice.

"These seats are taken. But you can stand at the corner of the table."

The man who answered is probably the head of the gang. I size him up. Cropped brown hair. A dangerous glint in Nordic-blue eyes. Tiny pupils that suggest he's on heroin. Weightlifter-type veins bulging from a sturdy neck. Political ink on arms crisscrossed with scars. About the same age as me, thirty-three.

"Thanks. I'm Shaun from England." I volunteer my origin to show I'm different from them but not in a way that might get me smashed.

"I'm Bullet, the head of the whites." He offers me his fist to bump. "Where you roll in from, wood?"

Addressing me as wood is a good sign. It's what white gang members on a friendly basis call each other.

"Towers jail. They increased my bond and re-classified me to maximum security."

"What's your bond at?"

"I've got two $750,000 bonds," I say in a monotone. This is no place to brag about bonds.

"How many people you kill, brother?" His eyes drill into mine, checking whether my body language supports my story. My body language so far is spot on.

"None. I threw rave parties. They got us talking about drugs on wiretaps." Discussing drugs on the phone does not warrant a $1.5 million bond. I know and beat him to his next question. "Here's my charges." I show him my charge sheet, which includes conspiracy and leading a crime syndicate – both from running an Ecstasy ring.

Bullet snatches the paper and scrutinises it. Attempting to pre-empt his verdict, the other whites study his face. On edge, I wait for him to respond. Whatever he says next will determine whether I'll be accepted or victimised.

"Are you some kind of jailhouse attorney?" Bullet asks. "I want someone to read through my case paperwork." During our few minutes of conversation, Bullet has seen through my act and concluded that I'm educated – a possible resource to him.

I appreciate that he'll accept me if I take the time to read his case. "I'm no jailhouse attorney, but I'll look through it and help you however I can."

"Good. I'll stop by your cell later on, wood."

After breakfast, I seal as many of the cracks in the walls as I can with toothpaste. The cell smells minty, but the cockroaches still find their way in. Their day shift appears to be collecting information on the brown paper bags under my bunk, containing a few items of food that I purchased from the commissary; bags that I tied off with rubber bands in the hope of keeping the cockroaches out. Relentlessly, the cockroaches explore the bags for entry points, pausing over and probing the most worn and vulnerable regions. *Will the nightly swarm eat right through the paper?* I read all morning, wondering whether my cellmate has died in his cocoon, his occasional breathing sounds reassuring me.

Bullet stops by late afternoon and drops his case paperwork off. He's been charged with Class 3 felonies and less, not serious crimes, but is facing a double-digit sentence because of his prior convictions and Security Threat Group status in the prison system. The proposed sentencing range seems disproportionate. I'll advise him to reject the plea bargain – on the assumption he already knows to do so, but is just seeking the comfort of a second opinion, like many un-sentenced inmates. When he returns for his paperwork, our conversation disturbs my cellmate – the cocoon shuffles – so we go upstairs to his cell. I tell Bullet what I think. He is excitable, a different man from earlier, his pupils almost non-existent.

"This case ain't shit. But my prosecutor knows I done other shit, all kinds of heavy shit, but can't prove it. I'd do anything to get that sorry bitch off my fucking ass. She's asking for something bad to happen to her. Man, if I ever get bonded out, I'm gonna chop that bitch into pieces. Kill her slowly though. Like to work her over with a blowtorch."

Such talk can get us both charged with conspiring to murder a prosecutor, so I try to steer him elsewhere. "It's crazy how they can catch you doing one thing, yet try to sentence you for all of the things they think you've ever done."

"Done plenty. Shot some dude in the stomach once. Rolled him up in a blanket and threw him in a dumpster."

Discussing past murders is as unsettling as future ones. "So, what's all your tattoos mean, Bullet? Like that eagle on your chest?"

"Why you wanna know?" Bullet's eyes probe mine.

My eyes hold their ground. "Just curious."

"It's a war bird. The AB patch."

"AB patch?"

"What the Aryan Brotherhood gives you when you've put enough work in."

"How long does it take to earn a patch?"

"Depends how quickly you put your work in. You have to earn your lightning bolts first."

"Why you got red and black lightning bolts?"

"You get SS bolts for beating someone down or for being an enforcer for the family. Red lightning bolts for killing someone. I was sent down as a youngster. They gave me steel and told me who to handle and I handled it. You don't ask questions. You just get blood on your steel. Dudes who get these tats without putting work in are told to cover them up or leave the yard."

"What if they refuse?"

"They're held down and we carve the ink off them."

Imagining them carving a chunk of flesh to remove a tattoo, I cringe. He's really enjoying telling me this now. His volatile nature is clear and frightening. *He's accepted me too much. He's trying to impress me before making demands.*

At night, I'm unable to sleep. Cocooned in heat, surrounded by cockroaches, I hear the swamp-cooler vent – a metal grid at the top of a wall – hissing out tepid air. Giving up on sleep, I put my earphones on and tune into National Public Radio. Listening to a Vivaldi violin concerto, I close my eyes and press my tailbone down to straighten my back as if I'm doing a yogic relaxation. The playful allegro thrills me, lifting my spirits, but the wistful adagio provokes sad emotions and tears. I open my eyes and gaze into the gloom. Due to lack of sleep, I start hallucinating and hearing voices over the music whispering threats. I'm at breaking point. Although I have accepted that I committed crimes and deserve to be punished, no one should have to live like this. I'm furious at myself for making the series of reckless decisions that put me in here and for losing absolutely everything. As violins crescendo in my ears, I remember what my life used to be like.

Prison Time by Shaun Attwood

Chapter 1

"I've got a padlock in a sock. I can smash your brains in while you're asleep. I can kill you whenever I want." My new cellmate sizes me up with no trace of human feeling in his eyes. Muscular and pot-bellied, he's caked in prison ink, including six snakes on his skull, slithering side by side. The top of his right ear is missing in a semi-circle.

The waves of fear are overwhelming. After being in transportation all day, I can feel my bladder hurting. "I'm not looking to cause any trouble. I'm the quietest cellmate you'll ever have. All I do is read and write."

Scowling, he shakes his head. "Why've they put a fish in with me?" He swaggers close enough for me to smell his cigarette breath. "Us convicts don't get along with fresh fish."

"Should I ask to move then?" I say, hoping he'll agree if he hates new prisoners so much.

"No! They'll think I threatened you!"

In the eight by twelve feet slab of space, I swerve around him and place my property box on the top bunk.

He pushes me aside and grabs the box. "You just put that on my artwork! I ought to fucking smash you, fish!"

"Sorry, I didn't see it."

"You need to be more aware of your fucking surroundings! What you in for anyway, fish?"

I explain my charges, Ecstasy dealing and how I spent twenty-six months fighting my case.

"How come the cops were so hard-core after you?" he asks, squinting.

"It was a big case, a multi-million-dollar investigation. They raided over a hundred people and didn't find any drugs. They were pretty pissed off. I'd stopped dealing by the time they caught up with me, but I'd done plenty over the years, so I accept my punishment."

"Throwing raves," he says, staring at the ceiling as if remembering something. "Were you partying with underage girls?" he asks, his voice slow, coaxing.

Being called a sex offender is the worst insult in prison. Into my third year of incarceration, I'm conditioned to react. "What you trying to say?" I yell angrily, brow clenched.

"Were you fucking underage girls?" Flexing his body, he shakes both fists as if about to punch me.

"Hey, I'm no child molester, and I'd prefer you didn't say shit like that!"

"My buddy next door is doing twenty-five to life for murdering a child molester. How do I know Ecstasy dealing ain't your cover story?" He inhales loudly, nostrils flaring.

"You want to see my fucking paperwork?"

A stocky prisoner walks in. Short hair. Dark eyes. Powerful neck. On one arm: a tattoo of a man in handcuffs above the word OMERTA – the Mafia code of silence towards law enforcement. "What the fuck's going on in here, Bud?" asks Junior Bull – the son of "Sammy the Bull" Gravano, the Mafia mass murderer who was my biggest competitor in the Ecstasy market.

Relieved to see a familiar face, I say, "How're you doing?"

Shaking my hand, he says in a New York Italian accent, "I'm doing alright. I read that shit in the newspaper about you starting a blog in Sheriff Joe Arpaio's jail."

"The blog's been bringing media heat on the conditions."

"You know him?" Bud asks.

"Yeah, from Towers jail. He's a good dude. He's in for dealing Ecstasy like me."

"It's a good job you said that 'cause I was about to smash his ass," Bud says.

"It's a good job Wild Man ain't here 'cause you'd a got your ass thrown off the balcony," Junior Bull says.

I laugh. The presence of my best friend, Wild Man, was partly the reason I never took a beating at the county jail, but with Wild Man in a different prison, I feel vulnerable. When Bud casts a death stare on me, my smile fades.

"What the fuck you guys on about?" Bud asks.

"Let's go talk downstairs." Junior Bull leads Bud out.

I rush to a stainless-steel sink/toilet bolted to a cement-block wall by the front of the cell, unbutton my orange jumpsuit and crane my neck to watch the upper-tier walkway in case Bud returns. I bask in relief as my bladder deflates. After flushing, I take stock of my new home, grateful for the slight improvement in the conditions versus what I'd grown accustomed to in Sheriff Joe Arpaio's jail. No cockroaches. No blood stains. A working swamp cooler. Something I've never seen in a cell before: shelves. The steel table bolted to the wall is slightly larger, too. *But how will I concentrate on writing with Bud around?* There's a mixture of smells in the room. Cleaning chemicals. Aftershave. Tobacco. A vinegar-like odour. The slit of a window at the back overlooks gravel in a no-man's-land before the next building with gleaming curls of razor wire around its roof.

From the doorway upstairs, I'm facing two storeys of cells overlooking a day room with shower cubicles at the end of both tiers. At two white plastic circular tables, prisoners are playing dominoes, cards, chess and Scrabble, some concentrating, others yelling obscenities, contributing to a brain-scraping din that I hope to block out by purchasing a Walkman. In a raised box-shaped Plexiglas control tower, two guards are monitoring the prisoners.

Bud returns. My pulse jumps. Not wanting to feel like I'm stuck in a kennel with a rabid dog, I grab a notepad and pen and head for the day room.

Focussed on my body language, not wanting to signal any weakness, I'm striding along the upper tier, head and chest elevated, when two hands appear from a doorway and grab me. I drop the pad. The pen clinks against grid-metal and tumbles to the day room as I'm pulled into a cell reeking of backside sweat and masturbation, a cheese-tinted funk.

"I'm Booga. Let's fuck," says a squat man in urine-stained boxers, with WHITE TRASH tattooed on his torso below a mobile home, and an arm sleeved with the Virgin Mary.

Shocked, I brace to flee or fight to preserve my anal virginity. I can't believe my eyes when he drops his boxers and waggles his penis.

Dancing to music playing through a speaker he has rigged up, Booga smiles in a sexy way. "Come on," he says in a husky voice. "Drop your pants. Let's fuck." He pulls pornography faces. I question his sanity. He moves closer. "If I let you fart in my mouth, can I fart in yours?"

"You can fuck off," I say, springing towards the doorway.

He grabs me. We scuffle. Every time I make progress towards the doorway, he clings to my clothes, dragging me back in. When I feel his penis rub against my leg, my adrenalin kicks in so forcefully I experience a burst of strength and wriggle free. I bolt out as fast as my shower sandals will allow and snatch my pad. Looking over my shoulder, I see him stood calmly in the doorway, smiling. He points at me. "You have to walk past my door every day. We're gonna get together. I'll lick your ass and you can fart in my mouth." Booga blows a kiss and disappears.

I rush downstairs. With my back to a wall, I pause to steady my thoughts and breathing. In survival mode, I think, *What's going to come at me next?* In the hope of reducing my tension, I borrow a pen to do what helps me stay sane: writing. With the details fresh in my mind, I document my journey to the prison for my blog readers, keeping an eye out in case anyone else wants to test the new prisoner. The more I write, the more I fill with a sense of purpose. Jon's Jail Journal is a connection to the outside world that I cherish.

Someone yells, "One time!" The din lowers. A door rumbles

open. A guard does a security walk, his every move scrutinised by dozens of scornful eyes staring from cells. When he exits, the din resumes, and the prisoners return to injecting drugs to escape from reality, including the length of their sentences. This continues all day with "Two times!" signifying two approaching guards, and "Three times!" three and so on. Every now and then an announcement by a guard over the speakers briefly lowers the din.

Before lockdown, I join the line for a shower, holding bars of soap in a towel that I aim to swing at the head of the next person to try me. With boisterous inmates a few feet away, yelling at the men in the showers to "Stop jerking off," and "Hurry the fuck up," I get in a cubicle that reeks of bleach and mildew. With every nerve strained, I undress and rinse fast.

At night, despite the desert heat, I cocoon myself in a blanket from head to toe and turn towards the wall, making my face more difficult to strike. I leave a hole for air, but the warm cement block inches from my mouth returns each exhalation to my face as if it's breathing on me, creating a feeling of suffocation. For hours, my heart drums so hard against the thin mattress I feel as if I'm moving even though I'm still. I try to sleep, but my eyes keep springing open and my head turning towards the cell as I try to penetrate the darkness, searching for Bud swinging a padlock in a sock at my head.

ABOUT THE AUTHOR

Michael Sheridan was the main screenwriter and co-producer of the Sky Pictures/Irish Film Board feature film *When the Sky Falls*, the story of the life and death of assassinated Irish crime reporter Veronica Guerin. He wrote and directed *Neil Jordan: A Profile* broadcast by RTE and WNET. He was a storyline consultant on the documentary *Sinatra and the Jack Pack* produced by David Harvey, and broadcast on one of the biggest cable channels in the US. He is working as a consultant on a five-part series for Sky, *Murder at the Cottage: The Search for Justice for Sophie*, directed by Jim Sheridan and produced by Donal McIntyre.

He adapted and directed a musical version of his best-selling Victorian true crime book *Murder at Shandy Hall*, which was a sell-out production at the Cork Opera House.

In addition, he is Ireland's most successful non-fiction author with combined sales of over 700,000 copies. He has been writing on the Sophie Toscan Du Plantier case as a journalist and author for seventeen years and his book published in 2002 on the subject, *Death in December* was a best seller. He was co-author and ghost-writer of the story of the Magdalen Laundry survivor Kathy O Beirne, *Don't Ever Tell* which spent 22 weeks in the UK's top ten and was an international hit published in twenty countries. Among his other best-selling books are *Murder at Shandy Hall*, *Frozen Blood* and *Sinatra and The Jack Pack*.

His second book on the Du Plantier case, *The Murder of Sophie: How I Hunted and Haunted the West Cork Killer* was researched and written with the exclusive and full backing and co-operation of the victim's family, the chief murder investigator and many witnesses.

www.ingramcontent.com/pod-product-compliance
Lightning Source LLC
Chambersburg PA
CBHW071728080526
44588CB00013B/1933